Rising Power, Limited Influence

Rising Power, Limited Influence

The Politics of Chinese Investments in Europe and the Liberal International Order

Edited by

Indrajit Roy
Jappe Eckhardt
Dimitrios Stroikos
and
Simona Davidescu

OXFORD
UNIVERSITY PRESS

Great Clarendon Street, Oxford, OX2 6DP,
United Kingdom

Oxford University Press is a department of the University of Oxford. It furthers the University's objective of excellence in research, scholarship, and education by publishing worldwide. Oxford is a registered trade mark of Oxford University Press in the UK and in certain other countries

Published in the United States of America by Oxford University Press198 Madison Avenue, New York, NY 10016, United States of America

British Library Cataloguing in Publication Data

Data available

Library of Congress Control Number: 2023939085

ISBN 9780192887115

DOI: 10.1093/oso/9780192887115.001.0001

Printed and bound by
CPI Group (UK) Ltd, Croydon, CR0 4YY

Acknowledgements

This volume would not have been possible without the support of colleagues at the University of York, the Political Studies Association, and Oxford University Press. A grant from the University of York Research Priming Fund allowed us to convene as a group and support the logistics and coordination of the project. Thanks are also due to the Open Research team at the University of York for supporting the Open Access publication of this work. Another grant from the Pushing the Boundaries Award funded by the Political Studies Association enabled follow-up meetings at which the present volume took shape. We are very grateful to all the participants of those two conferences, especially Professor Christopher R. Hughes of the London School of Economics and Political Sciences, for their insightful contributions. The diligence and efficiency of Dr Ran Hu, then a doctoral student at the University of York, seamlessly connected the editors with the contributors to ensure the timely delivery of this volume. At Oxford University Press, Adam Swallow's wisdom helped us navigate its numerous review processes, and Karen Bunn's patience and efforts steered the volume through production.

The usual disclaimers apply.

Contents

List of Figures

List of Tables

List of Abbreviations

AIIB	Asian Infrastructure Investment Bank
ANSA	Agenzia Nazionale Stampa Associata
ASEAN	Association of Southeast Asian Nations
BRI	Belt and Road Initiative
CCP	Chinese Communist Party
CEE	Central and Eastern Europe
CGN	China Guangdong Nuclear
Cosco	China Overseas Shipping Group Co
CPIA	Country Policy and Institutional Assessment
DAC	Development Assistance Committee
DECC	Department of Energy and Climate Change, UK
DfID	Department for International Development
EDF	Électricité de France
EEC	European Energy Community
EU	European Union
FDI	Foreign Direct Investment
Fidesz	Hungarian Civic Alliance
GVC	Global Value Chains
IMF	International Monetary Fund
LIO	Liberal International Order
M5S	Five Stars Movement, Italy
MoU	Memorandum of Understanding
MP	Member of Parliament
MSR	Maritime Silk Road
NATO	North Atlantic Treaty Organization
NDB	New Development Bank
OECD	Organization for Economic Co-operation and Development
OFDI	Outward Foreign Direct Investment
PRC	People's Republic of China
SASAC	State Owned Assets Supervision and Administration Commission
SAR	Special Administrative Region
SCP	Standing Committee of the Politburo
SOE	State-Owned Enterprise
SREB	Silk Road Economic Belt
SRF	Silk Road Fund
UK	United Kingdom
UNCTAD	United Nations Conference on Trade and Development
UNHRC	United Nations Human Rights Council
US	United States
V4	Visegrád Four
WB	World Bank

List of Contributors

Editors

Indrajit Roy, Department of Politics and International Relations, University of York

Jappe Eckhardt, Department of Politics and International Relations, University of York

Dimitrios Stroikos, Department of International Relations, London School of Economics and Political Science

Simona Davidescu, Department of Politics and International Relations, University of York

Contributors

Yu Jie, Chatham House

Ran Hu, School of Social Sciences and Global Studies, The Open University

Ágnes Szunomár, Center for Economic and Regional Studies Institute of World Economics, Hungary and Institute of Global Studies, Corvinus University of Budapest

Filippo Boni, School of Social Sciences and Global Studies, The Open University

Małgorzata Jakimów, School of Government and International Affairs, Durham University

Nicholas Crawford, International Institute for Strategic Studies

Jan Knoerich, Lau China Institute, King's College London

Catherine Jones, School of International Relations, University of St Andrews

Introduction

Chinese Investments in Europe

Power, Influence, and the Liberal International Order

Indrajit Roy and Ran Hu

As one of the world's largest economies, the influence of the People's Republic of China on the international order has generated much attention. Since its reform and opening-up in 1978, China has transformed itself from a poor and relatively isolated country into an economic powerhouse with a strong military capability and technological sophistication. With decades of strong economic growth, China surpassed Japan in 2010, becoming the world's second largest economy. It is predicted to overtake the United States (US) and become world's largest economy in 2028 (CEBR, 2020). China's rise[1] has been interpreted as the emergence of a Chinese world order or a Chinese century, at the expense of Western domination.[2] Though these visions of Chinese domination have yet to be realized (Kai, 2015; Thurow, 2007), China's rise seems to have taken on a new meaning: its long-established discourse of a 'peaceful rise' appears less tenable. For the first time since the Industrial Revolution, the West is confronted by a military and economic power that is not White.

[1] Publications referring to China's rise have proliferated over the last three decades. See, for example, Kristof's (1993) *The Rise of China*; Ikenberry's (2008) *The Rise of China and the Future of the West*; and De Graaff et al. (2020)'s *China's Rise in a Liberal World Order in Transition*, among others. More recently, Doshi's (2021) *The Long Game* claims to unearth 'China's grand strategy to displace American order'. China's Belt and Road Initiative (BRI) has offered the occasion for growing commentary of such purported grand strategies (Cavanna, 2019; Fallon, 2015; Macaes, 2018; Scobell et al., 2018)

[2] See, for example, *The Economist*, 2018; Jacques, 2009; Rees-Mogg, 2005; and Stiglitz, 2014. Others have described this process as a 're-emergence' of China, see (Nye, 1997; Rapkin and Thompson, 2003); or the rejuvenation of the Chinese nation (Yan, 2001).

Indrajit Roy and Ran Hu, *Chinese Investments in Europe*. In: *Rising Power, Limited Influence*. Edited by: Indrajit Roy, Jappe Eckhardt, Dimitrios Stroikos, and Simona Davidescu, Oxford University Press.
DOI: 10.1093/oso/9780192887115.003.0001

The Puzzle of Chinese Power: Growing Resources vs Limited Influence

The rise of China's economic, military, and political power and its likely impact on the behaviour of other states has been documented by several studies. These works suggest that China's rise is influencing not only the behaviour of other states, but also the character of the international order. Although this scholarship undoubtedly offers a crucial foundation for an enriched understanding of the global distribution of power, it tells us little about how effectively China uses its power, if at all. While much has been written about whether and how China seeks to influence the Liberal International Order (LIO), the debates tend to be bounded by assumptions of relative power shifts generating certain responses from others or claims about the resilience of the international order. Consequently, the ensemble of China's actions, other countries' responses, and the influence—if any—of these relationships on the international order remains neglected.

Indeed, as prescient observers of China's rise have noted, its growing economic and military might do not mechanically translate into either an enhanced influence on the international order or the ability to prevail over other countries. Despite its recent pandemic diplomacy, China was unable to exercise any meaningful leverage over the policies of recipient countries. Its sprawling investments across 120 countries via the Belt and Road Initiative have had limited impact in shaping host countries' attitudes towards China. In Europe, Africa, and South-East Asia, China's ascendance has hardly been welcomed with the enthusiasm that critics feared and supporters hoped for. Against neighbours with whom it has had long-standing territorial disputes—including Japan, the Philippines, Vietnam, and India—China's obvious military and economic superiority have not translated into any meaningful influence on them or the broader international order. Nevertheless, critical assessments (Segal, 1999) that China is no more than 'overrated', a 'second-rank middle power', or a 'theoretical power' do not account for the country's growing footprint across the globe (Doshi, 2021; Macaes, 2018; and Chhabra et al., 2021). As David Shambaugh (2013) notes in his much-acclaimed study, China's global spread in the realms of diplomacy, global governance, and economic, cultural, and security networks is a fact. And yet even he concludes that despite China's active presence in different parts of the globe, its inability to shape actors or events means that it is, at the end of the day, a partial power.

This volume is motivated by a significant puzzle that lies at the heart of China's ascendance: the gap between its growing economic, military, and cultural resources and the conversion of those resources into meaningful global influence. This puzzle in turn leads to at least three crucial questions: (1) Does China, in fact, intend to challenge the international order? (2) Do China's expanding overseas investments have unintended consequences for the international order? And (3) How does European agency interact with Chinese influence to (re-)shape the Liberal International Order? Answering these questions requires us to direct detailed attention to the ways in which China uses its power to affect the policy choices and decisions of other countries, instead of focusing on scorecards that enumerate its political, economic, and cultural resources. Reflecting on these questions on China's power requires us to move away from understandings of power as resource to power as influence, which relates resources to outcomes. The contributors to this volume assert that to assess China's impact on the international order, we must appreciate the ways in which its growing power resources are translated into actual policy influence. Here, we find helpful the crucial distinction offered by Evelyn Goh (2014; 2016) between an understanding of power that is limited to enumeration of resources and latent capability, towards an understanding of power that focuses on its effective exercise, or influence, on the preferences and behaviour of other actors.

Case Selection

In this volume we investigate the puzzle of China's growing resources against its limited influence on the international order. We do so by exploring the three questions noted above in the context of the politics of Chinese investments in Europe. Three core reasons motivate the selection of European countries as empirical cases for this study. First, Chinese investments in Europe upend the usual direction of financial flows from the 'developed countries' of the Global North to the 'developing countries' of the Global South, which have underpinned the international order. Second, the growing volume of overseas investments originating in China, which continues to be labelled a 'developing economy', is unabashedly authoritarian and, where the state permeates its economy, threatens to disrupt the liberal foundations of the international order. Third, Europe prides itself upon and is widely considered the champion of the Liberal International Order, if not its forebear. The increasing volume of economic investments originating in one of the world's most resilient authoritarian regimes towards a Europe where liberal values are increasingly besieged provide us with useful entry points into the ways in which China's actions interact with responses from other states to influence the international order.

China's OFDI in 2020 stood at USD 153.71 billion, ranking first globally for the first time.[3] Since 2012, China has come in the top three countries in terms of the OFDI flows. Driven by its 'Going Out' strategy and Belt and Road Initiative, China is expected to continue the expansion of its OFDI footprints. Through overseas investment, China can not only boost its economy, but also further project its power by leveraging its economic strength. Between 2003 and 2012, China's OFDI flow to Europe tripled with a general uptrend, standing at USD 7.04 billion in 2012. Between 2013 and 2019, the flow fluctuated. China's OFDI flow in Europe recorded its lowest of USD 5.95 billion in 2013 and the highest of USD 18.46 billion in 2017, but it still registered at USD 12.69 billion in 2021. Due to the opacity of the Chinese Communist regime, there is a serious concern that the Chinese OFDI may pose certain 'existential' political problems to Europe (Meunier, Burgoon, and Jacoby, 2014: 119). For instance, Godement and Parello-Plesner (2011: 1) sounded an alarm by asserting that China was 'buying up Europe', calling it a 'scramble for Europe'. Other narratives such as China 'invading' (L'Express, 2011) or 'taking over Europe' (Bordet, 2011) also emerged.

Despite these alarms, the *politics* of Chinese investment in Europe remains under-researched: most literature on China's OFDI has focused on the types of the Chinese OFDI and investors, investment behaviour, patterns, and rationale (Hanemann, 2014; Knoerich and Miedtank, 2018; Meunier, 2014b, 2014c; Meunier, Burgoon, and Jacoby, 2014; Pavlićević, 2019; Zhang and Van Den Bulcke, 2014). A preliminary research agenda on the politics of Chinese investments in Europe is emerging and growing (Meunier, Burgoon, and Jacoby, 2014). Meunier (2014a) discusses the most the issue concerning political implications with regards to European domestic politics, institutional process, and transatlantic relations. Zhang and Van Den Bulcke (2014) focus on security and institutions, and Burgoon and Raess (2014) on labour regulation.

The collection of papers in Meunier et al., (2014) are valuable for their granular perspectives on Chinese investments in Europe. Their volume is framed by five questions: (1) What is the true magnitude of Chinese FDI in Europe? (2) Should Europeans see Chinese investments as malign or benign?

[3] All the data for this introduction are taken from the Statistical Bulletin of China's Outward Foreign Direct Investment, an annual report compiled jointly by the Ministry of Commerce of the People's Republic of China, National Bureau of Statistics, and State Administration of Foreign Exchange. Data refers to mainland China only, Hong Kong and Macao excluded.

(3) Are national and European perspectives on Chinese FDI in conflict? (4) Are political reactions to Chinese FDI different in Western and in CEE countries? And (5) Is the influx of Chinese FDI into Europe a security threat? In responding to these questions, they lay the agenda for further research on the political impact of China's investments in Europe. However, the scope of the articles precludes an exploration of the influence of Chinese European investments *on the world order*, an important area of investigation in light of the vast and growing literature on the topic. This volume builds on the research agenda proposed by Meunier and her colleagues while also making distinct empirical, conceptual, and theoretical contributions outlined below.

China's Influence on the International Order: Prevalent Perspectives in IR

The growing attention being paid to China's influence on the international order has been motivated by a number of recent Chinese actions. Since 2012, the Chinese government led by President Xi Jinping has largely abandoned its traditional foreign policy strategy of *taoguang yanghui* (keeping a low profile) and embraced a new strategy of *fenfa youwei* (striving for achievement) (Foot, 2014; Renminwang, 2013; Sørensen, 2015; Yan, 2014). In recent years, the country has portrayed itself as a staunch champion of liberal globalization. The Belt and Road Initiative was, for instance, framed by the Chinese Foreign Minister Wang Yi (2018) as 'a public good China offers the world ... [that] has grown into the largest platform for international cooperation'. During the 2017 World Economic Forum, Chinese President Xi Jinping defended multilateralism, globalization, and free trade, and championed a commitment to 'growing an open global economy'. Four years later, Xi (2021) re-emphasized that 'upholding multilateralism' is the way to address the challenges and problems the world is facing.

At the same time, contradictions abound. China's domestic behaviour is not always an endorsement of liberal globalization, given its high degree of state intervention in the economy, the limited market access for foreign investors, and its human rights violations. Moreover, China has become more assertive, if not completely aggressive, particularly regarding the issues and events taking place in the Asia-Pacific region. A recent example is the growing tension between China and the US in the South China Sea, where China continues to build artificial islands and conduct military exercises whilst the US strengthens its cooperation with other countries in the region (Geaney, 2020; Tangen, 2020).

Meanwhile in Europe, a new consensus among EU members on China appears to have emerged (Oertel, 2020), frustrated by lack of progress on improvement in China's market access and human rights practices. A survey on the character of EU-China relations in 2020 shows that all but three EU member states now regard 'China, pragmatically, as rival and partner' (Busse et al., 2020).[4] In 2019 the EU labelled China as 'a systemic rival promoting alternative models of governance' (EU Commission, 2019: 1). Bilateral relations between China and different European nations are troubled. The UK-China relationship is now in a deep freeze, with the UK public opinion about China plunging (Ford and Hughes, 2020). France and Germany were also compelled to reappraise their ties with China, given China's growing assertive approach to international affairs (Oertel, 2020; Solomon and Chazan, 2020). According to Pew Research Centre, negative views of China prevailed in all fourteen countries surveyed (Silver, Devlin, and Huang, 2020). Public perceptions favourable to China have nosedived in the wake of the COVID-19 pandemic.

These contradictory dynamics have understandably led to a proliferation of studies on the influence of China's ascendance on the international order. Following Ikenberry (2018), we identify five features of the LIO. One concerns openness in trade and exchange. The second relates to rules-based relations between states. The third pertains to collective security. The fourth conviction that underpins the LIO is the belief that international society can be reformed: states can work together to achieve mutual gains rather than being embroiled in zero-sum power contests. Last but not least, the LIO is animated by a conviction that internationalization will nudge states towards liberal democracy: liberal democracies will become more liberal and authoritarian states will become democratic.

In broadest terms, studies on the influence of China's rise on the LIO fall into two categories. The first draws on realist theoretical approaches to analyse the motivations, actions, and reactions of individual states. Their considerations include China as well as other states with whom China interacts, considering their relative intentions, preferences, and actions. The second draws on liberal theoretical approaches to foreground the global institutions within which different states are embedded, with a focus on how these institutions shape the behaviour of states. As we shall see, both categories share an understanding of power that is limited to resources.

[4] Only Bulgaria, Greece, and Cyprus categorize China 'as strategic partner', according to the survey (Busse et al., 2020).

According to realists, China's rise is bound to trigger a conflict between itself and the West (Allan, Vucetic, and Hopf, 2018; Allison, 2017; Goh, 2014; Khalilzad, 2017; Krickovic, 2017; Layne, 2018; Liff, 2016; Mearsheimer, 2001, 2010, 2019; Schake, 2017; Yan, 2010), thus threatening the LIO. Analysts writing in this vein present two interlinked visions for the future of the LIO. The first vision focuses on China's challenges to regional orders in East and South-East Asia by establishing its predominance in the region and further pushing the US out of Asia (Larson, 2015; Mearsheimer, 2001, 2019; Montgomery, 2014; Shambaugh, 2004). The second vision looks beyond Asia and pivots to a worldwide systemic competition, signalling the return of great-power rivalry (Allison, 2017; Fravel, 2010; Schweller and Pu, 2011; Wright, 2018), this time 'between the U.S.-led and Chinese-led orders' (Mearsheimer, 2019: 47).

By contrast, liberals anticipate China's full integration into the LIO (Buzan, 2010, 2018; Deudney and Ikenberry, 2018; Ikenberry, 2008, 2009, 2011, 2014, 2017, 2018; Lieber, 2014; Zeng and Liang, 2013). Analysts writing in this vein make three claims. First, the LIO is highly institutionalized, open, and resilient (Ikenberry, 2017). Second, despite China's continued rise, the US and its Western allies remain highly influential players (Tang, 2018; Zakaria, 2020). Third, China is either unwilling or unable to offer an appealing alternative to the LIO (Breslin, 2013; Cooley and Nexon, 2020; Mitter, 2021). Therefore, scholars who focus on structures claim that the LIO will endure in an updated and reformed form and that China will continue being socialized into 'this broad framework of ordering rules and institutions' (Ikenberry, 2018: 24).

Despite their different assessments of the rise of China in relation to the LIO, both strands rely, explicitly and implicitly, on notions of power that focus on economic, military, and ideational resources. For realists, Chinese power, largely defined in material terms, is overwhelming and able to overcome the power of the LIO. A stronger China would translate its newly acquired economic and military power into geopolitical clout (Foot, 2006; Glaser, 2011). It will become 'bolder, more demanding, and less inclined to cooperate' (Roy, 1994: 160) and eventually overthrow the existing order and create a new one. For liberals, Chinese power, understood largely in economic terms, is derived from and subjected to the LIO. China derives its economic power from its embeddedness into this order. Should China renege on this rules-based order (Fravel, 2010; Glaser, 2011), its disruption would inflict wide-ranging costs, both politically and economically, upon it. Important differences between them notwithstanding, both groups of scholars rely on the relative distributions of resources as the starting point of their analysis.

Whilst these analyses—one drawing on realism and the other inspired by liberalism—shed light on the changing global distribution of power and the evolving LIO, their conclusions about the influence of China's rise on the LIO are, at best, speculative. For instance, against the scenarios predicted by realists, China and the US have managed to avoid war with each other. However, against the assumptions of liberal analysts who believe that economic growth and international socialization foment political democratization, China resolutely remains a one-party authoritarian state. As we have seen, despite its growing economic, military, and cultural resources, and the endurance of its political regime, China's rise has not, in practice, overthrown the LIO and established a new Chinese-led order. The overwhelming focus in the literature on the power possessed by China (or the LIO, for that matter) has led to a neglect of the effect of that power, or what it actually yields. The assumption in the literature is that China's material power or the ideational power of the LIO would automatically generate certain responses (Goh, 2014). Departing from such focus on power as resources, we investigate power as influence: How does China's influence over European states influence the LIO, if at all?

Our Arguments: Growing Resources, Limited Influence

The contributions to the volume interrogate assumptions of China's growing economy, bringing it into conflict with the LIO as well as presumptions about the LIO's resilience coopting China's rise. We caution against the widely prevalent assumption that growing Chinese investments in Europe inevitably challenge the LIO (Bhattacharya, 2016; Callahan, 2016; Chen, 2016; Du and Ma, 2014; Godement and Kratz, 2015; Fallon, 2015; Fasslabend, 2015; Leverett and Wu, 2017; Miller, 2017; Xu and Wang, 2016). Against such assumptions of inevitable conflict, we argue that China's European investments do not necessarily undermine liberal internationalism. At the same time, against assumptions celebrating the resilience of the LIO, we remain open to the possibility that China's growing economic footprint may well align with illiberal preferences of domestic European actors. Alternatively, its increasing economic might may allow it to induce players to behave in a certain way to the detriment of liberal internationalism. With scholars who contest flattened narratives that highlight conflict with or cooption into the LIO (de Graaff, 2020; de Graaff, ten Brink, and Parmar, 2020; Huo and Parmar, 2020; Jones and Zeng, 2019; Knoerich and Miedtank, 2018; McNally, 2020; Weinhardt and ten Brink, 2020), we offer a nuanced account of the influence of China's economic investments in Europe on the global order.

A related analytical argument has to do with the domestic factors threatening the liberal underpinnings of the international order. China's growing economic and military resources are often held to be directly responsible for the challenges to the LIO. Such analysis ignores the other notable sources of such challenges. The rising tide of authoritarianism, populism, and nationalism in the liberal heartlands of Europe and North America poses important ideational and political challenges to the LIO. The social and economic difficulties associated with neoliberal economic policies offer another set of challenges to the LIO. Our focus on the influence of China's European investments on the LIO recognizes these endogenous challenges, thereby foregrounding the importance of European agency.

These two arguments are based on a conceptual argument about power. We contend that assessments of China's impact on the international order require us to appreciate how its growing power resources are translated into actual influence. Such an endeavour entails focusing on the actual *effect* of resources rather than enumerating the latent capabilities of China's growing material and economic resources. Our conceptual argument contributes to broader discussions on power in global politics, and emphasizes its relational rather than material dimension.

An understanding of China's influence on different countries is impossible without appreciating the underlying relations between states and societies. This broader theoretical argument undergirds our conceptual argument. We depart from actor-orientated concepts as well as structural approaches to situate states within their broader social relations. In this vein, the volume directs attention to interactions between state-society relations in China and state-society relations in the countries towards which Chinese investments are directed: an exclusive focus on what the Chinese state wants or does is inadequate. State-society relations in the countries subject to Chinese influence matter. Our theoretical argument thus contributes to widening discussions on influence in global politics by incorporating the role of state-society relations.

Our Conceptual Framework: Power as Resources vs Power as Influence

To reflect on the influence of Chinese investments in Europe and their implications for the global order, we adopt a sharper and narrower focus on influence away from broader understandings of power. We draw on Max Weber's notion of power as the 'opportunity to have one's will prevail within a social relationship' (Berenskoetter and Williams, 2007: 3). Weber further reminds us that power may or may not be converted into influence: power may only partially translate into influence. Cox and Jacobson (1973: 465) add more specificity: for them, influence refers to the actual 'modification of one actor's behavior by that of another'.

Our reflections on power as influence build on, but also depart from, Bachrach and Baratz's (1962) landmark study. Departing from elitist (Mills, 1956), pluralist (Dahl, 1957), and hegemonic (Lukes, 1974) notions of power that emphasized the importance of (material, social, and symbolic) resources, their scholarship insists on highlighting the importance of influence in establishing and sustaining power. Agents wield influence by setting agendas, excluding potential decision items, and preventing opposition from emerging at all. Such an understanding of power is broad enough to consider circumstances where direct conflict is absent. It is also narrow enough to preclude structural and institutional operations of power where agents' actions don't matter.

These foundations enable us to outline two key components of influence (Dahl and Stinebrikner, 2003). First, causality: a causal relationship is discernible between the wielder of influence and their target. Second, attainment of consequences: the causal relationship results in behaviours that may or may not be consistent with the preferences, or wants, of those wielding influence. The attainment of consequences can be graded or partial, rather than dichotomous binaries: for this volume, the consequence we are interested in studying is the impact on the Liberal International Order. These two components of influence—viz. causality and attainment of consequences—frame the conceptual framework to enable us to examine our empirical cases and their impact on the LIO.

The conceptual framework of influence deployed in this volume is narrower than the vast spectrum of analysis on power that characterizes the scholarship in social theory, political science, and international relations. By focusing on causality and attainment of preferences as our starting point, we preclude meta-structural understandings of power relations. Our attempt to identify and trace the processes of change (or the lack thereof) on the subjects of influence generates a dynamic relational analysis, thereby allowing us the opportunity to explore in greater detail causal relationships that tend to be neglected in structural studies of power.

At the same time, the framework of influence adopted for this volume departs from understandings (including Bachrach and Baratz) that centre intentionality, or the concerted set of actions aiming to attain a certain preference. Such studies take as their starting point the intentionality of those who wield influence. They then proceed to trace the pathways through which influence-wielders effect the behaviour of subjects in line with their intentions. The identification of intentions is always a fraught project, since intentions are often unstated. Intentions of states and social actors are even more difficult to discern. Moreover, a focus on intentionality while studying China's influence on the international order is unnecessarily narrow: irrespective of whether China intends to overthrow, reshape, or comply with the LIO, its actions have consequences for this order.

Indeed, the relationship between intentionality and action is far from straightforward. This holds true for so-called Rising Powers that may seek a relatively limited set of goals but whose actions may result in different, and expansive, outcomes. A 'Rising Power' may intend to improve its status in the international system. Alternatively, it may intend to secure its neighbourhood. Or, the country might intend to better the economic prospects of key domestic constituencies. In each of these cases, its actions may, however, trigger broader processes that result in changing the status quo (or entrenching it) without the country in question intending to do so.

A second key departure from Bachrach and Baratz is our resistance to the assumption that influence always entails a conflict of interests, or preferences. We do not endorse the view that the exercise of influence requires that one agent prevails over the preferences of the other. It is possible that the preferences of two (or more) agents align, and the influence of one agent amplifies those aligned preferences. Alternatively, preferences may be undetermined. Under such circumstances, the influence of one agent may well shape the (as yet undetermined) agent or persuade them to adopt certain preferences over others. Such an agent may well attempt to shape broader institutions, which in turn could set the agenda that limits the remit within which individual subjects operate.

The approach adopted in this volume and the broader findings of the study resonate with recent research on the scope of China's power. Drawing on cases from Chinese engagements with South-East Asia, Evelyn Goh (2014) outlines three modes through which the country seeks to influence outcomes in its neighbouring region. The first, and most prominent, mode of influence is through a 'multiplier' effect that intensifies and mobilizes converging preferences. In this vein, China marshals its growing structural power to promote economic regionalism in the interest of its Association of Southeast Asian Nations (ASEAN) neighbours. The second mode of influence is through 'persuasion', which entails economic inducement: this helps China to influence perceptions in its favour when South-East Asian countries are undecided as to whether or not China is a threat. The third mode of influence, invoked when China confronts divergent or opposing interests, is the 'ability to prevail'. This is the approach to China's territorial disputes with its neighbours. A fourth approach, which is explored in the extended volume edited by Goh (2016), pertains to the ways in which China shapes regional and global institutions in its own favour (Ciorciari, 2016; Foot and Inboden, 2016).

Arguably, demonstrating China's influence on Europe and through it on the liberal world order invites very different challenges to undertaking a similar exercise in South-East Asia. China's South-East Asian neighbours are poorer and relatively weaker. The relationship between China and the Association of Southeast Asian Nations is imbalanced in China's favour. Furthermore, China has direct territorial conflicts with several of its neighbours. By contrast, the European cases discussed in this volume are richer and stronger than China's South-East Asian neighbours. The geographical distance rules out direct territorial disputes of the sort that China has with the Philippines, Vietnam, or Taiwan. The European countries can balance any Chinese transgressions by turning to the European Union in a way that ASEAN countries cannot turn either to the regional bloc or to the USA. As Goh demonstrates, Chinese actions in South-East Asia are intended to generate policies, norms, and public opinion in its own favour: this demonstration of intentionality is key to her argument. By contrast, whether China intends its investments in Europe to challenge the LIO is quite unnecessary to demonstrate for us to analyse its *effect* on this order.

This volume thus departs from the contributions to the excellent volume edited by Everlyn Goh (2016) in three key ways. *First*, its empirical focus on Europe is quite distinct from their focus on South-East Asia. *Second*, we are agnostic on the question of China's intentionality vis-à-vis the international order. To us, the effects of Chinese investments in Europe are not solely caused by its intentions: irrespective of whether China *intends* to overthrow, reshape, or comply with the LIO, the impacts of its investments in Europe are shaped by emerging alignments in European political economies. *Third*, we take seriously the complexes of 'state-society relations' while reflecting on the effects of China's investments in Europe on the LIO. In doing this, we depart from the otherwise insightful contributions to Goh's (2016) volume which singularly focus on state actors.

Blending these insights on power with emerging perspectives on agency in international relations (Lampert and Mohan, 2018), these contributions urge us not to neglect the accountability, intentionality, and subjectivity of actors in international relations. Such actors refer not only to political elites, bureaucrats, and others in government as the prevailing literature tends to assume (Wight, 2004); they also refer to diverse actors beyond formal state institutions such as business interests, civil society groups, and trade unions, among others (Hagmann and Péclard, 2010). Furthermore, an agent is also 'an agent of something' (Wight, 1999: 133), a perspective that recognizes the ways in which they are embedded in broader socio-cultural systems.

Europe (or any other region for that matter) cannot be seen as simply a passive space increasingly subject to intervention by and investments from China. Likewise, strains and stresses on the LIO cannot be simplistically attributed to the actions and attitudes of a singularly conceptualized Chinese state. Reinserting European agency into the dominant discourse of China-in-Europe exposes Sino-European relationships that tend to be more locally mediated and driven by domestic politics than is usually recognized. In a similar vein, the agency of diverse actors within China needs to be recognized in terms of how they shape that country's overseas investments.

Our Theoretical Foundations: The Role of State-Society Relations in IR

The contributions to this volume depart from prevailing interpretations of China's rise and its impact on the global order that tend to focus on the roles and motivations of state actors: our emphasis on the agency of domestic actors is analytically reliant on appreciating the underlying state-society relations. Our approach resonates with the work of scholars who draw on the Comparative Capitalism (Jackson and Deeg, 2006) literature and extend it to the study of emerging markets such as Brazil, Russia, India, China and South Africa (BRICS) and beyond (Nölke, 2012). In this vein, Nölke et al. (2015) highlight the extent to which states permeate the market economies of emerging markets such as China and the implications of such permeation on the global order. China's state-heavy form of development and its potential challenge to the norms preached by the Washington Consensus has invited much commentary (Arrighi, 2007; Breslin, 2013; McNally, 2012; Strange, 2011; Wade, 2003). An interesting question here is the extent to which the growing importance of China may be expected to lead to a 'more statist model of global capitalist regulation' (Nölke, 2015) and the stripping away of the liberal elements of the prevailing global order (Stephen, 2014a, 2014b). One useful response to this question has been offered by de Graaf et al. (2020), who argue that

> the outcome and future direction of China's interplay with the liberal order, first, should be seen in a longer-term historical perspective and not treated as static and uni-directional but as an essentially dynamic and contested transitory process, which, second, can best be conceptualized as leading to an increasingly hybrid

> order—more fragmented in certain respects, but not necessarily less integrated in other domains. (de Graaf et al., 2020: 200)

The focus on 'state-society relations' distinguishes our contributions from the established actor-orientated concepts (Helleiner and Malkin, 2012; Schirm, 2013) as well as the more widely used two-level game approach (da Conceição-Heldt, 2013; Putnam, 1988). Against the tendency of both approaches to limit attention to the roles and motivations of states abstracted from underlying social relations, our volume builds on a broader political economy literature that instead situates states within the 'broader field of social relations' (Overbeek, 2004: 114), thus lending them sociological depth. Such an approach corrects against the assumption that states are unrelated to social forces without, at the same time, presuming that states are merely a reflection of social struggles without any autonomy whatsoever. The concept of 'state-society complexes' (Stephen, 2014b: 919) emphasizes that states are embedded in

> configurations of social forces upon which state power ultimately rests. A particular configuration of social forces defines in practice the limits or parameters of state purposes, and the modus operandi of state action, defines, in other words, the raison d'etat for a particular state. (Cox, 1987: 105)

In emphasizing the value of state-society relations to the liberal world order, our contributors implicitly endorse 'second image' explanations that highlight domestic politics as a source of cooperation and conflict in global politics (Waltz, 1959). This approach contrasts with 'first image' and 'third image' perspectives which emphasize, respectively, the role of human nature and the structure of the international system. The second image approach has been elaborated by Katzenstein (1976, 1978, 1985) and recently favoured by scholars studying the importance of domestic politics in the emerging markets to the global order, with an understandable focus on China (de Graaf et al., 2020; Helleiner and Kirshner, 2014; Nölke, 2015).

Where scholars have incorporated state-society relations in their analyses, they have tended to focus exclusively on China and treated it as a monolith. We depart from this exclusive focus on state-society relations in China. Instead, we situate the implications of Chinese investments in Europe by drawing together reflections on state-society relations in *both* origin and destination contexts. In other words, our analysis reflects on the impact of Chinese investments on the LIO by considering their interaction with

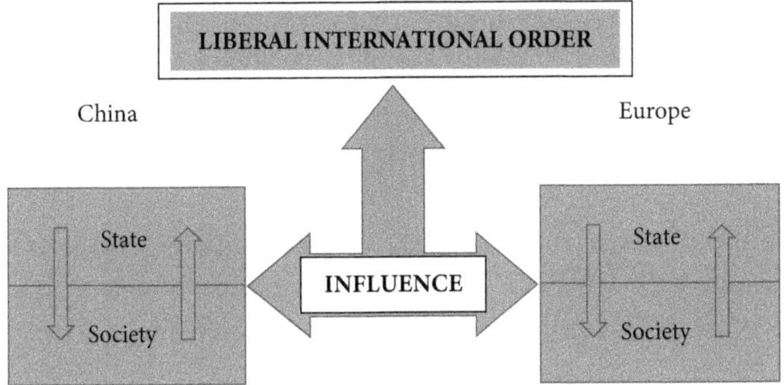

Figure I.1 State-society relations and the influence of Chinese investments in Europe on the LIO

state-society relations in *both* China and Europe. Such an approach not only brings China specialists into conversation with European country specialists; it enables us to reflect on the interactions between state-society complexes in China and state-society complexes in Europe in influencing the international order (see Figure I.1).

Methodology

The modes of influence explored in this volume emerged through empirical observation and process-tracing. Given the access to and knowledge of target actors, complex decision-making processes within states, and the underlying state-society complexes required by the analysis offered here, most of our contributors are country specialists. They investigate the impact of China's presence in their respective countries of specialization and chart the influence of these impacts on the LIO. Additionally, we have a group of China specialists among our contributors who help us understand China's intentions and the underlying state-society complexes. Far from aspiring to be comprehensive in our coverage, we have aimed to focus on one aspect of China's presence in Europe: its economic investments in the different countries of that continent. The reason for this focus is straightforward: China's overseas economic investments are the origin of the whole debate on its rise. As shown above, China's economic power is the key underlying assumption of the analyses of Chinese power in relation to the LIO, as it is fungible and can potentially be translated into other forms of power, most noticeably military power.

Contributing authors were tasked with six undertakings:

(1) Identify, based on their specialist knowledge of specific countries, the extent to which their *extant* preferences converge with, or diverge from, the LIO;
(2) Examine, based on their expertise on the bilateral relations between China and the relevant country, the extent to which Chinese investments in that country translate into political influence over the extant preference (whatever that is);
(3) Trace the processes through which key actors in states and societies of the target countries negotiate China's influence;
(4) Analyse whether political influence exerted by China results in the formation of new preferences or the consolidation of existing preferences within the target countries;
(5) Establish whether these new preferences (if any) diverge from or converge with China's preferences;
(6) Analyse their implications on the liberal underpinnings of the international order.

The aim through the contributions is to examine the implications of Chinese investments in Europe for the LIO. This aim is achieved by uncovering connecting and causal processes between applications of Chinese resources and the shaping of preferences among states and societies in Europe, where liberal ideals, norms, and practices are expected to be strongest. Each case study specifies the domain of Chinese investments, describes China's objectives, identifies the Chinese and European actors involved, and explores China's intentionality vis-à-vis the outcomes of its specific European investments and the broader Liberal International Order. In exploring causality, each study directs close attention to the *targets* of Chinese influence to examine the extent to which their extant preferences converge with, or diverge from, the LIO, and the specific ways in which these preferences may be consolidated, undermined, or unaffected by Chinese investments.

Two sets of dynamics recur throughout the chapters: the role of domestic state-society relationships in the bilateral relationships, and the broader question of Chinese intentionality vis-à-vis the international order. Each study analyses the role of state-society relations in shaping the influence of Chinese investments on bilateral relations. Every single one of the authors also reflects, side by side, on China's intentionality (if any) vis-à-vis the LIO, driving home the larger point that such intentionality cannot be taken for granted. Our methodological approach of studying influence through process-tracing alerts us to its mutually generative aspect rather than it being uni-directional. Influence does not always bring about new change, as the cases reveal, but it may reinforce continuity or consolidate changes already in progress.

The cases analysed in this volume range from major developed economies in western Europe, such as Britain and Germany, to other less developed economies in southern and eastern Europe, such as Hungary and Greece. These cases exemplify a 'diverse' approach to descriptive case studies (Gerring and Cojocaru, 2016) in which a small basket of diverse cases is selected from a larger population of potential cases in order to capture variations. The diversity of cases examined in this volume includes countries as varied as the Visegrad group, the Western Balkans, Italy, and Romania. The cases illustrate the impact of China's engagements with diverse 'varieties of capitalism' (Hall and Soskice, 2001).

The Contribution of this Volume

This volume is structured in three parts. Its structure is consistent with our conceptual framing of power as influence. The contributions by Yu Jie and Ran Hu in Part One reflect on the ways in which China's domestic politics influence its foreign investments and, by extension, the LIO. These two chapters adopt an inside-out approach and examine the actual policymaking process with reference to BRI. Yu's chapter utilizes a Bureaucratic Politics Model to explain the intricate relations among the party, policymaking institutions, and policy execution entities. Hu's chapter employs the concept of state transformation to lay bare the fragmented and contested emerging process of BRI. Both chapters recognize that the 'intricate' or 'contested' domestic politics have complicated China's effort to challenge the LIO and that how other states respond to China's strategies also shape the future of the LIO. These responses are explored by contributors in Parts Two and Three of the volume.

The contributions in Part Two investigate the ways in which China's bilateral investments in Europe contribute to straining the liberal aspects of the international order. Ágnes Szunomár's study of the 'special relationship' between China and Hungary demonstrates the 'alignment and amplification of preferences' between the illiberal rationales of the two countries. Filippo Boni's study finds an uptake among some (not all) political elites in Italy of China's narratives on key issues such as Xinjiang and Hong Kong, suggesting that the operation of 'discursive persuasion' is at work. Elements of 'preference multiplying' and 'persuasion' are evident in Dimitrios Stroikos's study of China-Greece relations from 2016 to 2019, when on a few occasions Greece's position diverged greatly from EU's China policy. Drawing on her study of China's involvement in the Visegrad group of Central and Eastern European (CEE) countries, Malgorzata Jakimów's study finds evidence of 'institutional shaping' through the adoption by these countries of some (not all) China-promoted norms. Similar evidence of 'institution shaping' is offered by Nicholas Crawford's study of the Western Balkans, although it is only Serbia's foreign policy that appears to converge with China's. Each of these studies is careful to point out the limits to China's influence: even as Chinese investments in Europe may be contributing to straining the liberal elements of the international order, they are (yet) far from successful.

The contributions in Part Three examine the alternative position: that China's bilateral investments in Europe strengthen, rather than strain, the international order, *including* its liberal aspects. Through an analysis of the bilateral energy relations between China and the UK and China and Romania, Simona Davidescu's study offers evidence of how China's investments were initially framed in purely economic terms, as a way to strengthen liberal institutional commitments to sustainability. Jan Knoerich's study on Chinese foreign direct investments demonstrates China's commitment to rules-based financial transactions. Taking a broader view, Catherine Jones's study shows that China's presence as a development actor means that it acts as a catalyst to enable the continuation of liberal patterns of aid and investment.

The conclusion distils key findings from across the three sections and explores ways in which the influence of Chinese investments entwines with the agency of state and social actors in Europe to impact the Liberal International Order. It reiterates the disjunctions between China's global intentions, its actions in Europe, and its effects on the LIO. The conclusion outlines these varied impacts, reminding us of the ways in which Chinese investments in Europe could strain as well as strengthen the LIO, without intending to do either. It will also propose areas of future focus based on the theoretical, conceptual, and empirical arguments of the contributions.

Bibliography

Allan, B., S. Vucetic, and T. Hopf. 2018. 'The Distribution of Identity and the Future of International Order: China's Hegemonic Prospects'. *International Organization* 72 (4): pp. 839–869.

Allison, G. 2017. *Destined for War: Can America and China Escape Thucydides's Trap?* Boston: Houghton Mifflin Harcourt.

Arrighi, G. 2007. *Adam Smith in Beijing: Lineages of the Twenty-First Century.* London: Verso.

Bachrach, P., and M. Baratz. 1962. 'Two Faces of Power'. *The American Political Science Review* 56 (4): 947–952.

Berenskoetter, F. 2007. 'Thinking about Power'. In *Power in World Politics*, edited by F. Berenskoetter and M. J. Williams. pp. 1–22. London: Routledge.

Berenskoetter, F., and M. J. Williams. 2007. eds. *Power in World Politics.* London: Routledge.

Bhattacharya, A. 2016. 'Conceptualising the Silk Road Initiative in China's Periphery Policy'. *East Asia* 33 (4): pp. 309–328.

Bordet, M. 2011. 'La Chine rachète l'europe'. *Le Point*, 22 September. Available at: https://www.lepoint.fr/economie/la-chine-rachete-l-europe-22-09-2011-1380187_28.php [Accessed 17 May 2021].

Breslin, S. 2013. 'China and the Global Order: Signaling Threat or Friendship?'. *International Affairs* 89 (3): pp. 615–634.

Burgoon, B., and D. Raess. 2014. 'Chinese Investment and European Labour: Should and Do Workers Fear Chinese FDI?'. *Asia Europe Journal* 12 (1–2): pp. 179–197.

Busse, C. et al. 2020. 'Policy Intentions Mapping'. European Council on Foreign Relations. Available at: https://ecfr.eu/special/eucoalitionexplorer/policy_intentions_mapping/ [Accessed 14 May 2021].

Buzan, B. 2010. 'China in International Society: Is "Peaceful Rise" Possible?'. *The Chinese Journal of International Politics* 3 (1): pp. 5–36.

Buzan, B. 2018. 'China's Rise in English School Perspective'. *International Relations of the Asia-Pacific* 18 (3): pp. 449–476.

Callahan, W. 2016. 'China's Belt and Road Initiative and the New Eurasian Order'. *Policy Brief* 22: pp. 1–4.

Cavanna, T. 2018. 'Unlocking the gates of Eurasia: China's Belt and Road Initiative and its implications for US Grand Strategy. *Texan National Security Review* 22 (3): 11–37.

Centre for Economics and Business Research (CEBR). 2020. World Economic League Table 2021. Available at: https://cebr.com/service/macroeconomic-forecasting/ [Accessed 13 May 2021].

Chen, H. 2016. '"Yidai yilu" jianshe: jiang zuowei wo duiwai kaifang dingceng sheji. [The Construction of Belt and Road Initiative: To Serve as the Top Design of China's Opening to the World]'. December. Available at: http://epaper.gmw.cn/gmrb/html/2016-12/27/nw.D110000gmrb_20161227_6-11.htm [Accessed 2 April 2021].

Chhabra, T. 2019. *The China Challenge, Democracy, and US Grand Strategy*. Washington DC: Brookings.

Ciorciari, J. 2016. 'China's Influence in Asian Monetary Policy Affairs'. In *Rising China's Influence in Developing Asia*, edited by E. Goh, pp. 217–235. Oxford: Oxford University Press.

Cooley, A., and D. H. Nexon. 2020. 'How Hegemony Ends: The Unravelling of American Power'. *Foreign Affairs* 99 (4): pp. 143–156.

Cox, R. 1987 *Production, Power, and World Order: Social Forces in the Making of History*. New York: Columbia University Press.

Cox, R., and H. Jacobson. 1973. *The Anatomy of Influence: Decision-Making in International Organization*. New Haven: Yale University Press.

da Conceição-heldt, E. 2013. 'Two-Level Games and Trade Cooperation: What Do We Now Know?'. *International Politics* 50 (4): pp. 579–599.

Dahl, R. 1957. 'The Concept of Power,' *Behavioral Science* 2(3): 201–215.

Dahl, R., and B. Stinebrickner. 2003. *Modern Political Analysis*. 6th edn. New Jersey: Prentice Hall.

Deudney, D., and G. J. Ikenberry. 2018. 'Liberal World: The Resilient Order'. *Foreign Affairs* 97 (4): pp. 16–24.

Doshi, R. 2021. *The Long Game: China's Grand Strategy to Displace American Order*. New York: Oxford University Press.

Du, D., and Y. Ma. 2014. 'Yidai yilu': zhonghua minzu fuxing de diyuan dazhanlue. [One Belt and One Road: The Grand Geo-Strategy of China's Rise]'. *Dili Yanjiu* [Geographical Research] 34 (6): pp. 1005–1014.

de Graaff, N. 2020. 'China Inc. Goes Global. Transnational and National Networks of China's Globalizing Business Elite'. *Review of International Political Economy* 27 (2): pp. 208–233.

de Graaff, N., T. ten Brink, and I. Parmar. 2020. 'China's Rise in a Liberal World Order in Transition—Introduction to the FORUM'. *Review of International Political Economy* 27 (2): pp. 191–207.

EU Commission. 2019. *EU-China—A Strategic Outlook*. Joint Communication to the European Parliament, the European Council and the Council. Strasbourg, 3 December 2019.

Fallon, T. 2015. 'The New Silk Road: Xi Jinping's Grand Strategy for Eurasia'. *American Foreign Policy Interests* 37 (3): pp. 140–147.

Fasslabend, W. 2015. 'The Silk Road: A Political Marketing Concept for World Dominance'. *European View* 14 (2): pp. 293–302.

Foot, R. 2006. 'Chinese Strategies in a US-Hegemonic Global Order: Accommodating and Hedging'. *International Affairs* 82 (1): pp. 77–94.

Foot, R. 2014. 'Doing Some Things' in the Xi Jinping Era: The United Nations as China's Venue of Choice'. *International Affairs* 90 (5): pp. 1085–1100.

Foot, R., and R. Inboden. 2016. 'China's Influence on Asian States During the Creation of the UN Human Rights Council: 2005–2007'. In *Rising China's Influence In Developing Asia*, edited by E. Goh, pp. 237–256. Oxford: Oxford University Press.

Ford, J., and L. Hughes. 2020. 'UK-China Relations: From 'Golden Era' to the Deep Freeze'. *Financial Times.* [Online] Available at: https://www.ft.com/content/804175d0-8b47-4427-9853-2aded76f48e4 [Accessed 11 May 2021].

Fravel, M. T. 2010. 'International Relations Theory and China's Rise: Assessing China's Potential for Territorial Expansion'. *International Studies Review* 12 (4): pp. 202–532.

Geaney, D. 2020. 'China's Island Fortifications Are a Challenge to International Norms'. *Defense News.* Available at: https://www.defensenews.com/opinion/commentary/2020/04/17/chinas-island-fortifications-are-a-challenge-to-international-norms/ [Accessed 14 May 2021].

Gerring, J., and L. Cojocaru. 2016. *Sociological Methods & Research.* 45(3): 392–423.

Glaser, C. 2011. 'Will China's Rise Lead to War? Why Realism Does Not Mean Pessimism'. *Foreign Affairs* 90 (2): pp. 80–91.

Godement, F., and A. Kratz. 2015. *'One Belt, One Road': China's Great Leap Outward.* European Council on Foreign Relations and Asia Centre.

Godement, F., and J. Parello-Plesner. 2011. *The Scramble for Europe.* European Council on Foreign Relations.

Goh, E. 2014. 'The Modes of China's Influence: Cases from Southeast Asia'. *Asian Survey* 54 (5): pp. 825–848.

Goh, E. 2016. 'Introduction'. In *Rising China's Influence in Developing Asia*, edited by E. Goh, pp. 1–23. Oxford: Oxford University Press.

Hagmann, T., and D. Péclard. 2010. 'Negotiating Statehood: Dynamics of Power and Domination in Africa'. *Development and Change* 41(40): 539–562.

Hall P., and D. Soskice. 2001. *Varieties of Capitalism: The Institutional Foundations of Comparative Advantage.* Oxford: Oxford University Press.

Hanemann, T. 2014. 'Chinese Direct Investment in the EU and the US: A Comparative View'. *Asia Europe Journal* 12 (1–2): pp. 127–142.

Helleiner, E., and J. Kirshner, eds. 2014. *The Great Wall of Money: Power and Politics in China's International Monetary Relations.* Ithaca and London: Cornell University Press.

Helleiner, E., and A. Malkin. 2012. 'Sectoral Interests and Global Money: Renminbi, Dollars and the Domestic Foundations of International Currency Policy'. *Open Economies Review* 23 (1): pp. 33–55.

Huo, S., and I. Parmar. 2020. '"A New Type of Great Power Relationship"? Gramsci, Kautsky and the Role of The Ford Foundation's Transformational Elite Knowledge Networks in China'. *Review of International Political Economy* 27 (2): pp. 234–257

Ikenberry, G. J. 2008. 'The Rise of China and the Future of the West: Can the Liberal System Survive'. *Foreign Affairs* 87 (1): pp. 23–37.

Ikenberry, G. J. 2009. 'Liberal Internationalism 3.0: America and the Dilemmas of Liberal World Order'. *Perspectives on Politics* 7 (1): pp. 71–87.

Ikenberry, G. J. 2011. 'The Future of the World Order: Internationalism after America'. *Foreign Affairs* 90 (3): pp. 56–68.

Ikenberry, G. J. 2014. 'The Illusion of Geopolitics: The Enduring Power of the Liberal Order'. *Foreign Affairs* 93 (3): pp. 80–91.

Ikenberry, G. J. 2017. 'The End of Liberal International Order?'. *International Affairs* 94 (1): pp. 7–23.

Ikenberry, G. J. 2018. 'Why the Liberal World Order Will Survive'. *Ethics and International Affairs* 32 (1): pp. 17–29.

Jackson, G., and R. Deeg. 2006. 'How Many Varieties of Capitalism? Comparing the Comparative Institutional Analyses of Capitalist Diversity'. *MPIfG Discussion Paper* 06/2, pp. 1–48.

Jacques, M. 2009. *When China Rules the World: The Rise of the Middle Kingdom and the End of the Western World*. London: Penguin Books.

Jones, L., and J. Zeng, 2019. 'Understanding China's "Belt and Road Initiative": Beyond "Grand Strategy" to a State Transformation Analysis'. *Third World Quarterly* 40 (8): pp. 1415–1439.

Kai, J. 2015. 'Are We Living in a 'Chinese Century?'. *The Diplomat*, 23 January. Available at: https://thediplomat.com/2015/01/are-we-living-in-a-chinese-century/ [Accessed 17 May 2021].

Katzenstein, P. J. 1976. 'International Relations and Domestic Structures: Foreign Economic Policies of Advanced Industrial States'. *International Organization* 30 (1): pp. 1–45.

Katzenstein, P. J. ed. 1978. *Between Power and Plenty: Foreign Economic Policies of Advanced Industrial States*. Madison: University of Wisconsin Press.

Katzenstein, P. J. 1985. *Small States in World Markets: Industrial Policy in Europe*. Ithaca: Cornell University Press.

Khalilzad, Z. 2017. 'The Case for Congagement with China'. *The National Interest*. Available at: https://nationalinterest.org/feature/the-case-congagement-china-21232. [Accessed 16 April 2021].

Knoerich, J., and T. Miedtank. 2018. 'The Idiosyncratic Nature of Chinese Foreign Direct Investment in Europe'. *CESifo Forum* 19 (4): pp. 3–8.

Krickovic, A. 2017. 'The Symbiotic China-Russia Partnership: Cautious Riser and Desperate Challenger'. *Chinese Journal of International Politics* 10 (3): pp. 299–329.

Kristof, N. 1993. 'The Rise of China'. *Foreign Affairs* 72 (5): pp. 59–74.

Lampert, B. and Mohan, G. (2018). 'A transformative presence? Chinese migrants as agents of change in Ghana and Nigeria'. In *Chinese and African Entrepreneurs: Social Impacts of Interpersonal Encounters.* edited by Giese, Karsten and Marfaing, Laurence. Leiden: Brill, pp. 147–169.

Larson, D. W. 2015. 'Will China Be a New Type of Great Power?', *The Chinese Journal of International Politics* 8 (4): pp. 323–348.

Layne, C. 2018. 'The US-Chinese Power Shift and the End of the Pax Americana'. *International Affairs* 94 (1): pp. 89–111.

Leverett, F., and B. Wu. 2017. 'The New Silk Road and China's Evolving Grand Strategy'. *The China Journal* 77: pp. 110–132.

Lieber, R. 2014. 'The Rise of the BRICS and American Primacy'. *International Politics* 51 (2): pp. 137–154.

Liff, A. P. 2016. 'Whither the Balancers? The Case for a Methodological Reset'. *Security Studies* 25 (3): pp. 420–459.

Lukes, S. 1974. *Power: A Radical View.* Basingstoke: Palgrave Macmillan.

Lukes, S. 2005. *Power: A Radical View.* 2nd edn. Basingstoke, Palgrave Macmillan.

L'Express. 2011. Comment la Chine envahit l'Europe. 4 February.

Macaes, B. 2018. *Belt and Road: A Chinese World Order.* London: Hurst and Company.

McNally, C. 2012. 'Sino-Capitalism: China's Reemergence and the International Political Economy'. *World Politics* 64 (4): pp. 741–776.

McNally, C. 2020. 'Chaotic Mélange: Neo-Liberalism and Neo-Statism in the Age of Sino-Capitalism'. *Review of International Political Economy* 27 (2): pp. 281–301.

Mearsheimer, J. 2001. *The Tragedy of Great Power Politics.* New York: W. W. Norton.

Mearsheimer, J. 2010. 'The Gathering Storm: China's Challenge to US Power in Asia'. *Chinese Journal of International Politics* 3 (4): pp. 381–396.

Mearsheimer, J. 2019. 'Bound to Fail: The Rise and Fall of the Liberal International Order'. *International Security* 43 (4): pp. 7–50.

Meunier, S. 2014a. 'A Faustian Bargain or Just a Good Bargain? Chinese Foreign Direct Investment and Politics in Europe'. *Asia Europe Journal* 12 (1–2): pp. 143–158.

Meunier, S. 2014b. '"Beggars Can't Be Choosers": The European Crisis and Chinese Direct Investment in the European Union'. *Journal of European Integration* 36 (3): pp. 283–302.

Meunier, S. 2014c. 'Divide And Conquer? China and the Cacophony of Foreign Investment Rules in the EU'. *Journal of European Public Policy* 21 (7): pp. 996–1016.

Meunier, S., B. Burgoon, and W. Jacoby. 2014. 'The Politics of Hosting Chinese Investment in Europe—An Introduction'. *Asia Europe Journal* 12 (1–2): pp. 109–126.

Miller, T. 2017. *China's Asian Dream: Quiet Empire Building Along the New Silk Road*. London: Zed Books.

Mills, C. 1956. *The Power Elite*. Oxford: Oxford University Press.

Mitter, R. 2021. 'The World China Wants: How Power Will—and Won't—Reshape Chinese Ambitions'. *Foreign Affairs* 100 (1): pp. 161–175.

Montgomery, E. 2014. 'Contested Primacy in the Western Pacific: China's Rise and the Future of U.S. Power Projection'. *International Security* 38 (4): pp. 115–149.

Nölke, A. 2012. 'The Rise of the "B(R)IC Variety of Capitalism": Towards a New Phase of Organized Capitalism?'. In *Neoliberalism in Crisis*, edited by H. Overbeek and B. Apeldoorn. Houndmills: Palgrave Macmillan, pp. 117–137

Nölke, A. 2015. 'Second Image Revisited: The Domestic Sources of China's Foreign Economic Policies'. *International Politics* 52 (6): pp. 657–665.

Nölke, A. et al. 2015. 'Domestic Structures, Foreign Economic Policies and Global Economic Order: Implications from the Rise of Large Emerging Economies'. *European Journal of International Relations* 21 (3): pp. 538–567.

Nye, J. 1997. 'China's Re-Emergence and the Future of the Asia-Pacific'. *Survival* 39 (4): pp. 65–79.

Oertel, J. 2020. 'The New China Consensus: How Europe Is Growing Wary of Beijing'. European Council on Foreign Relations. Available at: https://ecfr.eu/publication/the_new_china_consensus_how_europe_is_growing_wary_of_beijing/ [Accessed 14 May 2021].

Overbeek, H. 2004. 'Transnational Class Formation and Concepts of Control: Towards a Genealogy of the Amsterdam Project in International Political Economy'. *Journal of International Relations and Development* 7 (2): p. 113–141.

Pavlićević, D. 2019. 'Structural Power and the China-EU-Western Balkans Triangular Relations'. *Asia Europe Journal* 17 (4): pp. 453–468.

Putnam, R. 1988. 'Diplomacy and Domestic Politics: The Logic of Two-Level Games'. *International Organization* 42 (3): pp. 427–460.

Rapkin, D., and W. Thompson, 2003. 'Power Transition, Challenge and the (Re)Emergence of China'. *International Interactions* 29 (4): pp. 315–324.

Rees-Mogg, W. 2005. 'This Is the Chinese Century'. *The Times*. [Online]. Available at: 3 January 2005, https://www.thetimes.co.uk/article/this-is-the-chinese-century-3fbqb8qz7tk [Accessed 15 May 2021]

Renminwang. 2013. 'Xi Jinping zai zhoubian waijiao gongzuo zuotanhui shang fabiao zhongyao jianghua [Xi Jinping Makes Important Remarks at A Conference on the Diplomatic Work with Neighbouring Countries]'. Available at: http://politics.people.com.cn/n/2013/1025/c1024-23332318.html [Accessed 15 May 2021].

Roy, D. 1994. 'Hegemon on the Horizon? China's Threat to East Asian Security'. *International Security* 19 (1): pp. 149–168.

Schake, K. 2017. *Safe Passage: The Transition from British to American Hegemony*. Cambridge: Harvard University Press.

Schirm, S. 2013. 'Global Politics Are Domestic Politics: A Societal Approach to Divergence in the G20'. *Review of International Studies* 39 (3): pp. 685–706.

Schweller, R. L., and X. Pu. 2011. 'After Unipolarity: China's Visions of International Order in an Era of U.S. Decline'. *International Security* 36 (1): pp. 41–72.

Scobell, A., E, Burke, C., Cooper III, S. Lilly, C. Ohlandt, E. Warner and J. Williams. 2020. China's Grand Strategy: Trends, Trajectories and Long-term Competition. Santa Monica, California: RAND Corporation, accessed: https://www.rand.org/content/dam/rand/pubs/research_reports/RR2700/RR2798/RAND_RR2798.pdf

Segal, G. 1999. 'Does China Matter?'. *Foreign Affairs* 78 (5): pp. 24–36.

Shambaugh, D. 2004. 'China Engages Asia: Reshaping the Regional Order'. *International Security* 29 (3): pp. 64–99.

Shambaugh, D. 2013. *China Goes Global: The Partial Power*. Oxford: Oxford University Press.

Silver, L., K. Devlin, and C. Huang. 2020. *Unfavourable Views of China Reach Historic Highs in Many Countries*. Oct 2020 Pew Research Centre.

Solomon, E., and G. Chazan. 2020. '"We Need a Real Policy for China": Germany Ponders'. *Financial Times*. Available at: https://www.ft.com/content/0de447eb-999d-452f-a1c9-d235cc5ea6d9 [Accessed 11 May 2021].

Stephen, M. 2014a. 'States, Norms and Power: Emerging Powers and Global Order'. *Millennium* 42 (3): pp. 888–890.

Stephen, M. 2014b. 'Rising Powers, Global Capitalism and Liberal Global Governance: A Historical Materialist Account of the BRICS Challenge'. *European Journal of International Relations* 20 (4): pp. 912–938.

Stiglitz, J. 2014. 'The Chinese Century'. *Vanity Fair*. Available at: https://www.vanityfair.com/news/2015/01/china-worlds-largest-economy [Accessed 17 May 2021].

Strange, G. 2011. 'China's Post-Listian Rise: Beyond Radical Globalisation Theory and the Political Economy of Neoliberal Hegemony'. *New Political Economy* 16 (5): pp. 539–559.

Sørensen, C. 2015. 'The Significance of Xi Jinping's "Chinese Dream" for Chinese Foreign Policy: From "Tao Guang Yang Hui" to "Fen Fa You Wei"'. *Journal of China and International Relations* 3 (1): pp. 53–73.

Tang, S. 2018. 'China and the Future International Order(s)'. *Ethics and International Affairs* 32 (1): pp. 31–43.

Tangen, O. 2020. 'Is China Taking Advantage of COVID-19 to Pursue South China Sea Ambitions?'. *Deutsche Welle*. Available at: https://www.dw.com/en/is-china-taking-advantage-of-covid-19-to-pursue-south-china-sea-ambitions/a-53573918 [Accessed 14 May 2021].

The Economist. 2018. 'The Chinese Century is Well Under Way'. Available at: https://www.economist.com/graphic-detail/2018/10/27/the-chinese-century-is-well-under-way [Accessed 13 May 2021].

Thurow, L. 2007. 'A Chinese Century? Maybe It's the Next One'. *The New York Times*. Available at: https://www.nytimes.com/2007/08/19/business/yourmoney/19view.html [Accessed 17 May 2021].

Wade, R. 2003. *Governing the Market: Economic Theory and the Role of Government in East Asian Industrialization*. Princeton: Princeton University Press.

Waltz, K. 1959. *Man, the State, and War*. New York. Columbia University Press.

Wang, Y. 2018. 'Wang Yi zai di 73 jie lianheguo dahui yibanxing bianlun shangde jianghua. [Statement by Wang Yi at the General Debate of the 73rd Session of the UN General Assembly]'. Available at: http://www.gov.cn/guowuyuan/2018-09/29/content_5326793.htm [Accessed 14 May 2021].

Weinhardt, C., and T. ten Brink. 2020. 'Varieties of Contestation: China's Rise and the Liberal Trade Order'. *Review of International Political Economy* 27 (2): pp. 258–280.

Wight, C. 1999. 'They shoot dead horses don't they? Locating agency in the agent-structure problematique'. *European Journal of International Relations* 5 (1): 109–142.

Wight, C. 2004. 'State agency: social action without human activity', *Review of International Studies* 30 (20): 269–280.

Wright, T. 2018. 'The Return to Great-Power Rivalry Was Inevitable'. *The Atlantic*. [Online]. Available at: https://www.theatlantic.com/international/archive/2018/09/liberal-international-order-free-world-trump-authoritarianism/569881/ [Accessed 12 May 2021].

Xi, J. 2017. 'Xi Jinping zai shijie jingji luntan 2017 nianhui kaimushi shangde zhuzhi yanjiang'. [President Xi Addressed the Opening Ceremony of World Economic Forum Annual Meeting 2017]. [Online]. Available at: http://www.fmprc.gov.cn/web/ziliao_674904/zyjh_674906/t1431319.shtml [Accessed 17 May 2021].

Xi, J. 2021. 'Xi Jinping zai shijie jingji luntan "dawosi yicheng" duihuahui shangde tebie zhici [President Xi addresses the World Economic Forum Virtual Event of the Davos Agenda]'. Renmin Ribao [People's Daily], 26 January 2021, p. 2.

Xu, L., and X. Wang. 2016. '"Yidai yilu" yu Xi Jinping de waijiao zhanlue shixiang'. ["BRI" and Xi Jinping's diplomatic thought]. *Journal of Beijing University of Technology* 16 (4): pp. 34–44.

Yan, X. 2001. 'The Rise of China in Chinese Eyes'. *Journal of Contemporary China* 10 (26): pp. 33–39.

Yan, X. 2010. 'The Instability of China-US Relations'. *Chinese Journal of International Politics* 3 (3): pp. 263–292.

Yan, X. 2014. 'From Keeping a Low Profile to Striving for Achievement'. *The Chinese Journal of International Politics* 7 (2): pp. 153–184.

Zakaria, F. 2020. 'The New China Scare: Why America Shouldn't Panic about Its Latest Challenger'. *Foreign Affairs* 99 (1): pp. 52–69.

Zeng, K., and W. Liang, eds. 2013. *China and Global Trade Governance: China's First Decade in the World Trade Organization*. London: Routledge.

Zhang, H. and D. Van Den Bulcke. 2014. 'China's Direct Investment in the European Union: A New Regulatory Challenge?'. *Asia Europe Journal* 12 (1–2): pp. 159–177.

1

Country, Corporates, and the Construct of BRI

The Roles of Chinese State-Owned Enterprises

Yu Jie

Introduction

This chapter seeks to discuss to what extent Chinese companies, mostly state-owned enterprises (SOEs), have become formidable players in challenging the so-called Liberal International Order (LIO).[1] In particular, it aims to explore the evolving relationships between the Chinese companies and the Chinese central government as Beijing pursues its flagship Belt and Road Initiative (BRI).

It intends to analyse whether Chinese SOEs have become a source of destabilizing the existing Liberal International Order and acted as a vehicle of delivering Beijing's geopolitical ambition through the participation in the BRI.

The conventional wisdom from Europe is that those Chinese SOEs are acting on behalf of the state. Yet, this conventional wisdom needs to be challenged by examining what the Chinese SOEs have done in the process of pursing the BRI in Europe. This chapter departs from most existing literature on BRI in Europe, which mostly focuses upon the geo-economic and geo-political impacts of the BRI.

Instead, it adopts an 'inside-out' approach by examining the actual policy process with a primary focus on individual actors such as the Party, the government departments, and the Chinese state-owned companies. It also disentangles the intricate relations amongst the Party, the key decision-making institutions, and the policy execution entities in determining the final outcome of the BRI.

[1] The author is senior research fellow on China in the Asia-Pacific Programme at Chatham House, and associate fellow of LSE IDEAS.

Yu Jie, *Country, Corporates, and the Construct of BRI*. In: *Rising Power, Limited Influence*. Edited by: Indrajit Roy, Jappe Eckhardt, Dimitrios Stroikos, and Simona Davidescu, Oxford University Press.
DOI: 10.1093/oso/9780192887115.003.0002

After ten years of implementation, the BRI is riding high and low with numerous criticisms from both Western liberal democracies and some recipient countries. Much of the criticism has focused on the role of China's state capital in providing project finance, which put some Chinese state-owned companies in the limelight. Most of the existing literature concurs that the Chinese SOEs are unilaterally following the executive orders from central government to fulfil the Chinese leaders' ambition to project Beijing's political influence.

However, it is simplistic to draw the above conclusion given the numbers of SOEs already involved in infrastructure projects across different continents. Many of the existing projects are now considered under the umbrella of BRI; some others have been newly added either to fit into Beijing's wishes or to profit from the existing project networks on the ground.

As China gradually emerges from the COVID-19 pandemic into a tougher international environment, a new concept has emerged: the 'dual circulation' strategy, which promotes domestic demand to displace the old motors of the Chinese economy—capital investment and exports—as the source of growth and employment in decades to come. By implementing this strategy, it also requires state capital and SOEs to redistribute their financial resources and manpower back to the domestic market (SCMP, 2020). As a result, this will lead to a scale-back of the BRI investments by Chinese SOEs which have frequently made headlines across the world in recent years.

This chapter will firstly examine some elements of the Liberal International Order that are related to Chinese SOEs' overseas economic activities. Instead of examining the implications of Chinese SOEs' investments as most of the existing literature has done, it focuses on individual players within the Chinese political establishments, and investigates the process of decision-making in investments under the umbrella of the BRI. It utilizes the Bureaucratic Politics Model to analyse the evolving relationships amongst the Party, the central government, and the SOEs in the process of delivering BRI projects. This chapter also aims to offer a nascent assessment of the implementation of the 'dual circulation strategy' in determining future BRI investments by the Chinese SOEs.

What Is Order, What Does China Do?

'Order' is defined as an emergent property of interaction of many actors in a system. As Ikenberry and Nathan have noted, in the current international system 'order' includes norms, rules, institutions, and practices that are products of the behaviour of everything from state apparatus to the non-governmental organizations to multinational corporations to inter-governmental organizations to individual thought leaders (Ikenberry, 2018: 20; Nathan, 2016: 167).

Given this myriad of players with different interests and norms, the outcomes of their interactions are bound to be complex or even contradictory. One should expect to see 'issue-specific' orders where the key norms and institutions that regulate entities' behaviour vary depending on the issue area, such as territory integrity, trade, environment, and political rights.

Across many aspects of 'order', the dominant norms are substantially different or contested within each other. Many scholars have pointed out that 'China's compliance with "order" like that many other countries, largely varied depending on which order to be considered' (Foot and Walter, 2011; Johnston, 2019).

There is no singular 'liberal international order', but there are multiple orders, some of which China strongly supports, some of which it strongly opposes, and some of which China has shifted its position from one to the other. As a result, simply asserting that China seeks to challenge 'rule-based international order' is a binary conceptual misunderstanding.

When it comes to implementation of the Belt and Road initiative, China's behaviour has become equally difficult to assess in terms of whether it follows the 'rule-based international order' or seeks to overthrow it completely. Given the limited space of this chapter, it chiefly focuses on whether Chinese state-owned companies, in conducting the BRI, have acted as accelerators to help Beijing in overthrowing that 'order'.

The Party, BRI, and the Chinese Companies

The Party has an omnipresent role in every aspect of policymaking within the Chinese political system. Foreign policy and the advocacy of BRI are no exceptions. The seven members of the Standing Committee of the CCP Politburo and the State Council generally set key strategic guidelines, or long-term policy goals, for China's foreign affairs; however, more specific policy measures are mostly made and implemented by the various governmental ministries and state-owned corporations. The making of Chinese foreign policy has become an increasingly crowded playground for various equally powerful stakeholders competing for their departmental interests, like in any Western democracy.

China's foreign policy formulation has become increasingly pluralistic compared to the one of Mao's era. A process of decentralization in decision-making has occurred since the 1978 Economic Reforms. As a result, there has been no single bureaucratic body that has supreme authority over the others when it comes to making certain decisions. Almost all bureaucracies and other players have utilized their resources and expertise to gain access to the highest level of Party elites in the search for more political clout and greater budgetary power.

Vested interest groups have played a significant part in the Chinese political system since 1978. As Graham Allison argued in his interpretation of the Cuban Missile Crisis, whilst the rules of the game might play out very differently in a democratic elected government, the fundamental characteristics of bureaucratic competition remain the same regardless of the type of government (Allison, 1969: 689; Halperin and Claap, 1974: 23).

Bureaucratic Politics Model and China's Foreign Policy Decision-Making

One can argue that the Bureaucratic Politics Model (BPM) is largely applicable to liberal democracies with multiparty systems to satisfy the electorates' interests. Therefore, there are numerous interest groups across the whole political spectrum which are making many attempts to shape foreign policies according to their desired outcomes. China, as an authoritarian state, is conventionally perceived as monolithic, and therefore does not have interest groups which could oppose or influence decisions made by the Standing Committee of the Politburo (SCP).

However, the phenomenon of bureaucratic politics, as described by Graham Allison and Morton Halperin, has not restricted its application to a particular political system, and vested interest groups do play a significant part across the Chinese political system (Ibid; Ibid).

The relevance of BPM to interpreting the Chinese political system and the formation of BRI is twofold. Firstly, almost every domestic or external affairs decision made is based on a desire to achieve a consensus amongst the seven or nine members of the SCP, even if such consensus is sometimes merely an illusion. This consensus-seeking model has provided a unique opportunity to those potential interest groups seeking to influence the opinions of SCP members. Bargaining scenarios have often occurred in a process of consensus seeking amongst interest groups.

These interest groups may be located both inside and outside of the formal foreign policymaking process. They mainly consist of governmental institutions, Chinese companies, and even some foreign corporate organizations to a smaller extent. They attempt to formulate Chinese foreign policy based on their departmental preferences and corporate interests respectively. More importantly, none of the current seven members of the SCP have much experience in foreign policymaking. This in turn has provided relevant Chinese foreign-policy actors with more channels and alternatives with which to shape Beijing's agenda.

Secondly, Chinese foreign policy has increased in scope and content, which has created fertile ground for the various stakeholders and interest groups to compete to shape the policy agenda via various channels.

Like the implementation of any Chinese policy, the cornerstones are laid on the domestic front. Dramatic changes in the distribution of power and devolution of authority within Chinese bureaucracies have been happening since Deng Xiaoping's momentous economic reforms.

Competing Interests in the Formation of the Belt and Road Initiative

The BRI is one of the best illustrations, perhaps the best, of institutional power distribution below the top Party leadership. Central ministries and provincial governments have scrambled to give BRI a meaning, gauge what it means for them, and, most importantly, ascertain how BRI could be used to get hold of or justify the use of project funds.

Many old 'China hands' in the West and home-grown Chinese scholars still dispute who makes Chinese foreign policy and why there are so many new institutions with obscure names proliferating across the Chinese foreign-policy formation process (Economy, 2014: 82; Lieberthal and Lampton, 1992; Miller, 2015; Zhang, 2021). The answers to these questions are far from clear. Neither China specialists in the West nor the home-grown scholars in China have given satisfactory responses over a long period of time (Lu, 1997; Zhang, 2014; Zhao, 2022).

The advocacy of the BRI has also triggered the same confusion as some previous foreign affairs initiatives did in Beijing. It is suffering from a lack of policy and bureaucratic coordination. Xi's ambitious initiative raises two key questions for Beijing and its BRI partners and loan providers: Which departments or ministries carry the overall responsibility for BRI? What are the selection criteria for categorizing infrastructure projects as parts of the initiative? There are no clear answers from Beijing on those two important and necessary questions which could potentially assure foreign investors and policymakers alike.

Besides setting broad policy priorities, the top leadership can determine the survival of any particular institution or a SOE. The Party can create a new bureaucratic framework, or assign and redistribute responsibilities and budgetary powers between existing agencies. However, such a restructuring process has not occurred on a regular basis.

What is more common are 'reshuffles' driven by issues and policy priorities. More often than not, an existing institution challenges the authority of any newly established organization which may share competencies and budgetary powers. The Party will 'award' or 'punish' the challengers according to the situation and policy domains. This case has also largely applied to the pursuit of BRI.

Chinese State-Owned Enterprises and Their BRI Engagements

Despite Chinese SOEs are determined to profit from Beijing's BRI and become some of the most important players in world economic affairs. However, their close association and somewhat submissive relationship with the CCP and the Chinese government has impeded their overseas business plans.

As established in the introduction, Chinese companies, in particular the SOEs, have an unusual structural characteristic that involves a combination of corporate organization and governmental ministry. Their relations with the Party and the central governmental apparatus have not always been submissive.

In recent years, large Chinese SOEs, in particular energy, construction, and utility companies, have had subsidiaries listed on foreign stock exchanges, and with an eye on the pursuit of profits, their corporate interests do not always coincide with those of the Party-state. As a result, bargaining between the central governmental institutions and the SOEs has been a frequent occurrence.

Literature on the Chinese SOEs' relations with the central governmental ministries and the Party has recently gained great popularity in the field of China studies. A number of scholars have argued that conflicts between the SOEs and their superiors, such as the Party and the central ministries, are pervasive and trigger severe policy discoordination both in domestic politics and external affairs (Downs, 2008; Garrison, 2009; Jakobson and Knox, 2010; Lampton, 2001; Leutert, 2018).

As one scholar nicely summarized, there are two types of bargaining taking place between the central governmental institutions and the SOEs, 'namely a bargain over redistribution and a bargain over planning' (Naughton, 1992: 268). This process of bargaining does not only operate between SOEs and the central government institutions, but also extends to other types of Chinese companies' relations with the state. In relation to the implementation of the BRI, bargains are happening both at the policy-planning stage as well as the resource-redistribution stage.

It is important to distinguish the SOEs' relations with the Party from those with the central ministries. The former is a rather submissive relationship as the Party has power and authority over the central ministries in terms of personnel appointments and resource distribution. As some scholars have observed, the latter relationship is less submissive, for while the central ministries have the power to regulate the SOEs' activities, 'their regulatory power has often been undermined due to the SOEs' enormous capacity to alter policy outcomes' (Brodsgaard 2012: 625).

This is because the SOEs often bypass the governmental institutions to communicate directly with the Standing Committee members of the CCP Politburo. Some SOEs and central governmental institutions share the same bureaucratic ranking within the CCP. Also, SOEs do not always follow the decisions that are made by relevant ministries. Rather, the SOEs treat the government institutions as their intermediaries to express their preferences, or as useful allies when seeking to influence the Party.

In recent years, the CCP has established a regulatory framework designed to set the parameters for the economic activities of SOEs. Even more importantly in terms of authority and power relations, as indicated by a few scholars the CCP controls the appointment of CEOs and the Party secretaries of the most important SOEs, such as CNPC, CNOOC, China Telecom, and CGNPC (Brodsgaard, 2012; Leutert, 2018; Li, 2009: 20; Rosen and Hanemann, 2009: 6). The CCP appoints the heads of those SOEs through two regulatory bodies. One of these is handled solely by the Central Department of Organization (CDO); the other involves recommendations by the State-Owned Assets Supervision and Administration Commission (SASAC). The CCP does pay great attention to the CDO's assessments of certain personnel, but it also uses the latter as a complement to the former.

Unlike in the conventional understanding, 'the SASAC does not hold a decisive position in the appointment of the heads of those most important SOEs', according to SASAC's own functional description (SASAC website). Instead, CEOs from those SOEs that I mentioned above (and not only those, there are fifty-three in total) are 'directly appointed and assessed by the Party' (SASAC website; Brodsgaard, 2012: 625). These CEOs have ministerial or vice-ministerial status and, in terms of rank, are equal to State Council ministers and the most provincial governors. Within the Chinese political system, political ranking is the ultimate benchmark for selecting personnel. It is a system where one's personal capacity to fulfil the task becomes far less important than one's political rank. To this extent, one can argue that 'certain commercial decisions made by the SOEs are mostly dependent on whether the CEOs of the enterprises either want to improve their assessment results from the CDO or wish to enhance their bureaucratic positions' 91. This view is also echoed by some other scholars who suggest that successful commercial decisions and outcomes will offer CEOs a chance to improve their political ranking within the Party as well as the bureaucratic status of the whole company in the government apparatus' (Rosen and Haneman, 2009: 21).

As China has experienced more than forty years of economic reform, a process of decentralization has taken place across every aspect of its national economy. This process of decentralization has become a double-edged sword. On the one hand, both the governmental departments and enterprises have accumulated the necessary skills and improved professional experience by operating in an economy with some market-orientated elements. On the other hand, the governmental institutions and the companies are locked into various lengthy bargaining scenarios. On some occasions, the interests of the governmental institutions are in direct contrast to those of the companies. Bargaining amongst relevant stakeholders takes place during the policy formulation and execution process, and here this chapter draws on Barry Naughton's categorization, namely the 'redistribution bargain' and the 'plan bargain' (Naughton, 1992: 268).

In the process of the redistribution bargain, the bureaucratic agencies still retain the power to distribute financial and physical resources to fulfil their own policy priorities. As Naughton notes, 'the central government uses the redistribution exercises to reach down the administrative hierarchy and shape the bargaining between the enterprises and in ways that reflect central-government priorities' (Naughton, 1992: 269). Certainly, both the SOEs and other enterprises can benefit by appealing to patrons at the central and provincial agencies. In doing so, they will have to make investments or launch new projects in the industries that the government institutions decide to support. The enterprises will then be rewarded by the distribution of extra financial and physical resources. For example, China Rail International and China Communications Construction Corporation made a reasonably successful bid to Beijing in completing the reconstruction of the Belgrade-Stara Pazova railway section in Serbia by September 2021 (SEE News, 2021). This project is seen by Beijing as one of the flagship BRI projects that China has managed to build in Europe (Xinhua, 2021).

However, as some scholars have observed, and several Chinese SOEs concur, 'conflicts have often arisen when the government's priorities are contrary to those of the enterprises' (Downs, 2008: Kong, 2009: 805). Even worse, sometimes following the policy priorities of the government will undermine the economic well-being of the enterprises or threaten the very survival of the companies. As these distributed resources from the government are not sufficient to keep up business as usual, the enterprises will argue back and forth with the relevant institutions to change policy priorities, or ignore the policy priorities as some powerful SOEs have been able to do in the past.

In other words, the central institutions have the authority to distribute financial and physical resources, but the enterprises will always ask for more to be given as a trade-off for their following of the government's priorities. Neither the governmental resource distribution nor the enterprises' bargaining have always been smooth transactions. Their bargaining outcomes have gravely affected international collaborations and have damaged the reputation of both the Chinese government and the companies, as one can observe from a number of BRI-related projects in Europe. It also leads to some countries, such as Italy, reconsidering the existing Memorandum of Understanding on BRI, which was signed in 2019 (*Financial Times*, 2021).

Another bargaining process that will be analysed is the so-called Plan Bargain (Naughton, 1992: 268). This often derives from the policy-formation process where the enterprises aim for their preferred policies or business models to be endorsed and adopted by the governmental institutions. This type of bargain involves the enterprises seeking to persuade the key personnel in both governmental departments and at the highest level of the Party.

As one scholar observed, 'science and politics are heavily intertwined in China, this has given the enterprises with the knowledge of cutting-edge technologies sufficient room to persuade their superior or the key decision maker' (Wubbeke, 2013: 713, 715). This thesis will draw on what Nina Halpern has described as the 'Competitive Persuasion' model to disentangle these bargaining relationships between the companies and governmental institutions (Halpern, 1992:125).

'Competitive Persuasion' and BRI Investments

Beside the conventional bargaining scenario, the bargaining process between the SOEs and the central government can be summarized as a 'competitive persuasion' model. This model has been widely applied across many BRI project investments. Within this model, the SOEs attempt to formulate persuasive arguments about appropriate policy or investment projects in competition with other companies. The SOEs will benefit from the policy outcomes once the policy persuasions are endorsed by the governmental institutions.

A competitive persuasion model neither focuses on the SOEs' subordination to the central government, nor does it explain the exchanges and mutual veto power between the government and the SOEs as discussed previously. Instead, it pays a great deal of attention to expertise and area-specific policymaking processes. It is therefore intended to 'apply only to the normal bureaucratic decision-making process where information and expertise are regarded as important' (Halpern, 1992: 126).

This particular model suits very well attempts to analyse Chinese SOEs' influence over formulating the BRI as well as the content of international collaborations amongst the relevant SOEs. The relevance of this model can be explained from two perspectives. Firstly, BRI involves numerous countries and industrial sectors. Both central and provincial governments do not have sufficient capacity to assess the feasibility of every project applied by SOEs. In some cases, Beijing's foreign affairs agenda is converging with SOEs' commercial interests. SOEs and the state do not always involve irreconcilable disputes under the umbrella of BRI.

Secondly, many countries' sectors that involve BRI projects are relatively unknown to the governmental players. Based on my own previous research interviews and some other scholars' published work, governmental departments often lack sufficient expertise and administrative capacity to offer thorough due diligence on the project feasibilities (Yu, 2015; Li and Zeng, 2019).

As a result, their lack of capacity has offered SOEs room to manoeuvre policy objectives and outcomes. As Halpern points out, 'lacking the information and expertise necessary to evaluate the recommendation of lower-level units, political leaders will often permit those units to become de-facto decision makers in their own policy spheres' (Halpern, 1992: 127).

The word 'competitive' in this formula suggests a sense of competition by the relevant stakeholders to persuade the core decision-makers. Therefore, there are winners and losers in every process of policy persuasion and execution.

Unlike Western multinational companies, the CCP and the government either at central or province level determine the Chinese SOEs' corporate strategies and investments plans under the BRI. Instead, each company's party secretary usually possesses final decision-making power to initiate corporate strategies. The Party's involvements in major business decisions of

SOEs have been further strengthened since President Xi came to power in 2012 (Yu, 2021).

Given the centrally controlled SOEs' direct ties to the government, it is difficult to judge whether SOEs' BRI investment plans are political decisions or based purely on commercial merit. Their close links with the state has become a double-edged sword for Chinese SOEs, providing financial support for potential BRI projects but also hindering growth and profit-making in foreign markets, where their direct links with Beijing have often provoked suspicions and hostility.

Most of the senior management teams of large Chinese SOEs who may potentially engage with BRI-related projects are appointed by the Party's Organization Department[2] and equipped with industrial expertise, but not the necessary management skills and general market knowledge of the host countries. For example, they are usually unfamiliar with the market environment of host countries with little understanding of local labour union politics, as COSCO experienced in Greece (Nikki Asian Review, 2020). This has further exacerbated some European political elites' mistrust in participating in the BRI led by Beijing.

SOEs may hire leading global professional services firms to develop their potential BRI projects. Some Chinese companies believe that outsourcing professional services firms is equivalent to possessing sound project-management skills themselves and therefore readiness to pursue BRI projects. Chinese companies utilize professional services firms mostly on the basis of their reputations rather than their specific know-how. In part, this reflects the fact that engaging such major multinationals is often primarily a signal of their determination to pursue BRI projects in line with central government objectives.

Dual Circulation Strategy and the Recalibration of BRI

Since its launch, the BRI envisages funding and building infrastructure in about 120 countries. No other developmental initiative has stirred such international debate, yet not all is going well.

Beijing has realized that its passion for BRI may be unrequited abroad, partly because the programme includes serious risks. China should not automatically assume that growth through gigantic infrastructure investments—the model that drove its own economic miracle—is a panacea applicable

[2] An administrative department run by the CCP to appoint the most senior ministerial-level officials and CEOs of most important SOEs and state-owned banks.

everywhere. Nor should it relentlessly seek recognition from its neighbours and great powers for its foreign investments. In this Five-Year Plan, the BRI is rarely mentioned, and no fresh state capital has been raised for its projects since 2019 (Xi, 2019).

Behind an exuberant chorus of pandemic diplomacy performed by senior Chinese diplomats in 2020, the tone of the Chinese leaders is sombre on international challenges posed by the pandemic (Ang, 2021; Yu, 2020). It signals a diplomatic scaling back to serve China's age-old foreign affairs priority—creating a stable external environment for domestic economic development and a return to diplomacy focused on its immediate neighbours in the South and the East. Under the new priorities, Beijing needs to narrow down its objectives and focus on East Asia and the wider region.

The signature of the Regional Comprehensive Economic Pact, a free-trade agreement among fifteen Asia-Pacific nations including China, provides Beijing with further economic and political incentives to pivot its foreign affairs priorities to its neighbours and away from Eastern Europe and the Middle East. And Xi's recent announcement 'to favourably consider joining CPTPP, a trade agreement originally proposed by the United States but from which Trump withdrew, is a further step to narrowing down its priorities and creating greater economic interdependence with China's neighbours (Xinhua, 2020).

It is clear that China's economic survival takes precedence in determining Beijing's foreign policy agenda in years to come. With no sign of improvement in its relations with the West, Beijing must find markets and partners that are willing and big enough to complement its economy. As a result, many of the existing and new BRI investments will recalibrate according to this shift in China's macro-economic policies to combat further geopolitical headwinds. Many of SOEs will have to redistribute their financial resources and manpower to fit into the overall transition to become more domestically focused.

Conclusion

This chapter looks at the evolving relationships amongst the Chinese SOEs, the Party, and the government institutions in determining some of the BRI investments decisions. It contends with some of the existing literature that argues the Chinese SOEs have become a significant vehicle to accelerate the Chinese government's ambition in challenging the Liberal International Order. Instead, it suggests that the LIO consists of many aspects of institutions, trade, rules, and organizations. China's words and deeds should be reviewed in an 'issue-specific' manner. In particular, it is overly simplistic to conclude that all overseas investments made by the Chinese SOEs are fulfilling Beijing's geopolitical gambit under the BRI. The relationships amongst the Party, the SOEs, and the central government institutions are not strictly top-down, as many observers concur.

It does not deny that the Party remains omnipresent across different aspects of the Chinese political establishments. And the Chinese SOEs will follow the overall objectives decided by the Party and the central governmental apparatus.

Given the increase in breath and width of Chinese foreign policy priorities, this requires top leaders in Beijing to equip themselves with sufficient time and expertise in making decisions that are beyond the traditional realm of diplomacy. But the reality is that there is simply neither enough time nor sufficient expertise on specific issues, such as infrastructure project management and development assistance related to the BRI, amongst the Standing Committee of Politburo within the Party. As a result, this reality provides a myriad of opportunities for relevant SOEs and other institutions to persuade the central government in selecting BRI projects as well as formulating investments strategies according to their preferences. And the 'winners' of the persuasions have often earned greater political capital as well as being offered more generous state capital accordingly. In other words, it is less about following the political executive orders because such orders are often vague in terms, fluid in nature, and opaque in practice. The Chinese leadership relies on those SOEs and government apparatus to interpret and implement those orders; therefore, some SOEs and institutions have become the de-facto decision-makers.

In addition, Chinese leaders have their minds set for the precarious geopolitical environment. Worsening Sino-US relations and tougher access to overseas markets for Chinese companies has prompted a fundamental rethink of growth drivers by the leadership. In the past eight years, much attention has been given to promote the BRI. However, this current radical external environment will require China to recalibrate its model to engagements with the rest of the world. This recalibration also leads to SOEs reallocating their existing financial resources and manpower in order to implement the 'dual circulation' strategy introduced under the 14th Five-Year Plan. One would expect less overseas economic activities from SOEs as their plans begin to focus on China's domestic market.

Assuming China to be a monolithic entity with every decision made by a single person has always been detached from the reality on the ground.

Dealing with Beijing and its SOEs requires an enhanced understanding of its complexities in decision-making processes. This also applies to an honest assessment of whether the Chinese government utilizes its SOEs in challenging the overall Liberal International Order. As found in many China policy analyses, it is always easier said than done.

Bibliography

Allison, T. G. 1969. 'Conceptual Models and Cuban Missile Crisis'. *American Political Science Review* 63 (3): pp. 689–718

Ang, Y.Y. 2021. 'Chinese Leaders Boast about China's Rising Power. The Real Story Is Different'. *The Washington Post*, 13 April. Available at: https://www.washingtonpost.com/politics/2021/04/13/chinese-leaders-boast-about-chinas-rising-power-real-story-is-different/ [Accessed 15 April 2021].

Brodsgaard, K. 2012. 'Politics and Business Group Formation in China: The Party in Control'. *The China Quarterly* 211: pp. 624–648.

Downs, E. 2008. 'Business Interests Groups in Chinese Politics: The Case Studies of the Oil Companies'. In *China's Changing Political Landscape*, edited by C. Li, pp. 121–141. Washington DC: The Brookings Institution.

Economy, E. 2014. 'China's Imperial President, Xi Jinping Tightens His Grip'. Foreign Affairs 93 (6): pp. 80–93.

Financial Times. 2021. 'Mario Draghi Sets Tone in Cooling EU-China Relations'. *Financial Times*, 6 June. Available at: https://www.ft.com/content/4d7bf8ad-f585-44b2-9250-790ec430de4b [Accessed 7 June 2021].

Foot, R., and A. Walter. 2011. *China, the United States and Global Order*. New York and Cambridge: Cambridge University Press.

Gerrison, J. 2009. *China and the Energy Equation in Asia: The Determinants of Policy Choice*. Boulder: First Forum Press.

Halperin, M., and Claap. 1974. *Bureaucratic Politics and Foreign Policy*. Washington D.C: Brookings Institution Press.

Halpern, N. 1992. 'Information Flows and Policy Coordination in the Chinese Bureaucracy'. In *Bureaucracy, Politics and Decision Making in Post-Mao China*, edited by K. Lieberthal and D. Lampton, pp. 125–148. Berkeley: University of California Press.

Ikenberry, G. 2018. 'The End of Liberal International Order'. International Affairs 94 (1): pp. 7–23

Jakobson, L., and D. Know. 2010. *New Foreign Policy Actors in China*. Stockholm: SIPRI, SIPRI Policy Paper No. 26.

Johnston, A. I. 2019. 'The Failures of the 'Failure of Engagement' with China'. *The Washington Quarterly* 42 (2): pp. 99–114.

Kong, B. 2009. 'China's Energy Decision-Making: Becoming More Like the United States'. *Journal of Contemporary China* 18 (62): pp. 780–812.

Leutert, W. 2018. 'The Political Mobility of China's Central State-Owned Enterprise Leaders'. *China Quarterly* 233: pp. 1–21.

Li, X. J., and K. Zeng. 2019. 'Geopolitics, Nationalism, and Foreign Direct Investment: Perceptions of the China Threat and American Public Attitudes toward Chinese FDI'. *Chinese Journal of International Politics* 12 (4): pp. 495–518.

Lieberthal, K., and D. Lampton, eds. 1992. *Bureaucracy, Politics, and Decision-Making in Post Mao China.* Berkeley: University of California.

Lu, N. 1997. *The Dynamics of Foreign Policy in China.* Boulder: Westview Press.

Miller, A. 2015. 'The Trouble with Factions'. *China's Leadership Monitor*, No. 46, p. 3. Available at: https://www.hoover.org/sites/default/files/research/docs/clm46am-2.pdf [Accessed 14 April 2021].

Nathan, A. 2016. 'China's Rise and International Regimes: Does China Seek to Overthrow Global Norms'. In *China in the Era of Xi Jinping*, edited by R. Ross and J. Bekkvold, pp. 165–195. Washington D. C.: Georgetown University Press.

Naugton, B. 1992. 'Hierarchy and Bargaining Economy, Government and Enterprises in the Reform Process'. In *Bureaucracy, Politics, and Decision-Making in Post Mao China*, edited by K. Liberthal and D. Lampton, pp. 245–279. Berkeley: University of California.

Nikki Asian Review. 2020. 'COSCO Faces Backlash as It Moves to Tighten Grip on Greek Port'. Nikki Asian Review, 29 December. Available at: https://asia.nikkei.com/Business/Transportation/COSCO-faces-backlash-as-it-moves-to-tighten-grip-on-Greek-port [Accessed 14 April].

Rosen, D., and T. Hanemann. 2009. *China's Changing Outbound Foreign Direct Investment Profile: Drivers and Policy Implications.* Petersen Institute for International Economics Policy Brief: June 2009, No. PB09–14. Washington D. C.: Petersen Institute.

SASAC. 2021. 'State Owned Assets Supervision Commission of the PRC State Council—What Do We Do'. *SASAC official website*. Available at: http://en.sasac.gov.cn/2018/07/17/c_7.htm [Accessed 14 April 2021].

SCMP. 2020. 'What is China's Dual Circulation Economic Strategy and Why Is It Important?'. *South China Morning Post*, 20 November. Available at: https://www.scmp.com/economy/china-economy/article/3110184/what-chinas-dual-circulation-economic-strategy-and-why-it [Accessed 2 March 2021].

SEE News. 2021. 'China's CRI, CCCC to Complete Railway Reconstruction Project in Serbia by Sept'. *SEE News*, 26 March. Available at: https://seenews.com/news/chinas-cri-cccc-to-complete-railway-reconstruction-project-in-serbia-by-sept-735912 [Accessed 15 April 2021].

Wubbeke, J. 2013. 'China's Climate Change Expert Community-principles, Mechanisms and Influence'. *Journal of Contemporary China* 22 (82): pp. 712–731.

Xi, J. 2019. 'Working Together to Deliver a Brighter Future for Belt and Road Cooperation'. Keynote Speech by H. E. Xi Jinping, President of the People's Republic of China, at the Opening Ceremony of the Second Belt and Road Forum for International Cooperation, 26 April 2019. Available at: https://www.fmprc.gov.cn/mfa_eng/zxxx_662805/t1658424.shtml [Accessed 14 April 2021].

Xinhua News Agency. 2020. 'China Positive to Joining CPTPP: Xi'. *Xinhua News*, 20 November. Available at: http://www.xinhuanet.com/english/2020-11/20/c_139530869.htm [Accessed 14 April 2021].

Xinhua News Agency. 2021. 'Serbian President Inspects Belgrade-Budapest Railway Project'. *Xinhua News*, 26 March. Available at: http://www.xinhuanet.com/english/2021-03/26/c_139836275.htm [Accessed 15 April 2021].

Yu, J. 2014. 'Partnership or Partnerships? An Assessment of China-EU Relations between 2001 and 2013 with Case Studies on Their Collaboration on Climate Change and Renewable Energy'. LSE PhD Thesis. Available at: http://etheses.lse.ac.uk/3294/ [Accessed 14 April 2021].

Yu, J. 2020. 'Coronavirus and Trade War Pushing China to Focus on Fixing Economy Rather Than Leading World Order'. *The South China Morning Post*, 8 June. Available at: https://www.scmp.com/comment/opinion/article/3087713/coronavirus-and-trade-war-pushing-china-focus-fixing-economy-rather [Accessed 15 April 2021].

Yu, J. 2021. 'China's Communist Century: An Ongoing Balancing Act'. *The World Today*, June/July issue, 4 June. Available at: https://www.chathamhouse.org/publications/the-world-today/2021-06/chinas-communist-century-ongoing-balancing-act [Accessed 5 June 2021].

Zhang, Q. 2014. 'Towards an Integrated Theory of Chinese Foreign Policy: Bringing Leadership Personality Back In'. *Journal of Contemporary China* 23 (89): pp. 902–922.

Zhang, Q. M. 2021. 'Diplomacy with Chinese Characteristics'. *The Hague Journal of Diplomacy* 16 (2–3): pp. 358–369.

Zhao, S. 2022. 'Top-level Design and Enlarged Diplomacy: Foreign and Security Policymaking in Xi Jinping's China'. Journal of Contemporary China, https://doi.org/10.1080/10670564.2022.2052440.

2
State Transformation and China's Belt and Road Initiative

Ran Hu

Introduction

After decades of economic, political, and societal turmoil such as the Great Leap Forward (1958–1962) and the Cultural Revolution (1966–1976), the Chinese government announced its economic reform and opening-up programme in late 1978, aiming to transform its isolated economy and turbulent society.[1] China has since enjoyed an economic boom and become the world's second largest economy, with a potential to overtake the world's largest economy, the US, in a decade (CEBR, 2020). The recent soaring of China's overseas investments and the emergence of China-led regional financial institutions and development strategies have further generated greater interest in China's regional and global economic power, as highlighted in the introduction of this volume.

To assess and understand China's growing power and, by extension, its implications regarding the liberal international order (LIO), there is no better case in this area than China's most recent and, probably, most contested trillion-dollar development strategy, the Belt and Road Initiative (BRI). As the centrepiece of Chinese President Xi Jinping's foreign policy, BRI has been widely discussed and debated regarding a variety of themes and issues such as the contents and features of BRI (Johnson, 2016; Summers, 2016); its goals and motivations (Fallon, 2015; Wang, 2016; Ye, 2019; Zhou and Esteban, 2018); and underlying difficulties and possible solutions (Bondaz, 2015; Cohen, 2015). This chapter joins in the debate on BRI with the focus on its formulation process and explores what the making of China's BRI implies

[1] The author would like to thank Indrajit Roy, Jappe Eckhardt, Nick Ritchie, and Joao Nunes for their helpful comments on earlier drafts. The chapter has also benefitted from the feedback received at the workshop 'The Politics of Chinese Investment in Europe' at the University of York in 2019, and at the Political Studies Association annual conference in 2021.

Ran Hu, *State Transformation and China's Belt and Road Initiative.* In: *Rising Power, Limited Influence.* Edited by: Indrajit Roy, Jappe Eckhardt, Dimitrios Stroikos, and Simona Davidescu, Oxford University Press.
DOI: 10.1093/oso/9780192887115.003.0003

regarding the Chinese power and the future of LIO. Put differently, unlike most IR-based literature that assumes BRI to be China's coherent global strategy a priori, this chapter problematizes that assumption and investigates the formulation process of BRI between 2013 and 2015 from an inside-out perspective of state transformation.

The chapter demonstrates that the existing IR-based literature has exaggerated the monopoly of the Chinese state and has ignored China's fragmented policymaking process characterized by decentralization and recentralization. It first argues that BRI started with incoherent and messy practices and discourses concerning two separate (sub-)regional proposals (the Belt initiative and the Road initiative). It then argues that a series of recentralizing measures initiated by the central government transformed those two initiatives into one relatively coherent, but still very vague and broad, initiative with general principles to achieve China's strategic goals. Thus, the chapter suggests that the fragmented policymaking process caused by the interplay between decentralization and recentralization emasculates the Chinese government to make a precise and coherent strategy, here BRI, so as to challenge the LIO.

The chapter is divided into three sections. The first section concentrates on a concise review of the dominant debates of BRI with the purpose of highlighting the need for an inside-out approach, that is, domestic politics, to understand BRI. The second section introduces the conceptual framework that is based on the state transformation with Chinese characteristics. The third section is devoted to the empirical investigation of the impact of the state transformation on the development of BRI.

The Rationale behind BRI

What motivated China to propose BRI, a megaproject with an estimated worth of around US$1 trillion (Chatzky and McBride, 2020), is a major issue regarding BRI. Two explanations dominate the debate. The first explanation argues that the purpose of BRI was to address economic and development problems concerning China and the Eurasian region, whilst the second contends that BRI aimed to reposition China in the established international order, or even challenge the order by adapting it to China's empowerment. These conceptualizations were based on an assumption that BRI was a linear and rational strategy. Here, 'linear' refers to both the one-way process (either top-down or bottom-up) and a rational and teleological development of BRI. However, what happened with regard to BRI suggests the opposite: the formulation of BRI was non-linear, incoherent, and multicausal. In other words, the existing literature has assumed BRI to be an unproblematic coherent strategy and undervalued the actual formulation process of BRI, which contained various underlying assumptions, specific discourses, and practices. This section reviews what has been discussed about BRI in terms of its rationale and implications and explains why the existing literature is insufficient to understand BRI in relation to the LIO.

First, BRI was understood as China's spatial-temporal fix for domestic and regional problems, such as industrial overaccumulation and unbalanced economic development (Johnson, 2016; Summers, 2016; Ye, 2019). China's economy suffered from industrial overaccumulation caused by excess production and inadequate domestic demand (Hung, 2008). This problem has been compounded by flaccid overseas consumption and rising trade protectionism worldwide since the 2008 global financial crisis (Johnson, 2016; Pu, 2016; Wang, 2016). Therefore, it is argued that BRI could, if implemented successfully, open up new territories and integrate them into the Chinese market, given its championing of closer international economic cooperation. For instance, inland western provinces such as Xinjiang and Yunnan can benefit economically from having access to better-integrated transport networks, port facilities, and open markets in neighbouring countries (Pu, 2016; Xue, 2017).

Second, from a geostrategic perspective, BRI was interpreted as being China's grand strategy to increase its regional economic leverage and political influence that could be utilized and transformed to develop its own sphere of influence and challenge the LIO (Benabdallah, 2019; Swaine, 2015). China's security calculations and hegemonic ambitions were often foregrounded in this strand of analysis. Its growing security concerns are partially derived from its increasing reliance on imported energy, which is mostly transported through maritime routes, for economic development (Wang, 2016). The infrastructure linking advocated by BRI could, as suggested by Ljungwall and Bohman (2017), expand regional transport networks and facilitate the flows of investment and trade, thus diversifying its energy sources and embedding China's neighbouring states into its economic sphere. On that account, China's economy might suffer less if a sudden and continued interruption in energy supply were to happen (Dannreuther, 2011). Moreover, the accumulation of the economic and security benefits brought by BRI is likely to transform China into 'a normative power' (Zhou and Esteban, 2018: 488) so as to challenge and shape the prevailing US-dominated international order (Aoyama, 2016; Benabdallah, 2019; Johnson, 2016), or, in Fallon's (2015: 140) words, 'rewrit[e] the current geopolitical landscape'.

These two broad strands of explanations are critical, exploring BRI beyond China's official explanations which framed it as a global public good, and shedding light on the difficulties China faced and international power shifting. Despite their different perspectives and analyses, both lack a critical engagement with the policymaking process of BRI. In other words, both explanations are an outside-in approach which focuses on the causal relationship between external issues (e.g. economic problems and international structure) and China's responses. Therefore, they seldom question the underlying assumptions, the discursive performances, and the actual practices through which BRI was made possible. Instead, they overwhelmingly assume, a priori, that BRI was, for instance, a 'well thought-out grand strategy' (Bhattacharya, 2016: 310), imposed by the Chinese central government and implemented by local actors (Aoyama, 2016; Benabdallah, 2019; Johnson, 2016; Zhou and Esteban, 2018).

This particular assumption—the linear development of BRI—contradicts, however, the 'disjointed' political history of BRI, particularly the messy period between late 2013 and early 2015. As demonstrated below, BRI understood as *one coherent initiative* did not exist in the so-called origin of BRI, that is, Xi's two 2013 speeches where he introduced the Silk Road Economic Belt (SREB) and the 21st-Century Maritime Silk Road (MSR) in his state visits to Kazakhstan and Indonesia respectively. Rather, before Beijing's first policy paper on BRI in March 2015, the BRI practices were incoherent and fragmented, as local actors all acted on their own interpretations of Xi's two 2013 speeches. More importantly, disregarding this messy period, or simply omitting it, in the literature distorts the analysis of what BRI is, how it came to be, and, by extension, what impacts it may have on the LIO.

Furthermore, the assumption that a strong top-down approach in an authoritarian China is the norm is also problematic, as the decades of decentralization have left China's policymaking more fragmented than is often assumed. It is predominantly acknowledged that China is an authoritarian state under the rule of the Chinese Communist Party (CCP). However, being an authoritarian one-party state does not necessarily imply that China is a monolithic state solely with the philosophy and practice of top-down governance (Jones, 2019; Jones and Zeng, 2019; Su, 2012; Yu, 2018). On the contrary, policymaking in China is less of a chain of command, and more of a coalition or consensus-building resulting from multiparty and multifront negotiations (Jakobson and Knox, 2010; Jones and Zeng, 2019).

To sum up, the assumption that BRI was a coherent strategy formulated by the central government alone created a blind spot in the perception of BRI. The analyses based solely on that assumption lost sight of the dynamic and evolving process of BRI and failed to explain and understand BRI in relation to the LIO. Therefore, this chapter brings back the centrality of domestic politics in China's foreign policymaking, as the international structure does not dictate a precise state behaviour and/or policy outcome of states, for great powers in particular (Foot, 2013).

China's Foreign Policymaking and State Transformation

After decades of China's Open-Door policy with an emphasis on economic reform, phenomena such as interdepartmental rivalries, party–government competition, and central–local conflicts became more apparent. The Chinese state became 'riddled with competing state agencies, problems of cross-department coordination, and mismatch between central and local policies' (Su, 2012: 504). This phenomenon has been conceptualized as state transformation characterized by fragmentation, decentralization, and internationalization (Hameiri and Jones, 2016; Hameiri et al., 2019; Jones, 2019; Jones and Zeng, 2019; Su, 2012). This conceptualization, however, seems to concentrate too much on the decentralizing process so as to discount the fact that the CCP always demands and makes every effort to be in command and stay in power. In other words, too much emphasis on fragmentation and decentralization leaves a misperception that the CCP and, by extension, the central government are losing control and allowing any breach of their centrality and authorities.

Built on the literature on state transformation and its applications (Hameiri and Jones, 2016; Hameiri et al., 2019; Su, 2012; Jones, 2019; Zheng, 2006), the chapter conceptualizes state transformation in the Chinese context as an interactive and continuous process of decentralization and recentralization, a tug of war between the central government and local actors. Decentralization that leads to fragmentation empowers local actors, whilst recentralization aims to maintain the power and authority of the central government. Thus, Chinese foreign policymaking is a double movement, complex, multilevel, and contingent on various factors working through the pull and push between decentralizing and recentralizing forces.

First, decentralization refers to the delegation of authority in terms of resource control, policymaking, and policy implementation from a central level to a local level and/or from state to society. This phenomenon is also conceptualized by Zheng Yongnian (2006: 107) as a '*de facto* federalism'. Given the Chinese one-party political system, decentralization remains much more about central-local relations than state-society relations

(Zheng, 2006). Through decentralization, local governments gain more power or autonomy in terms of making independent decisions in certain policy areas and interpreting and executing 'national' policies based on local circumstances and interests (Zheng, 2006). Thus, it has generated multilevel and multiparty bargaining and negotiation for policymaking and, sometimes, different implementation plans (He, 2019; Jones and Zeng, 2019). For instance, provincial governors could manage their own external economic relations and engage in external economic activities, which sometimes creates issues and problems for China's central foreign policy (Jones and Zeng, 2019). In other words, national policymaking is not simply a unidirectional, top-down process. Instead, it is a two-way process in which local actors also exert their influence on policymaking (Zheng, 2006).

At the same time, the state-society evolution via decentralization, subtle as it may be, does continue and leads to a fragmented state, known as fragmentation, which means that a wider range of actors is involved in policymaking, with some actors empowered whilst others are disempowered. Regarding foreign policymaking, not only traditional official actors such as governmental departments and institutions, but also non-traditional ones, such as state-owned enterprises and transnational and national networks in knowledge and business, all attempt to influence policymaking to suit their own interests (de Graaff, 2020; Huo and Parmar, 2020; Jakobson and Knox, 2010; Jakobson and Manuel, 2016; also see Yu in this volume).

Moreover, fragmentation implies struggles for power and resources, thus sometimes leading to contradictory guidance and practices, as decision-making is relegated to multiple agencies at the same level (He, 2019; Jones and Zeng, 2019; Pieke, 2013). In other words, responsibilities for some issues are shared among different departments which compete as well as cooperate with one another for greater influence (Pieke, 2013). This is also, to a certain degree, inflamed by globalization, as China increasingly integrates itself into the international society through socialization (Su, 2012) and more domestic actors tend to obtain an international role (Jones and Zeng, 2019). In terms of foreign policy at the central level, the Ministry of Foreign Affairs (MOFA) is joined and, sometimes, bypassed by other actors such as the Ministry of Defence, the People's Liberation Army, and the CCP's International Department (Jones and Zeng, 2019; Pieke, 2013; Zhang, 2016). For instance, regarding maritime affairs, twenty-two different agencies have some jurisdiction over it or some aspects of it, 'with inter-agency rivalry directly generating clashes with neighbouring countries' (Jones and Zeng, 2019: 1416). In short, decentralization leads to fractured authority with regard to foreign policymaking, and China is more fragmented and decentralized than it is often assumed (Jakobson and Manuel, 2016; Yu, 2018).

Second, recentralization is a critical part of the process as China remains an authoritarian one-party state in which '[t]he Party exercises overall leadership over *all areas* of endeavour in *every part* of the country' (CCP, 2017: 10, emphasis added). Since taking power, Xi has gradually amassed more power than either of his two predecessors (Jakobson and Manuel, 2016) and transformed China into a more repressive and ideological-orientated regime (Blackwill and Campbell, 2016). As Cabestan (2009: 64) forcefully argues, political power and policymaking 'have consistently been highly centralised and concentrated in the supreme CCP leading bodies'. This means that the CCP's power is paramount and takes charge of all critical issues (Jakobson and Manuel, 2016). The government led by the CCP has, for instance, been making every effort to maintain its authority and reclaim power over certain issues through all sorts of—often less explicit—techniques such as establishing ad hoc working groups to 'monitor' and 'discipline' local implementations of national policies, and personnel appointment (*reshi guanli*) in provincial governments and large SOEs (Hameiri and Jones, 2016). In short, China's centralized power could be perceived through its absolute controls over the industries critical to China's economy and its prerogative to appoint heads of all SOEs and public universities.

This state transformation with Chinese characteristics has a significant impact on foreign policymaking in China. Decentralization empowers local actors by further delegating central decision-making power to local governments or other non-state actors, and, by extension, it leads to a fragmented phenomenon, or simply fractured authority, in which central authority is partially weakened in certain issues areas (Jakobson and Knox, 2010). Thus, to formulate a coherent and consistent policy is difficult, especially at the beginning, as local actors compete to skew policy interpretation in their favour. At the same time, recentralization through mobilization, guidance, and steering aims to take control of the direction of policy and make sure ultimate goals are accomplished and in line with the CCP's interests (Zhang, 2016). Here, recentralization does not necessarily mean going back to Maoist China when the personality cult was rampant, or taking all decision-making power back to the central government. It only means that the central government led by the CCP attempts to ensure that its centrality and authority are undamaged and that it has multiple ways to realize that. These particular domestic political dynamics determine that it is difficult for the central government to formulate a coherent and detailed grand strategy. Rather, only vague and broad strategies can work in China, as they allow the central government to manage and achieve its goals whilst keeping local and departmental interests satisfied.

A Double Movement of Decentralization and Recentralization

As discussed above, BRI was often assumed to be *one coherent initiative* to achieve China's economic and/or geostrategic goals, and it contained two complementary parts: the Belt and the Road. However, a careful examination of the speeches made by senior Chinese officials and the practices billed by the Chinese government as BRI projects reveals a rather different story. Concentrating on the period between 2013 and 2015, this section finds that there was no BRI to begin with, and that the Belt and the Road were not, at least at the very beginning, interconnected. Based on the concept of state transformation, it argues that a relatively coherent BRI emerged out of a messy and fragmented state of two (sub-)regional projects through a series of recentralizing moves. It demonstrates that the policymaking in China is not a straightforward process (top-down), but rather a dialect process of decentralization and recentralization that is contested and complex.

A fragmented BRI: contradictions, multiple actors, and limited success

After the decades of reform and opening up, policymaking in China has become more decentralized, with more power being devolved to local governments, and also more fragmented, with an increasing number of actors involved. This is manifested via the unfolding of SREB and MSR. Right after the announcement, the governments at both central and local levels and non-state actors of various types started their activities straight away based on their own interpretations. Whilst the central government and state institutions focused on the grand design of SREB and MSR, local actors tended to concentrate on their pragmatic aspects. At the local level, the understandings and ways of enacting SREB and MSR were more diversified than, and sometimes contradictory to, those at the central level. Therefore, this subsection argues that real SREB and MSR projects were sporadic, and that their implementation at an early stage could only be characterized as being incoherent and inconsistent. The incoherent state demonstrates the necessity of not assuming what BRI is, a priori.

First, there was no BRI, but SREB and MSR, in Xi's original speeches. They were two separate regional projects as they aimed at different (sub-)regions, and no evidence in the original speeches indicates that they were two parts of one project (Xi, 2013a, 2013b). Whilst SREB was an independent regional strategy aiming to strengthen China's cooperation with mainly Asian countries (Xi, 2013a), MSR was a project subjected to Xi's other broader vision of 'build[ing] a more closely-knit China-ASEAN community of common destiny', aimed at 'develop[ing] maritime partnership' (Xi, 2013b) with Southeast Asian countries.

Until the second half of 2014, SREB and MSR were still referred to as two distinct projects, in the same way that senior Chinese officials such as Yang Jiechi (2014) and Xi Jinping (2014c) referred to them. Meanwhile, other than '*changyi*' (initiative), other designations such as '*zhanlue*' (strategy), '*jihua*' (plan), '*zhengce*' (policy) etc. were also employed to refer to the Belt and the Road. For instance, BRI was explicitly addressed as one of three national strategies (*zhanlue*) in the 2014 Central Economic Work Conference (Xinhua, 2019). These different designations were most often seen among local-level governments, and the word 'strategy' was often seen in academic journals.

Second, various actors were involved in the making of BRI, as actors are empowered as the result of fragmentation. At the central level, the Chinese government and the Central Committee of the CCP focused on strategic planning within China and policy coordination with other states. Just one month after the announcement of SREB and MSR, both projects were integrated into China's domestic strategy of deepening its domestic economic reforms (Zhu, 2017). As *The Decision of the CCCPC on Some Major Issues Concerning Comprehensively Deepening the Reform and Opening-up* (CCCPC, 2013) declared, 'we [the Chinese government] will ... work hard to build a Silk Road Economic Belt and a Maritime Silk Road, so as to form a new pattern of all-round opening'. Later that year, at China's highest-level economic conference, the annual Central Economic Work Conference, President Xi called for a strategic planning for SREB and MSR to promote infrastructural linkages within Eurasia (Tian, 2015).

However, these high-level internal meetings could not conceal the fact that there was no dedicated government agency designated to manage daily routines concerning SREB and MSR, as those meetings were annual events to discuss and debate all general issues. The National Development and Reform Commission (NDRC) had taken the lead in preparing a few SREB and MSR workshops, supported by the Ministry of Foreign Affairs (MOFA). But there is no evidence showing that they were the leading agencies for Xi's two regional projects.

Meanwhile, the Chinese government rebranded some previous projects as SREB or MSR projects, making them sound like coherent and well-developed ones. A webpage on the Renminwang site (people.cn),[2] a website affiliated to the CCP's news outlet *People's Daily*, can illustrate this point. The page listed some projects finished between 2013 and 2016 and claimed that they were all BRI projects. But a closer scrutiny of some early projects listed there indicates otherwise. Some of these so-called BRI projects could clearly be dated prior to SREB and MSR. The site lists, for instance, China's delivery of a remote sensing satellite system to Venezuela as a BRI project. But the system was in fact delivered on 4 September 2013, a few days earlier than the announcement of SREB on 7 September 2013 (Wu, 2013). Another example is the China-Myanmar Gas Pipeline; it was launched in 2010 and completed in June 2013 (Renminwang, 2013), but it was still listed as a BRI project (Renminwang, 2017). Put differently, BRI-related activities at this early stage were sporadic and unsystematic, both inside and outside China.

At the local level, governments, state-owned enterprises, and private businesses began vying for a seat at the table and provided their own interpretations with the purposes of not only gaining funding, but also embedding their interests and interpretations into the national one. However, those seemingly organized central-level practices, as shown above, have not been passed down to the local level. Instead, local-level activities, in terms of their understandings and ways of enacting SREB and MSR, could be only characterized as incoherent, disorganized, and even contradictory.

One of the most compelling examples of how indeterminant and incoherent SREB and MSR were is the debate about which city is the start of either land-based or maritime Silk Roads. Several local governments from coastal to inland cities began their campaigns to name themselves the start of either Silk Road (Liu, 2014; Wang, et al., 2015). For instance, other than Xi'an and Luoyang, which had long been rivals for the start of the ancient land-based Silk Road, and now SREB, there were three more contenders: Zhengzhou, Lianyungang, and Chongqing (Liu, 2014). Zhengzhou, the provincial capital of Henan Province, should be named as the starting point of SREB, argued the Party Secretary of Henan Province, because of its strategic location in Central China connecting China's eastern and western regions (Liu, 2014). The Lianyungang government made a similar argument and aimed to become the eastern bridgehead of SREB, built on its advantages as a

[2] http://world.people.com.cn/GB/8212/191616/409002/index.html.

port city (Liu, 2014). Chongqing, on the other hand, made its most ambitious move by tabling a proposal during the annual meetings of China's national legislature (National People's Congress) and top political advisory body (Chinese People's Political Consultative Conference) in March 2014 to designate Chongqing as the starting point of SREB, so as to tap its potential in contributing to both SREB and the Yangtze River Economic Belt (Liu, 2014; Wang and Zhong, 2014).

This domestic rivalry, or, in other words, messiness, was largely caused by the lack of central guidance of the implementation of SREB and MSR and the decentralization of state institutions that allowed more actors to participate in policymaking. Other than two speeches made by Xi in 2013, there were no documents on SREB and MSR before 2015. Without detailed guidance, participants had plenty of room to manoeuvre, to be precise, to interpret these two projects based on their individual needs. To actively promote or aggrandize senior leaders' pet projects, in this case SREB and MSR, is a common practice among provincial or municipal party leaders and the surest way for them to curry favour from their bosses and prepare for their own future career advancement (He, 2019). At the same time, doing so allows those party bosses to access newly available central funds to pursue their own local projects and/or save or relaunch their previous dead ones under the name of SREB and MSR.

As shown above, the unclear and tangled relationships among SREB, MSR, and BRI, the domestic institutional rivalry, and limited real achievements challenge the traditional assumption of a hard top-down approach in the Chinese governance and demonstrate the possibility of a strong presence and influence of the decentralizing movement in policymaking. Moreover, the existence of multiple designations was not simply a rhetorical problem about how BRI should be addressed. Rather, it undoubtedly shows that even the central government at that time was not sure of their positioning of SREB and MSR (later BRI), and had no specific plans for them. They all were important evidence of the 'indeterminacy' of SREB and MSR. Put differently, as there was no BRI to begin with, it is problematic to analyse BRI by simply taking it for granted that it was a coherent initiative. Instead, more attention shall be paid to understanding how BRI developed out of this messy period.

An ordered BRI: reclaiming the authority

As explained in the conceptual framework, decentralization and recentralization are two accompanying phenomena. This subsection focuses on the recentralizing process that has brought together what BRI is now. Here recentralization is more about reclaiming the authority of the central government and reasserting its influence, rather than explicitly taking back the decision-making power from local actors. To be specific, whilst allowing these incoherent and competing practices to take place, the central government also began to assemble thoughts from the local level, (re-)define what BRI is, and discipline what it regards as 'wrong' BRI practices.

The first recentralizing move was to reconceptualize SREB and MSR as *one initiative* through discourses. Starting from late 2014, the central government began to purposefully address SREB and MSR as one initiative. In November 2014, the Belt and Road *initiative* (*yidai yilu changyi*), singular not plural, appeared for the first time, when Xi (2014b, emphasis added) stated that '[t]he "Belt and Road" *initiative* and the connectivity endeavour are compatible and mutually reinforcing'. One initiative, *not two*, was undoubtedly asserted. This was a clear departure from the previous discourses on SREB and MSR that they were two separate initiatives. Meanwhile, the central government standardized the name for BRI by insisting that '*changyi*' (initiative, a singular not plural word) was the only legitimate title for BRI and no other words such as *strategy*, *project*, *programme*, and *agenda* should be used (BRI office, n.d.). At the same time, the Chinese government has never publicly clarified BRI's ambiguous relations with SREB and MSR, but it plainly used BRI in its later documents and pretended that the issue had never existed. This pretence was China's strategy to reinforce a narrative that BRI composed of SREB and MSR had always been the original design, and it did in fact reinforce that misleading narrative among the public. Many scholars have, as discussed earlier, based their arguments on Beijing's official narrative of BRI's origin.

Moreover, reconceptualizing BRI included the move of issuing the first national policy paper on BRI, that is, *Vision and Actions on Jointly Building the Silk Road Economic Belt and 21st Century Maritime Silk Road*. In this document, the principles, key areas of cooperation, cooperative mechanisms, and the planning for local regions concerning BRI were elaborated. In other words, the central government tried to explicitly determine what BRI is by defining the nature of BRI and setting boundaries for what should and should not be included in it and in what way. The release of *Vision and Actions* represented a significant act from the central government in the recentralizing processes because, after months of staying less active in shaping SREB, MSR, and BRI, it officially intervened and attempted to rein in all these disparate actors and activities and bring some coherence, as to how it should be understood, to the messy and incoherent period through documentation. This reconceptualizing move was not simply about rhetoric, but more importantly about politics; that is, asserting its authority and reclaiming its centrality.

One of the major steps this document took to recentralize BRI policymaking was political directives. It was first reflected through the central government's regulation of the previous responses at the local level to SREB and MSR. The central government outlined its expectations for local governments, namely, what their role(s) would be in BRI (NDRC, MOFA, and MOC, 2015). These chosen provinces and cities were all assigned different goals. For instance, to the north, Xinjiang was named as 'a core area on the Silk Road Economic Belt'; to the east, Fujian was entitled as 'a core area of the 21st-Century Maritime Silk Road'; and to the west, Yunnan was designated as 'a pivot of China's Opening-up to South and Southeast Asia' (NDRC, MOFA, and MOC, 2015: 4). This contrasted with the central government's earlier approach of staying away from issuing directives to local governments.

The second recentralizing move was institutional design at both domestic and international levels. There were two types of institution for the task of 'recentralizing': policymaking agencies and funding agencies. The former set goals and basic rules for SREB and MSR projects, utilized different resources to support some and suppress others, and supervised their implementation. The latter executed them and 'guided' future practices by using their funded projects to visually demonstrate what SREB and MSR (later BRI) projects should look like. In other words, SREB and MSR (later BRI) practices were disciplined through institutional monitoring based on political procedures, norms, and protocols, and regulated by releasing or withholding funding. By doing so, the central government recentralized the process of BRI decision-making and implementation not by directly controlling it, but by taking charge of the direction of BRI and disciplining practices that were perceived by the central government as 'wrong' practices.

The first funding agency was the Silk Road Fund (SRF), which was specifically established to serve BRI only and wholly sponsored by China's central government. The SRF is, with China's initial contribution of US$40 billion, 'designed to provide investment and financing support for countries along the "Belt and Road" [regions] to carry out infrastructure, resources, industrial cooperation, financial cooperation and other projects related to connectivity' (Xi, 2014b).[3] The second funding agency was a multilateral financial institution, the Asian Infrastructure Investment Bank (AIIB). Despite not being an

[3] In 2017, Xi announced an additional RMB 100 billion (148 billion USD as of 2019) to be injected into the Silk Road Fund.

intrinsic part of BRI, the AIIB can be, and indeed was utilized to facilitate the implementation of BRI mainly through financing infrastructure-related projects in Asia and beyond, either on its own or in partnership with other international financial institutions. As Laurel Ostfield (quoted in Shepard, 2017), the head of communications for the AIIB, explained, 'we are not connected to One Belt, One Road. [But] obviously, we will be playing a part in it'. In short, they regulate the BRI practices of other local actors.

Other than the SRF and AIIB, China also established a policymaking organization at the domestic level, that is, the Leading Small Group on Advancing the Construction of the Belt and Road (BRI LSG for short). Based in the State Council, it has been established to guide, monitor, and promote BRI (BRI office, n.d.). Under the BRI LSG, there was a permanent office called the Office of the Leading Small Group for BRI (BRI office for short). It was based in the National Development and Reform Commission (NDRC) and set up to carry out the daily work of the BRI LSG that convenes every six months (BRI office, n.d.).

Establishing a Leading Small Group (*lingdao xiaozu*, LSG) is regularly and widely practised in the Chinese political system to monitor and coordinate the implementation of policies concerning almost all areas (Johnson et al., 2017; Miller, 2008; Zhang, 2015). Although LSGs are still established on an ad hoc basis and disbanded after the mission, some of them are kept *de facto* permanently and become more formal (Zhang, 2015). More importantly, LSGs have been strengthened and become more involved in the policymaking process over the years, particularly under Xi's supervision (Johnson et al., 2017).

Although the BRI LSG is an ad hoc working group that convenes only twice a year (BRI office, n.d.), its establishment is significant in two aspects. First, the official establishment of the BRI LSG corresponded to the central government's reconceptualization of SREB and MSR as one coherent initiative because by then it had already frequently employed the term '*yidai yilu*' (the Belt and Road) and officially confirmed that they belonged to *one coherent initiative*. Second, it also addressed the previous 'messy' situation in which no dedicated central government agency was in charge of these two projects, or the problem of lacking 'an effective leadership structure' (He, 2019: 185). Chaired by Zhang Gaoli, who sat in the Standing Committee of the CCP Politburo, China's highest-ruling council, the BRI LSG is high in China's political system and has more power and resources than many other departments. In other words, the BRI LSG became the BRI network builder which had access to different resources and facilitated different agencies.

Looking Forwards

Instead of assuming BRI to be one coherent strategy a priori, this chapter has questioned the taken-for-granted assumption and investigated the development of BRI between 2013 and 2015 from the inside-out perspective of state transformation. It has demonstrated that rather than being a coherent strategy, BRI was derived from two separate (sub-)regional projects through discursive construction, political directives, and institutional design. Due to China's decades of decentralization, more local actors became involved in the making of BRI whilst competing for resources and interpretations. Thus, largely incoherent interpretations and practices followed the announcement of the Belt and the Road initiatives. Meanwhile, the CCP and its central government continuously asserted their power and authority over national policymaking by unifying the discourses and practices concerning SREB, MSR, and BRI, and by establishing dedicated agencies to guide the implementation process. This is how BRI as one coherent initiative emerged.

This chapter has argued that policymaking in China is greatly impacted by the interplay between decentralization and recentralization and, by extension, fragmented. That is, whilst continuing to allow a wider participation of local state and non-state actors and empower them in policymaking, the Chinese central government still makes every effort to dominate and dictate through more implicit and discrete means, such as setting general goals, monitoring implementation processes, and disciplining local implementations. Therefore, any national strategy design in China can only be vague, broad, and even flexible, so as to accommodate as many local or departmental interests as possible whilst assuring overarching goals are served.

So, what does this inside-out approach to BRI imply about China's growing power and its impact on the LIO? First, from the perspective of state transformation, this chapter suggests that China's ability, manifested through BRI, to challenge the LIO is rather limited, as BRI is so broad that different actors could, to a certain degree, use it to their own advantages, thus shaping its future development. To be precise, like BRI, China's other grand policies need to be broad and vague so as to accommodate the interests of both the central and local actors due to its fragmented policymaking being derived from the dialect process of decentralization and recentralization. That said, BRI could, as Jones (2020) cautioned, unintentionally pose some challenges to the LIO by simply providing an alternative funding source to developing countries. Second, and perhaps more importantly, BRI will not be China's last strategy regarding the LIO, as its growing economic power indeed is the foundation of its trillion-dollar investment project, vague and broad as it is. How other states respond to BRI will directly influence the outcome of China's future strategies. Merely blaming China's hegemonic ambition or isolating it will not, therefore, provide a satisfactory answer to the question of the future of the LIO.

Bibliography

Aoyama, R. 2016. '"One Belt, One Road": China's New Global Strategy'. *Journal of Contemporary East Asia Studies* 5 (2): pp. 3–22.

Benabdallah, L. 2019. 'Contesting the International Order by Integrating It: The Case of China's Belt and Road Initiative'. *Third World Quarterly* 40 (1): pp. 92–108.

Bhattacharya, A. 2016. 'Conceptualising the Silk Road Initiative in China's Periphery Policy'. *East Asia* 33 (4): pp. 309–328.

Blackwill, R., and K. Campbell. 2016. 'Xi Jinping on the Global Stage: Chinese Foreign Policy Under a Powerful but Exposed Leader'. *Council on Foreign Relations Special Report* Issue 74: pp. 1–47.

Bondaz, A. 2015. 'Rebalancing China's Geopolitics'. In *'One Belt, One Road': China's Great Leap Outward*, edited by François Godement and Agatha Kratz, pp. 6–8. European Council on Foreign Relations and Asia Centre.

BRI office. n.d. 'Zuzhi lingdao he gongzuo jizhi. [BRI's Organisation Structure, Leadership, and Working Mechanisms]'. Available at: https://www.yidaiyilu.gov.cn/info/iList.jsp?tm_id=540 [Accessed 21 April 2020].

Cabestan, J.-P. 2009. 'China's Foreign- and Security-policy Decision-making Processes under Hu Jintao'. *Journal of Current Chinese Affairs* 38 (3): pp. 63–69.

CCCPC (Central Committee of CPC). 2013. 'Zhonggong henhuag guanyu quanmian henhua gaige ruogan zhongda wenti de jueding. [Decision of the CCCPC on Some Major Issues Concerning Comprehensively Deepening the Reform and Opening-up]'. [Online]. Available at: http://www.china.org.cn/chinese/2014-01/17/content_31226494.htm [Accessed 5 April 2020].

CCP. 2017. 'Constitution of Communist Party of China'. Available at: http://www.xinhuanet.com/english/special/2017-11/03/c_136725945.htm [Accessed 20 April 2020].

Centre for Economics and Business Research (CEBR). 2020. 'World Economic League Table 2021'. Available at: https://cebr.com/service/macroeconomic-forecasting/ [Accessed 13 May 2021].

Chatzky, A., and J. McBride. 2020. 'China's Massive Belt and Road Initiative'. Council on Foreign Relations. Available at: https://www.cfr.org/backgrounder/chinas-massive-belt-and-road-initiative [Accessed 13 May 2022].

Cohen, D. 2015. 'China's "Second Opening": Grand Ambitions but a Long Road Ahead'. In *'One Belt, One Road': China's Great Leap Outward*, edited by François Godement and Agatha Kratz, pp. 3–5. European Council on Foreign Relations and Asia Centre.

Dannreuther, R. 2011. 'China and Global Oil: Vulnerability and Opportunity'. *International Affairs* 87 (6): pp. 1345–1364.

De Graaff, N. 2020. 'China Inc. Goes Global. Transnational and National Networks of China's Globalizing Business Elite'. *Review of International Political Economy* 27 (2): pp. 208–233.

De Graaff, N. et al. 2020. 'China's Rise in a Liberal World Order in Transition—Introduction to the FORUM'. *Review of International Political Economy* 27 (2): pp. 191–207.

Fallon, T. 2015. 'The New Silk Road: Xi Jinping's Grand Strategy for Eurasia'. *American Foreign Policy Interests* 37 (3): pp. 140–147.

Foot, R. 2013. 'Introduction: China Across the Divide'. In *China Across the Divide: The Domestic and Global in Politics and Society*, edited by Rosemary Foot, pp. 1–16. Oxford: Oxford University Press.

Hameiri, S., et al. 2019. 'Reframing the Rising Powers Debate: State Transformation and Foreign Policy'. *Third World Quarterly* 40 (8): pp. 1397–1414.

Hameiri, S., and L. Jones. 2016. 'Rising Powers and State Transformation: The Case of China'. *European Journal of International Relations* 22 (1): pp. 72–98.

He, B. 2019. 'The Domestic Politics of the Belt and Road Initiative and Its Implications'. *Journal of Contemporary China* 28 (116): pp. 180–195.

Hung, H. 2008. 'Rise of China and the Global Overaccumulation Crisis'. *Review of International Political Economy* 15 (2): pp. 149–179.

Huo, S., and I. Parmar. 2020. '"A New Type of Great Power Relationship"? Gramsci, Kautsky and the Role of the Ford Foundation's Transformational Elite Knowledge Networks in China'. *Review of International Political Economy* 27 (2): pp. 234–257.

Jakobson, L., and D. Knox. 2010. 'New Foreign Policy Actors in China'. *SIPRI Policy Paper* No. 26: pp. 1–51.

Jakobson, L., and R. Manuel. 2016. 'How are Foreign Policy Decisions Made in China'. *Asia & the Pacific Policy Studies* 3 (1): pp. 101–110.

Johnson, C. K. 2016. *President Xi Jinping's 'Belt and Road' Initiative: A Practical Assessment of the Chinese Communist Party's Roadmap for China's Global Resurgence*. Washington: Centre for Strategic & International Studies.

Johnson, C. K., S. Kennedy, and M. Qiu. 2017. 'Xi's Signature Governance Innovation: The Rise of Leading Small Groups'. Washington: Centre for Strategic & International Studies. [Online]. Available at: https://www.csis.org/analysis/xis-signature-governance-innovation-rise-leading-small-groups [Accessed 16 April 2020].

Jones, L. 2019. 'Theorizing Foreign and Security Policy in an Era of State Transformation: A New Framework and Case Study of China'. *Journal of Global Security Studies* 4 (4): pp. 579–597.

Jones, L. 2020. 'Does China's Belt and Road Initiative Challenge the Liberal, Rules-Based Order?'. *Fudan Journal of the Humanities and Social Sciences* 13: pp. 113–133.

Jones, L., and J. Zeng. 2019. 'Understanding China's "Belt and Road Initiative": Beyond "Grand Strategy" to a State Transformation Analysis'. *Third World Quarterly* 40 (8): pp. 1415–1439.

Liu, Y. 2014. 'Wushi zhengqiang xinsichou zhilu jingjidai qidian. [Five Cities Eyeing for the Starting Point of Silk Road Economic Belt]'. *Fenghuangwang*. Available at: http://finance.ifeng.com/a/20140315/11895702_0.shtml [Accessed 9 April 2020].

Ljungwall, C., and V. Bohman. 2017. 'Mending Vulnerabilities to Isolation: How Chinese Power Grows Out of the Development of the Belt and Road Initiative'. *The RUSI Journal* 162 (5): pp. 26–33.

Miller, A. 2008. 'The CCP Central Committee's Leading Small Groups'. *China Leadership Monitor* Issue 26: pp. 1–21.

NDRC, MOFA, and MOC. 2015. 'Tuidong gongjian sichou zhilu jingjidai he 21 shiji haishang sichou zhilu de yuanjing yu xingdong. [Vision and Actions on Jointly Building Silk Road Economic Belt and 21st Century Maritime Silk Road]'. *Renmin Ribao* [People's Daily], 29 March, 4.

Pieke, F. 2013. 'Immigrant China'. In *China Across the Divide: The Domestic and Global in Politics and Society*, edited by Rosemary Foot, pp. 97–121. Oxford: Oxford University Press.

Pu, X. 2016. 'One Belt, One Road: Visions and Challenges of China's Geoeconomic Strategy'. *Mainland China Studies* 59 (3): pp. 111–132.

Renminwang 2013. 'Zhongmian tianranqi guandao quanxian guantong ke raokai maliujia jinkou zhongdong yuanyou. [China-Myanmar Gas Pipeline Opens; Crude Oil Could Be Imported by Detouring the Strait of Malacca]'. Available at: http://finance.people.com.cn/n/2013/0605/c1004-21741624.html [Accessed 5 April 2019].

Renminwang 2017. 'Shida shijian jianzheng yidai yilu. [Ten Major Events Witnessed the Development of BRI]'. Available at: http://politics.people.com.cn/n1/2017/0514/c1001-29273580.html [Accessed 16 April 2020].

Shepard, W. 2017. 'The Real Role of the AIIB in China's New Silk Road'. *Forbes*. Available at: https://www.forbes.com/sites/wadeshepard/2017/07/15/the-real-role-of-the-aiib-in-chinas-new-silk-road/#69f51a637472 [Accessed 29 April 2020].

Su, X. 2012. 'Rescaling the Chinese State and Regionalisation in the Great Mekong Subregion'. *Review of International Political Economy* 19 (3): pp. 501–527.

Summers, T. 2016. 'China's "New Silk Roads": Sub-national Regions and Networks of Global Political Economy'. *Third World Quarterly* 37 (9): pp. 1628–1643.

Swaine, M. D. 2015. 'Chinese Views and Commentary on the "One Belt, One Road" Initiative'. *China Leadership Monitor* Issue 47: pp. 1–24.

Tian, S. (2015). *Chronology of China's belt and road initiative*. [Online]. Available at: http://news.xinhuanet.com/english/2015-03/28/c_134105435.htm [Accessed 8 April 2020].

Wang, H., et al. 2015. 'Haishang sichou zhilu 'qidian' zhizheng beihou. [What Is Behind the Debates of the Starting Point of Maritime Silk Road]'. *Zhongguo Shehui Kexuewang*. [Online]. Available at: http://www.cssn.cn/zx/201508/t20150809_2111775.shtml [Accessed 12 April 2020].

Wang, J., and Z. Shaoju. 2014. 'Yangshiwang diaocha: Yichang "sichou zhilu" qidian de kuasheng zhengduozhan. [CNTV Investigation: Provinces Vying to Become a Starting Point of Silk Road]'. *China Network Television*. Available at: http://news.cntv.cn/2014/07/15/ARTI1405392360592136.shtml [Accessed 12 April 2020].

Wang, Y. 2013. 'Wang Yi waizhang zai 'xinqidian, xinlinian, xinshijian—2013 zhongguo yu shijie' yantaohui shangde yanjiang. [Address by Foreign Minister Wang Yi at the Symposium 'New Starting Point, New Thinking and New Practice 2013: China and the World]'. Available at: http://www.fmprc.gov.cn/web/ziliao_674904/zyjh_674906/t1109156.shtml [Accessed 24 April 2020].

Wang, Y. 2016. 'Offensive for Defensive: The Belt and Road Initiative and China's New Grand Strategy'. *The Pacific Review* 29 (3): pp. 455–463.

Weinhardt, C., and T. ten Brink. 2020. 'Varieties of Contestation: China's Rise and the Liberal Trade Order'. *Review of International Political Economy* 27 (2): pp. 258–280.

Wu, Z. 2013. 'Zhongguo xiang weineiruila jiaofu yaogan weixing xitong. [China Delivered the Remote Sensing Satellite System to Venezuela]'. *Renmin Wang*. Available at: http://finance.people.com.cn/n/2013/0905/c1004-22810489.html [Accessed 2 April 2019].

Xi, J. 2013a. 'Xi zai nazhaerbayefu daxue de yanjiang. [Xi Delivers a Speech at Nazarbayev University]'. Available at: http://www.fmprc.gov.cn/mfa_chn/ziliao_611306/zyjh_611308/t1074151.shtml [Accessed 12 April 2020].

Xi, J. 2013b. 'Xi zai yindunixiya guohui de yanjiang. [Xi Delivers a Speech at the Indonesia Parliament]'. Available at: http://www.fmprc.gov.cn/mfa_chn/ziliao_611306/zyjh_611308/t1084354.shtml [Accessed 12 April 2020].

Xi, J. 2014a. 'Xi zai yatai jinghe zuzhi gongshang lingdaoren fenghui kaimushi shangde jianghua. [Xi Addresses the Opening Ceremony of the APEC CEO Summit]'. Available at: http://www.fmprc.gov.cn/web/ziliao_674904/zyjh_674906/t1208842.shtml [Accessed 12 April 2020].

Xi, J. 2014b. Xi zai "jiaqiang hulian hutong huoban guanxi" dongdaozhu huoban duihuahui shangde jianghua. [Xi Addresses the Dialogue on Strengthening Connectivity Partnership]'. Available at: http://www.fmprc.gov.cn/web/ziliao_674904/zyjh_674906/t1208702.shtml [Accessed 21 April 2020].

Xi, J. 2014c. 'Xi zai yindu shijie shiwu weuyuanhui de yanjiang. [Xi Addresses the Indian Council of World Affairs]'. Available at: http://www.fmprc.gov.cn/web/ziliao_674904/zyjh_674906/t1192744.shtml [Accessed 24 April 2020].

Xi, J. 2017. 'Xi zai "yidaiyilu" guoji hezuo gaofeng luntan yuanzuo fenghui shangde kaimuci [Opening Remarks by Xi at the Leader's Roundtable of the Belt and Road Forum for International Cooperation]'. Available at: http://www.xinhuanet.com/world/2017-05/15/c_1120976082.htm [Accessed 12 April 2020].

Xinhua 2019. 'Zhejiushi "yidai yilu" jianshi. [This is the Brief History of "BRI"]'. Available at: http://www.xinhuanet.com/world/2019-04/26/c_1124418156.htm [Accessed 12 April 2020].

Xue, L. 2017. '"Yidai yilu" yu zhongguo de "xin gaige kaifang". ["One Belt One Road" and China's "New Reform and Opening-up"]'. *Financial Times (Chinese)*. Available at: http://www.ftchinese.com/story/001075165?full=y [Accessed 8 March 2020].

Yang, J. 2014. 'Yang Jiechi zai boao yazhou luntan 2014 nianhui "sichou zhilu de fuxing: duihua yazhou lingdaoren" fenluntan shangde yanjiang. [Yang Jiechi Delivers a Speech at the Session of "Reviving the Silk Road: a Dialogue with Asian Leaders" at the Boao Forum for Asia Annual Conference 2014]'. Available at: http://www.fmprc.gov.cn/web/ziliao_674904/zyjh_674906/t1145772.shtml [Accessed 21 April 2020].

Ye, M. 2019. 'Fragmentation and Mobilisation: Domestic Politics of the Belt and Road in China'. *Journal of Contemporary China* 28 (119): pp. 696–711.

Yu, J. 2018. 'The Belt and Road Initiative: Domestic Interests, Bureaucratic Politics and the EU-China Relations'. *Asia Europe Journal* 16 (3): pp. 223–236.

Zhang, D. 2017. 'China Becomes World's Second-Largest Source of Outward FDI: Report'. *Xinhua News*. Available at: http://www.xinhuanet.com/english/2017-06/08/c_136350164.htm [Accessed 9 April 2020].

Zhang, F. 2015. 'Dangnei lingdao xiaozu changyu zhongde zuzhi zhiduhua. [Institutionalising Leading Small Groups Within the CCP]'. *Lilun yu gaige*. [Theory and Reform] Issue 4: pp. 10–14.

Zhang, Q. 2016. 'Bureaucratic Politics and Chinese Foreign Policy-making'. *The Chinese Journal of International Politics* 9 (4): pp. 435–458.

Zheng, Y. 2006. 'Explaining the Sources of *de facto* Federalism in Reform China: Intergovernmental Decentralisation, Globalisation, and Central-Local Relations'. *Japanese Journal of Political Science* 7 (2): pp. 101–126.

Zhou, W., and M. Esteban. 2018. 'Beyond Balancing: China's Approach Towards the Belt and Road Initiative'. *Journal of Contemporary China* 27 (112): pp. 487–501.

Zhu, Z. 2017. '"Yidai yilu" jinzhan quanshuli. [An Overview of the Progress of BRI]'. *Minsheng Securities*: pp. 1–40.

3

Illiberal Rationalism?

The Role of Political Factors in China's Growing (Economic) Footprint in Hungary

Ágnes Szunomár

Introduction

In parallel with its increasing global engagements, hallmarked by the 'Going global' (*zhou chu qu*) policy and the Belt and Road Initiative, China has become more active in the Central and Eastern European (CEE) region in the past two decades. Similarly to China's relations with developing and emerging regions, Chinese presence in CEE is characterized by developing trade relations, growing inflows of foreign direct investment (FDI), and recently also infrastructure projects carried out by Chinese companies, financed by Chinese loans (see Knoerich's chapter in this volume). Although when compared to China's economic presence globally or in the developed world its economic impact on CEE countries is still small, it has increased significantly over the past two decades. Since the relationship between China and the CEE region had a rather low profile in previous decades, this was quite a new phenomenon, but not an unexpected one. On the one hand, the transformation of the global economy and restructuring of China's own economy are responsible for growing Chinese interest in CEE, and on the other hand CEE also represents new challenges and new opportunities for China. In line with these challenges and opportunities, China created the 16+1 (later 17+1) platform in 2012—strongly connected to the Belt and Road Initiative (BRI) announced in 2013—to increase cooperation with and its influence in the CEE region. Hence, in addition to economic expansion, China has started to gain a foothold in political terms too.

These trends have inevitably drawn the attention of EU officials and Western European diplomats, scholars, and media to these intensifying efforts and the potential implications on the EU or even globally. According to EU fears, China woos CEE nations, which could result in the EU becoming even more

Ágnes Szunomár, *Illiberal Rationalism?* In: *Rising Power, Limited Influence.* Edited by: Indrajit Roy, Jappe Eckhardt, Dimitrios Stroikos, and Simona Davidescu, Oxford University Press.
DOI: 10.1093/oso/9780192887115.003.0004

divided (Karásková et al., 2020). The CEE countries' eagerness for cooperation with China is, however, far from being the same throughout the CEE region: the majority of countries are either cautious of engaging with non-EU players or have reservations about a growing Chinese presence, while a few—such as Hungary or Serbia—welcome the resulting economic and/or political opportunities.

For Hungary, integration to the 'West', into the Liberal International Order (LIO), has been a dream for decades, and has finally come true with NATO (1999) and EU membership (2004). Today, this LIO is in crisis as a result of various political and economic tendencies, including the rise of the 'new authoritarianism' (Ikenberry, 2018: 7) that appears to have become an attractive alternative to liberal democracy, one of the major pillars of the LIO (Mearshimer, 2019: 8). While China has embraced authoritarian rule from the very beginning, Hungary is one of the countries where liberal democracy appears to be in retreat only in the past decade. As many scholars (Buzogány, 2017; Cianetti et al., 2018; Csaba, 2019; Innes, 2015; Wilkin, 2018) point out, Hungary—one of the prominent players in the pro-democracy revolutions of 1989 and the CEE region's liberal transition—has recently shifted from democracy to autocracy. Among other reasons, the fall-out from the new core-periphery cleavage which has emerged in Europe in the wake of the global economic and financial crisis (Bohle, 2018; Gambarotto and Solari, 2015) also pushed the Hungarian government towards illiberalism, as well as towards China (and Russia).

This chapter examines China's growing presence in Hungary by investigating the economic relationship between the two countries, including trade relations and Chinese FDI, as well as infrastructure-related projects. Since the economic rationale seems to be missing in the majority of cases on the Hungarian side, considering the widening of the trade deficit, the low level of Chinese FDI, and an unnecessary but very expensive railway project, the chapter analyses the role of political factors connected to the aforementioned economic relationship. In line with Roy and Hu's (this volume) introduction, the chapter aims to understand the 'illiberal rationale', that is, the genuine motivation behind such a strong commitment of a declaredly illiberal democracy towards an authoritarian political system controlled by the Chinese Communist Party (CCP).

Viktor Orbán, the Prime Minister of Hungary, officially declared in 2014 that Hungary should 'go against the spirit of the age and build an illiberal political and state system' and that this—the thesis of illiberal democracy—'is an acceptable, viable and rational decision not only intellectually, but also from the point of view of a political programme', proclaiming loud and clear that Christian democracy is not necessarily a liberal but an illiberal democracy (Orbán 2014). This new, illiberal way of thinking that has emerged since 2010 resulted in—among others—centralizing measures pertaining to the whole economy and a shift in Hungary's foreign policy focus to the East.

Hungary, while being historically, geographically, and politically bounded to Europe and highly dependent on both trade and investment relations with developed, mainly-EU member states, has historically had good political relations with China since the People's Republic of China (PRC) was established. Moreover, Hungary seems to be committed to Beijing (rather than fellow European countries) even amidst growing European concerns about the various challenges China poses to Europe. Although Hungary is a small country with limited ability to influence global processes, with its illiberal rationalism—including the unduly appreciated and praised China relation—it does contribute to the uncertainties and fragmentation of Europe. Consequently—and ironically—it has a flatly destroying impact on the LIO, to which, not so long ago, it wanted to belong.

When mapping out the rationale behind the above-mentioned Hungarian engagement, it has to be emphasized that although Hungary hosts the majority of Chinese foreign direct investment stock in the CEE region, with a huge trade deficit and decreasing FDI flows, the Chinese-Hungarian relation has been—in the economic sense—less profitable in the past few years. In the meantime, however, the relationship has become more important politically, both for Hungary and for China, which provides a unique interpretation of the Chinese 'win-win' concept. The strong China-friendly stance of the Hungarian government provides a valuable European (and member of the EU) partner for China on the one hand, while, on the other hand, Hungary is also happy to have strong non-EU allies—such as China or Russia—that may contribute to the survival of the current political elite. Hungary's China relation is sometimes used as a bargaining chip when Budapest has tensions with Brussels (see Ferchen et al., 2018; Matura, 2018; Moreh, 2015; Szunomár, 2020), that is, for example, Hungary declaredly considers Chinese capital as an alternative if Brussels takes a firmer stance on Budapest.

Overall, political considerations seem to be more relevant to understanding the Chinese-Hungarian relationship than economic ones, particularly after the formulation of Orban's illiberal democracy. However, as Roy and Hu (this volume) suggest in their introduction, the politics of Chinese investment in Europe remains under-researched. To this end, the chapter is structured as follows: the first section gives a brief overview of the history of the relations between Hungary and China; the second part presents the main trends and patterns of economic relations; while the third section analyses the motivations of both China and Hungary, with a special focus on political rationale. Finally, conclusions will be drawn in order to evaluate the past developments and the future of the relation.

Chinese-Hungarian Relations in Retrospect

After the Second World War, both the People's Republic of China and the Hungarian People's Republic were established in 1949 (20 August and 1 October, respectively). Hungary formally recognized the PRC on 4 October 1949. In the 1950s the relationship began to develop, with a huge number of high-level visits followed by the improvement of economic, political, and cultural ties. Although the Hungarian-Chinese relationship was basically within the Soviet sphere of interest, Hungarian foreign policy did not follow, but rather differed from the policy of Moscow: in international affairs Budapest cooperated closely with Beijing and supported the Chinese position on Tibet, the One China Policy, and the United Nations Security Council membership from the very beginning (Vamos, 2006).

By the end of the 1950s, in line with the Sino-Soviet split, deep ideological differences emerged between the two countries, and in the 1960s—during the Chinese 'cultural revolution'—the relationship became increasingly colder. Later on, with the reorientation of the Chinese Communist Party in 1978 (economic reforms and opening up), the two countries were brought closer together again. The Chinese leadership was genuinely interested in the experiences of the Hungarian economic reform of 1968 (Bod, 2021); therefore a series of expert delegations visited Hungary to study the process of the reform. In the 1980s, state and inter-party relations were normalized, and high-level delegations were reinitiated too. After the democratic transition of Hungary in 1989, the level of contact between the two countries declined again, primarily as a result of the reorientation of Hungarian foreign policy, as more attention was given to Euro-Atlantic interests. For more than a decade, the degree of contact declined to a minimum; however, the relations were still free of tensions, within the framework of cordiality (Szunomár, 2015).

A new fruitful period began after the turn of the millennium, after the Hungarian Prime Minister, Péter Medgyessy, visited Beijing in 2003. In the early 2000s, the Hungarian economy showed a rapid catch-up in regional comparison, the government pursued a policy of stimulating demand, and in addition to developing existing economic relationships with the West it began to look East. This new wave of development was initiated independently by Hungary, as the government recognized that China is an unavoidable player in the global economy and international politics, while EU membership made Hungary more attractive to China as well (Szunomár, 2015). The government took several confidence-building measures and gestures towards China, including the creation of a new special envoy position within the Prime Minister's Office for the development of Hungarian-Chinese relations and for the coordination of the China-related work of governmental institutions and the public administration. The first results of the new policy were the arrival to Hungary of a branch of the Bank of China (2003), the creation of the Bilingual Chinese-Hungarian Primary School in Budapest (2004), and the launch of a direct flight connection between Budapest and Beijing (2004). Cultural contacts have deepened as well: the first Confucius Institute was established in Budapest in 2006, and four more were opened in the following years.

Although China was neglected by the first Orbán government (1998–2002), it has been receiving special attention from the more populist second, third, fourth, and fifth (2010–2014, 2014–2018, 2018–2022, 2022–) Orbán administrations.[1] Prime Minister Orbán first visited China at the end of 2010. This meeting was returned by premier Wen Jiabao's visit to Budapest in the summer of 2011. Wen made a European tour to three countries only: Hungary, Great Britain, and Germany. His journey started in Budapest and was designed to buy European debts and 'help' Europe by shoring up its investments. These meetings of high-ranking officials were followed by several other visits from both sides in the coming years (Matura, 2018; Szunomár, 2015).

After these visits and steadily strengthening relations, expectations on the Hungarian side were higher than ever. Prime Minister Orbán kept emphasizing the importance of the East even before the elections (and the already mentioned 'illiberal democracy' speech) of 2014 and said that although Hungary's 'ship is sailing in Western waters, the wind blows from the East' (Szunomár, 2015). The domestic media echoed the importance of the country's role as a gateway to China, while the international media reported on the new Chinese-Hungarian 'special relationship', causing mixed feelings among Hungary's neighbours and the EU institutions. Against this background, Hungary launched a new foreign economic policy in the spring of 2012, which aimed to diversify Hungary's foreign economic relations: the 'Eastern opening policy'. Although the Orbán government has emphasized

[1] The illiberal turn as well as the foundations of the current, populist Orbán regime go back to Fidesz's overwhelming success at the 2010 elections, and were consolidated when the Hungarian parliament adopted a new constitution that came into effect on the first day of 2012 (Buzogány, 2017; Krekó-Enyedi, 2018).

that it would like to maintain Hungary's strong and important economic relations with its traditional Western (European) partners, the main objective of this policy has been to reduce Hungary's economic dependence on trade with the West by improving economic relations with the East, particularly China.

Politically Driven Warming Up Resulting in Modest Economic Pay-off

As mentioned above, since the early 2000s Hungary has increasingly perceived China as a country which could bring economic benefits through developing trade relations, growing inflows of Chinese investments, and, recently, also through infrastructure projects carried out by Chinese companies and financed by Chinese loans. This perception, however, does not necessarily reflect the reality when it comes to actual data on trade volume, stock of Chinese FDI, or implemented infrastructure projects (Karásková et al., 2020).

Trade between Hungary and China indeed increased from the early 2000s onwards (relatively fast, from a very low base), coinciding with the accession of CEE countries to the European Union in 2004. When China created the 16+1 initiative (2012), trade volumes went somewhat higher all around the region, including in Hungary, although this increase was not balanced at all: while imports from China increased substantially, the growth of exports to China remained rather modest, and even decreased slightly for a few years after 2014 and 2017, respectively. In 2019, Hungary's exports to China were even below the 2012 level. Consequently, trade deficit increased rapidly, reaching almost 5,500 million USD, meaning that Chinese imports were more than four times higher than exports.

Regarding the structure of trade, the main imports of products from China are similar to most European countries: machinery and electronics. On the export side, Hungary exports to China product groups such as vehicles, machinery, and electronics, mainly produced by multinational companies located in Hungary and not by local Hungarian companies. Although China's hunger for high-quality agricultural products has recently been growing globally, the share of agricultural export is not significant for Hungary, as it is below 3%.

When it comes to FDI, as has been already mentioned, China's economic impact on Hungary, although accelerated significantly in the past decade, is relatively small, with Chinese investments dwarfed, for example, by German companies' investments. When calculating percentage shares based on

OECD statistics, we found that Chinese FDI stocks are around 2.5–3% of total inward FDI stocks in Hungary. It is worth mentioning that (Western) European investors are still responsible for more than 70% of total FDI stocks, while among non-European investors, companies from the United States, Japan, South Korea, or India are typically more important players than those from China.

The main Chinese investors targeting Hungary are primarily interested in telecommunication, electronics, the chemical industry, and transportation. Initially, Chinese investments flowed mostly into manufacturing (assembly), but over time, services have attracted more investment as well. Major investors are Wanhua, Huawei, ZTE, Lenovo, and BYD. The ownership structure of the investing Chinese companies is rather mixed: some are state-owned companies (such as Wanhua or ZTE), some are private firms (such as Huawei or BYD). However, the majority of private companies are so-called national champion companies of China, which assumes the home country's support (and a possible subordination) even if the owner is not directly the Chinese state (ten Brink, 2013).

Considering infrastructure, China has been planning and negotiating several construction projects in Hungary for at least a decade now: a train connection between downtown Budapest and Budapest airport; a bypass ring railway around Budapest; and two airports, in Eastern Hungary (Debrecen) and in Western Hungary (Szombathely), respectively. Yet none of these were realized (Brînză, 2020; Matura, 2018). The Budapest-Belgrade railway—a total section of 350 kilometres of railway between the Hungarian and the Serbian capital cities—seems to be the first project that will finally be implemented. However, several administrative procedures—including the European Commission's probing of Hungarian procurement processes—have delayed the project, which will not be ready before 2023. This is relatively surprising considering the fact that the Hungarian government was very keen on the railway project, and that when it signed the construction agreement in 2014 Prime Minister Orbán called it the most important moment in the cooperation between the European Union and China (Keszthelyi, 2014). The railway modernization is indeed important as well as costly, since Hungary signed a 2.1 billion USD loan agreement with China for this purpose (Ewing, 2020), making it one of the most expensive construction projects in Hungary. So far it seems that Chinese engineers will be responsible for carrying out planning, land surveying, and preparatory work, with Chinese contractors or subcontractors involved in the construction work. The CRE consortium responsible for the design and the reconstruction of the railway consists of three companies, two of them being companies founded for this purpose by the Chinese in Hungary, and the other one being the holding company Opus Global, controlled by an associate of Prime Minister Orbán (Than-Kőműves, 2020).

Exploring the Evolution and Rationale of Engagement on Both Sides

In 2000, the Chinese government initiated its 'Going global' policy aimed at encouraging domestic companies to become globally competitive. It introduced new policies to encourage firms to engage in overseas activities in specific industries, particularly in relation to trade. In 2001 this was integrated and formalized under the 10th Five-Year Plan, which also echoed the importance of 'going global' (Buckley et. al., 2007). This policy shift was part of the continuing reform and liberalization of the Chinese economy, and also reflected the Chinese government's desire to create internationally competitive and well-known companies and brands.

As China's economic growth has been slowing since 2010, the economy is facing new challenges and its economic strategy is transforming. New challenges require new answers, particularly regarding the fact that China has chosen not to stimulate its economy by turning inwards, but by opting for diplomacy, trade, and investment to broaden China's sphere of interest and business opportunities. In this way, it can promote economic relations, people-to-people links, and political influence, whilst strengthening the legitimacy of the ruling party and Xi Jinping (ten Brink, 2013). Thus, the focus on new directions, referred to as the already mentioned Belt and Road Initiative, is the result of domestic politics, geopolitics, and historical and economic rationales.

When the CEE countries became members of the European Union, China developed an interest in strengthening ties with them. Xi Jinping's 2009 vice-presidential tour to Europe signalled a real shift in the Chinese leadership's attitude towards the Central and Eastern European region and marked the beginning of a new stage in bilateral relations (Szunomár, 2018). Xi made an extended tour of Europe, visiting Belgium, Germany, Bulgaria, Romania, and Hungary (and spent more days in Budapest than anywhere else). The tour was framed as a visit to consolidate and develop economic cooperation between China and these five countries, but Xi's visit to CEE was more about China's evolving 'going out' investment strategy.

Beijing sees Central and Eastern Europe not only as one of its new frontiers for export expansion, but also as a strategic entry point for the wider

European market. Although the majority of EU member Central and Eastern European countries 'offer' the same economic and institutional characteristics and attracting factors—such as institutional stability, a qualified labour force that is cheaper compared to Western Europe, proximity to more affluent European markets, access to European/global value chains, etc.—Hungary is regarded as occupying a more prominent place in the (fictitious) ranking by the Chinese government than its geopolitical position would indicate. Consequently, the rationale behind China choosing Hungary as a host or hub for several projects and investments is not just economic or geographical, but also political.

In fact, Hungary is a country open to many types of cooperation, taking every opportunity to promote bilateral relations with Beijing, while its government supports China over many sensitive issues, such as lifting the arms embargo or granting market economy status. Hungary was the first European country to sign a memorandum of understanding with China on promoting the BRI. In 2016, Hungary (and Greece) prevented the EU from backing a court ruling against China's expansive territorial claims in the South China Sea, while in 2018 Hungary's ambassador to the EU was alone in not signing a report criticizing China's BRI for benefitting Chinese companies and Chinese interests. At the end of 2019, in the middle of the Huawei scandal, the Hungarian government even announced that Huawei is building a 5G network in Hungary. After the COVID-19 outbreak in 2020, Hungary was the loudest in Europe to praise Chinese support in supplying medical equipment (testing kits and medical masks) to European countries, while other EU countries had concerns about (and rejected to buy) these as many of the products tested were below standard or defective. Similarly, Hungary was the first in approving the Chinese Shinopharm (as well as the Russian Sputnik V) vaccine to speed up vaccination in the country. In response to criticism and mistrust from the Hungarian society, the government went even further and published a rather controversial table to prove that the 'Eastern' vaccines are far better than the 'Western' ones (Vaski, 2021).

In CEE as compared to Western Europe, there are fewer political expectations and economic complaints (or rather these are expressed more quietly) concerning China than in Western Europe. Hungary is a frontrunner in this regard, as governments never met government-level diplomatic delegations from Taiwan or Tibet, and anti-China protests are not allowed either. In addition, the critical approach does not characterize the Hungarian media (Bajomi-Lázár, 2013): its independence from the government is limited, thus the media discourse on China seems to be one-sided as it focuses overwhelmingly on economic data and developments, while topics like political values, human rights, minorities, or democracy are almost completely missing from the agenda (Turcsanyi et al., 2019). Turcsanyi et al. (2019) believe that a productive and useful discourse on China and on bilateral relations has never evolved in Hungary, and that the public sentiment is mostly influenced by a handful of agenda-setters, who are mostly politicians (from the government's side) and not experts on the matter.

China's relationships are deepening with countries such as Serbia, Greece, and Italy, and—as described above—Hungary has proved to be a true friend and supporter of China too. This might explain why China preferred this location instead of other countries in the CEE region from the very beginning of its presence there. But what makes Hungary so deeply engaged with China? As in the case of China, the answer is typically not of an economic nature anymore.

Economic interests in building relations with China used to be important for Hungary when the first prime ministerial visit took place after forty-four years, in 2003. As mentioned above, this period was characterized by modest prosperity in Hungary: the economy was able to show dynamic growth in the early 2000s, a growth advantage of 2% over the EU average. This period allowed the Hungarian government to look outside the Euro-Atlantic sphere in the hope of gaining economic benefits. Political alliance-building was not on the agenda since relations with the EU (and the US) were progressing, free of tensions and full of opportunities.

Conditions gradually began to change from 2006 onwards, as a result of the indebtedness of the 2000s and the forced but poorly structured fiscal adjustment before the global economic and financial crisis of 2008 (Andor, 2009). As Hungary is a very open economy, the global economic crisis had an enormously deep effect, further aggravated by the W-shaped recession caused by the European debt crisis. Between 2006 and 2012, Hungary's growth was on average 3.3% slower per year than the regional average (Portfolio, 2018).

The Fidesz party, led by Viktor Orbán, began its current string of victories in 2010 as a result of the Hungarian society's disillusionment with the socialist government and the effects of the crisis that were still painful in Hungary at that time (Bíró-Nagy, 2018). Rogers (2019: 101) characterizes the post-2010 Hungarian system as a 'resurgent political agency with an increased capacity to determine economic outcomes and subsequently the trajectory of Hungarian economic development'. Indeed, soon after coming into power, Prime Minister Orbán declared that the country's foreign policy would be taking a new direction. This was the already mentioned Eastern opening policy. Beijing and Moscow quickly rose to prominence, and relations began to evolve into an ever-closer partnership, hallmarked by high-level visits on a yearly basis, joint statements, and Memoranda of Understanding (Karásková et al., 2020). Various politically induced foreign capital dimensions have emerged in the past decade (Rogers 2019), originating from non-European, mainly Russian and Chinese actors, further complicated by the lack of transparency.

This process—that is, Hungary's turning towards the East—however, was not really justified by economic benefits in the decade that has passed since then. Hungary is still highly dependent on both trade and investment relations with developed, mainly EU-member states, while China represents a minor (although increasing) share. As far as trade or investment statistics are concerned, Hungary is also far from being among the most important partners for China. Trade relations remain relatively low and unbalanced, leading to increased trade deficit. Chinese FDI is also modest, representing less than 3% of total FDI stock in Hungary, concentrated in a few sectors, typically in manufacturing. The one and only infrastructure project so far, the Budapest-Belgrade railway, will be built from a record-high loan, while the benefits on the Hungarian side are often questioned.

As detailed above, economic benefits have been minor in the past decade compared to the enthusiasm of the Hungarian government for building further relations with China. Other countries in the region, such as Poland or Czechia, have already become disappointed or even suspicious about engagement with China, but Hungary continues to insist on the importance of the relationship. Consequently, economic rationale is not the major motivating factor, while the political rationale is more prevalent. Although there may not be a causal relation, a clear link can be found between Hungary's illiberal rationalism and the growing Chinese footprint in the Central and Eastern European country (Rogers 2019, 2020; Turcsanyi et al., 2019). Illiberal tendencies in Hungary are certainly not stemming from the development of Hungarian-Chinese relations, while Chinese economic presence is growing in countries with more liberal political regimes, too—but the two tendencies seem to be mutually reinforcing each other.

Since there are no clear indications that Chinese initiatives such as the Budapest-Belgrade railway project would bring future economic benefits to Hungary, the reason for the country being more open to Chinese initiatives is perhaps that this fits well into the logic of illiberalism both in domestic as well as foreign politics. Domestically, announcements via the Hungarian government-backed media about the flourishing Chinese-Hungarian relations—such as the 'Chinese' railway or China giving a helping hand during the COVID-19 pandemic with masks and vaccinations—provide positive legitimation for Orbán's politics. And on the foreign policy front, Hungary may expect that this 'alliance' could serve as a backup—a bargaining chip—when Budapest and the ruling Hungarian political elite has tensions with Brussels (and it does, relatively often) over various issues ranging from the rule of law to media independence, or when trying to silence critics amongst academics and non-governmental organizations.

Hungary indeed wants strong partners outside the EU because Orbán sees the EU as being in decline and not meeting its targets. He explained this at a conference in 2017, saying that 'Brussels became addicted to a utopia ... that is called a supranational Europe', while there are independent nations in Europe, with their own politics, intention, and will (Orbán, 2017). He added that in order to be successful, Europe needs new types of cooperation, where, for example, China must be treated with respect. Hungary—as he interpreted—is a front-runner in this regard, since this nation is 'of Eastern origin into whom Christianity has been grafted, that allows a special angle, so as we understand everything that is happening in China' (Orbán, 2017).

The above-mentioned developments may also embolden Hungary's illiberal turn by serving as a reference for the government to show that Hungary is not dependent on the EU. Although that is not the case—Hungary depends substantially on investments from developed countries, especially from EU member states, and has also received significant EU funding—the government can use these cases of Chinese investments to support its foreign economic policy both domestically and internationally.

Conclusion

This chapter has investigated China's growing presence in Hungary by evaluating the economic relationship between the two countries, with specific focus on the importance of the political rationale, while showing that the economic rationale is not always prevalent. Since 2010, Chinese-Hungarian (economic) relations seem to be driven by political rationale, since the lack of (major) economic benefits doesn't seem to dissuade Hungarian decision-makers from pursuing them, while the political commitment has become more visible and stronger in the past decade, both domestically and internationally.

This chapter shows that the enhanced cooperation between China and Hungary is quite a new phenomenon, but not an unexpected one. As many chapters of this volume suggest, the transformation of the global economy and the restructuring of China's economy are responsible for growing Chinese interest in the developed world, including the European Union. Hungary represents a dynamic, largely developed, less saturated economy, a new frontier for export expansion, a new entry point for Europe, and a cheap but qualified labour force. This adds up to fewer political or national security concerns and economic complaints compared to other European countries. At the same time, Hungary has become more open to Chinese business opportunities, too, especially after the global economic and financial crisis, with the intention of decreasing its economic dependency on Western (European) markets. Disappointment coming from the slower-than-expected catching-up processes to Western Europe also resulted in the country's turning towards the East, which has been further reinforced by populistic tendencies in the past decade. Be it a new investment of a Chinese automotive company, the Shanghai-based Fudan university opening a campus in Budapest, or the arrival of half a million vaccines from China, the Hungarian government as well as the government-backed media is praising the results achieved, commending the deepening ties, and also adding that the relations are of particular importance for Hungary.

While China often emphasizes that it offers a friendly partnership and a win-win cooperation with European countries, the growing Chinese presence in Europe is increasingly contested. Chinese investments into strategic sectors and infrastructure developments are perceived to threaten the competitiveness, strength, security, and unity of Europe, both economically and politically. Yet it is difficult to respond without a common European stance on China. And by 'dangling the spectre of China as an alternative partner' (Tucker, 2019), Hungary definitely makes it difficult to achieve a common European position. Since China is looking for allies in Europe, particularly within the EU, to promote its agenda, it engages with countries—EU member states or EU candidate countries (see Crawford, this volume)—with which it is able to find shared interests or a common ground. Hungary, which started an illiberal turn two decades after its democratic transition, is therefore an ideal springboard for the emerging East Asian power. However, in order to delve deeper into the root causes of such 'maverick' behaviour of Hungary, future research may investigate why some countries in Europe's periphery turn to China (for example Hungary), while others (for example Czechia, Poland, etc.) do not.

Acknowledgement

The chapter was written in the framework of the research project "China and Russia's infrastructure push in Central and Eastern Europe" (FK_138317) sponsored by the National Research, Development and Innovation Office. The author is also grateful for the support provided by the Bolyai János Research Fellowship of the Hungarian Academy of Sciences and the New National Excellence Program (ÚNKP-23-5-CORVINUS-153).

Bibliography

Andor, L. 2009. 'Hungary in the Financial Crisis: A (Basket) Case Study'. *Debatte Journal of Contemporary Central and Eastern Europe* 17 (3): pp. 285–296.

Bajomi-Lázár, P. 2013. 'The Party Colonisation of the Media: The Case of Hungary'. *East European Politics and Societies: and Cultures* 27 (1): pp. 69–89.

Bíró-Nagy, A. 2018. 'Why Orban Won? Explaining Fidesz's Dominance in Hungary'. *Foreign Affairs*, 10 April. Available at: https://www.foreignaffairs.com/articles/hungary/2018-04-10/why-orban-won [Accessed 20 December 2020].

Bod, P. A. 2021. 'Does a "Reform" Socialist Legacy Serve as an Asset or a Liability for Democratic Transformation? Considering Some Roots of "Orbanism"'. *Post-Communist Economies* 34 (6): pp. 736–755.

Bohle, D. 2018. 'European Integration, Capitalist Diversity and Crises Trajectories on Europe's Eastern Periphery'. *New Political Economy* 23 (2): pp. 239–253.

Brînză, A. 2020. 'China and the Budapest-Belgrade Railway Saga'. *The Diplomat*, 28 April. Available at: https://thediplomat.com/2020/04/china-and-the-budapest-belgrade-railway-saga/ [Accessed 20 December 2020].

Buckley, P. J., L. J. Clegg, A. R. Cross, X. Liu, H. Voss, and P. Zheng. 2007. 'The Determinants of Chinese Outward Foreign Direct Investment'. *Journal of International Business Studies* 38 (4): pp. 499–518.

Budapest Business Journal. 2019. 'Hungary Issues Panda Bonds for RMB 1 Bln'. 26 July 2017. Available at: https://bbj.hu/economy/hungary-issues-panda-bonds-for-rmb-1-bln_136406 [Accessed 20 December 2020].

Buzogány, A. 2017. 'Illiberal Democracy in Hungary: Authoritarian Diffusion or Domestic Causation?'. *Democratization* 24 (7): 1307–1325.

Cianetti, L., J. Dawson, and S. Hanley. 2018. 'Rethinking "Democratic Backsliding" in Central and Eastern Europe—Looking Beyond Hungary and Poland'. *East European Politics* 34 (3): pp. 243–256.

Clegg, J., and H. Voss. 2012. 'Chinese Overseas Direct Investment in the European Union'. Available at: http://www.chathamhouse.org/sites/default/files/public/Research/Asia/0912ecran_cleggvoss.pdf [Accessed 20 December 2020].

Csaba, L. 2019. 'Unorthodoxy in Hungary: An Illiberal Success Story?'. *Post-Communist Economies* 34 (1): pp. 1–14.

Ewing I. 2020. 'Hungary Signs $2.1bn Loan Agreement with China for Budapest-to-Belgrade Rail Link, CGTN Europe'. Available at: https://newseu.cgtn.com/news/2020-06-22/Hungary-signs-2-1bn-loan-with-China-for-Budapest-to-Belgrade-railway-Rx4Aiq8DHq/index.html [Accessed 20 December 2020].

Ferchen M., F. N. Pieke, F.-P. van der Putten, T. Hong, and J. de Blécourt. 2018. *Assessing China's Influence in Europe through Investments in Technology and Infrastructure.* Leiden Asia Centre. https://www.clingendael.org/publication/assessing-chinas-influence-europe-through-investments

Gambarotto F., and S. Solari. 2015. 'The Peripheralization of Southern European Capitalism within the EMU'. *Review of International Political Economy* 22 (4): pp. 788–812.

Ikenberry, G. J. 2018. 'The End of Liberal International Order?'. *International Affairs* 94 (1): pp. 7–23.

Innes, A. 2015. 'Hungary's Illiberal Democracy'. *Current History* 114 (770): pp. 95–100.

Karásková, I., A. Bachulska, Á. Szunomár, and S. Vladisavljev, eds. 2020. 'Empty Shell No More: China's Growing Footprint in Central and Eastern Europe. Prague, Csehország: Asociace Pro Mezinárodní Otázky (AMO)'. Available at: https://chinaobservers.eu/wp-content/uploads/2020/04/CHOICE_Empty-shell-no-more.pdf [Accessed 20 December 2020].

Keszthelyi, C. 2014. 'Belgrade–Budapest Rail Construction Agreement Signed'. *Budapest Business Journal*, 17 December. Available at: https://bbj.hu/budapest/belgrade-budapest-rail-construction-agreement-signed_89894 [Accessed 20 December 2020].

Krekó P., and Z. Enyedi. 2018. 'Explaining Eastern Europe: Orbán's Laboratory of Illiberalism'. *Journal of Democracy* 29 (3): pp. 39–51.

Matura, T. 2018. 'The Belt and Road Initiative Depicted in Hungary and Slovakia'. *Journal of Contemporary East Asia Studies* 7 (2): pp. 174–189.

Mearshimer, J. J. 2019. 'Bound to Fail—The Rise and Fall of the Liberal International Order'. *International Security* 43 (4): pp. 7–50.

Morck, R., B. Yeung, and M. Zhao. 2008. 'Perspectives on China's Outward Foreign Direct Investment'. *Journal of International Business Studies* 39 (3): pp. 337–350.

Moreh, C. 2015. 'The Asianization of National Fantasies in Hungary: A Critical Analysis of Political Discourse'. *International Journal of Cultural Studies* 19 (3): pp. 341–353.

Orbán, V. 2014. 'Speech at Băile Tuşnad (Tusnádfürdő) of 26 July 2014'. Available at: https://visegradpost.com/en/2019/07/29/orbans-full-speech-at-tusvanyos-political-philosophy-upcoming-crisis-and-projects-for-the-next-15-years/ [Accessed 20 December 2020].

Orbán, V. 2017. 'Speech at the Lámfalussy Lecture Series, 23 January 2017'. Available at: http://www.miniszterelnok.hu/orban-viktor-beszede-lamfalussy-lectures-szakmai-konferencian/ [Accessed 20 December 2020].

Portfolio. 2018. Összeomlás vagy sikersztori?—Így teljesített a magyar gazdaság 2000 óta'. *Portfolio*, 28 March. Available at: https://www.portfolio.hu/gazdasag/20180328/osszeomlas-vagy-sikersztori-igy-teljesitett-a-magyar-gazdasag-2000-ota-280426 [Accessed 20 December 2020].

Rogers, S. 2019. 'China, Hungary, and the Belgrade-Budapest Railway Upgrade: New Politically-Induced Dimensions of FDI and the Trajectory of Hungarian Economic Development'. *Journal of East-West Business* 25 (1): pp. 84–106.

Rogers, S. 2020. 'Hungarian Authoritarian Populism: A Neo-Gramscian Perspective'. *East European Politics* 36 (1): pp. 107–123.

Szunomár. Á. 2015. 'Blowing from the East'. *International Issues & Slovak Foreign Policy Affairs* 24 (3): pp. 60–78.

Szunomár, Á. 2018. 'One Belt, One Road: Connecting China with Central and Eastern Europe?'. In *The Belt & Road Initiative in the Global Arena: Chinese and European Perspectives*, edited by Y. Cheng, L. Song, and L. Huang, pp. 71–85. Singapore: Palgrave Macmillan.

Szunomár, Á. 2019. 'China's Investments and Infrastructural Expansion in Central and Eastern Europe'. In *Opportunities and Challenges: Sustainability of China-EU Relations in a Changing World*, edited by Jian Shi and Guenter Heiduk, pp. 84–103. Beijing, China: China Social Sciences Press.

Szunomár, Á. 2020. 'Home and Host Country Determinants of Chinese Multinational Enterprises' Investments into East Central Europe'. In *Emerging-market Multinational Enterprises in East Central Europe*, edited by Á. Szunomár, pp. 51–86. Palgrave Macmillan.

ten Brink, T. 2013. *China's Kapitalismus. Entstehung, Verlauf, Paradoxien/China's Capitalism: Emergence, Trajectory, Paradoxes.* Frankfurt and New York, NY: Campus.

Than, K., and A. Kőműves. 2020. 'Hungary, China Sign Loan Deal for Budapest-Belgrade Chinese Rail Project'. *Reuters*, 24 April. Available at: https://www.reuters.com/article/us-hungary-china-railway-loan-idUSKCN226123 [Accessed 20 December 2020].

Tucker, J. 2019. 'Avenues to Europe: China's Relationship with Hungary, ISDP Voices 25 February 2019'. Available at: https://isdp.eu/chinas-relationship-with-hungary/ [Accessed 20 December 2020].

Turcsanyi, R. Q., I. Karásková, T. Matura, and M. Simalcik. 2019. 'Followers, Challengers, or By-Standers? Central European Media Responses to Intensification of Relations with China'. *Intersections EEJSP* 3(5): pp. 49–67.

Vamos, P. 2006. 'Sino-Hungarian Relations and the 1956 Revolution. Woodrow Wilson International Center for Scholars'. Working Paper No. 54, p. 44. Available at: http://www.wilsoncenter.org/publication/sino-hungarian-relations-and-the-1956-revolution [Accessed 20 December 2020].

Vaski, T. 2021. 'Gov't Publishes Controversial Data to Prove Sinopharm and Sputnik Better Than Pfizer'. *Hungary Today*, 26 April. Available at: https://hungarytoday.hu/hungary-vaccines-vaccine-effectiveness-inoculation-vaccine-effectiveness-comparison-pfizer-sputnik-sinopharm/ [Accessed 20 December 2020].

Wilkin, P. 2018. 'The Rise of "Illiberal" Democracy: The Orbánization of Hungarian Political Culture'. *Journal of World-Systems Research* 24 (1): pp. 5–42.

4

China's Normative Influence in Europe

The Case of Sino-Italian Relations under the Belt and Road Initiative

Filippo Boni

Introduction

China's rise has been one of the most consequential developments of the past twenty years.[1] The announcement of the Belt and Road Initiative (BRI) in 2013, with the promise to create a New Silk Road from China to Europe through massive infrastructure investment, has accelerated China's ascendance to the world stage, and it has expanded its economic and political footprint globally. Starting from the Global South, and moving progressively towards Europe and more developed economies, Beijing's inroads into the political, economic, and social fabric of partner countries have garnered the attention of academics, journalists, and government officials concerned with understanding the motives and impacts of China's international behaviour. The main question, to which a burgeoning body of literature has devoted its attention, is whether China and, more generally, non-Western, rising powers are undermining and challenging the US-led, Liberal International Order (LIO) (Bettiza and Lewis, 2020; Economy, 2022; Ikenberry et al., 2018; Lee et al., 2020; Rolland, 2020).

The literature on China's relationship with the LIO can be summarized around three main strands. First, there are those who argue that China is not going to replace the US as the world's dominant power. The prominent Chinese scholar Yan Xuetong, for instance, notes that 'Beijing has no clear plan for filling this [the US'] leadership vacuum and shaping new international norms from the ground up' (2019: 40). Similarly, Fareed Zakaria points

[1] The author would like to thank Indrajit Roy, Jappe Eckhardt, Giles Mohan, and Ran Hu for their helpful comments on earlier drafts. The chapter has also benefitted from the feedback received at the workshop 'The Politics of Chinese Investment in Europe' at the University of York in 2019, and at the Political Studies Association annual conference in 2021.

Filippo Boni, *China's Normative Influence in Europe*. In: *Rising Power, Limited Influence*. Edited by: Indrajit Roy, Jappe Eckhardt, Dimitrios Stroikos, and Simona Davidescu, Oxford University Press. © Oxford University Press (2024). DOI: 10.1093/oso/9780192887115.003.0005

out that China 'has not gone to war since 1979. It has not used lethal military force abroad since 1988. Nor has it funded or supported proxies or armed insurgents anywhere in the world since the early 1980s. That record of non-intervention is unique among the world's great powers' (2019).

Opposed to these views, there are scholars and analysts who instead suggest that the BRI is a deliberate attempt by the Chinese Communist Party (CCP) to build a 'Sinocentric "community of shared destiny" in Asia' which will eventually turn China into a normative power capable of setting the rules of the game in global governance (Callahan, 2016: 3). Echoing this more sceptical approach to China's global outreach, in the 'Strategic Outlook' Joint Communication of 12 March 2019, the European Commission for the first time termed China a 'systemic rival' (EU Commission, 2019: 1). Along similar lines, the NATO Strategic Concept in 2022 mentioned for the first time that China's 'stated ambitions and coercive policies challenge our [the Alliance's] interests, security and values' (NATO Strategic Concept, 2022). Finally, there is also a third strand in the literature which takes a middle ground, arguing that China partly integrates and partly challenges existing rules and norms (De Graaf et al., 2020; Glaser, 2019). The essence of this strand is perhaps best captured by Lina Benabdallah, who observes that Beijing's approach is one that 'simultaneously supports/integrates the international order and also changes parts of the order that do not match its preferences' (2019: 93).

Situated within these debates, this chapter's contribution is two-fold: first, the analysis assesses the extent of China's normative influence in Europe by investigating how Chinese narratives on key issues pertaining to the LIO are entering the Italian political discourse and whether political elites take on board such narratives. The chapter argues that while Italy's historic, Western-orientated strategic posture has not been altered as a result of a deepening Sino-Italian entente—as shown for instance by Italy's endorsement of the G7's proposal of an alternative to the BRI (Meacci, 2021)—there has been an uptake among some of the elites (for example, members of parliament, bureaucrats) of China's narratives on key issues, including human rights in Xinjiang and Hong Kong's democratic status.

Second, the analysis presented here contributes to the burgeoning, yet still relatively limited, literature assessing the role that populist parties play in shaping foreign policy while in government (Coticchia and Vignoli, 2020; Chryssogelos, 2017; Destradi and Plagemann, 2019). In doing so, the analysis focuses on Italy's Five Star Movement, as they were the party that won the 2018 elections and obtained 33% of the seats in Parliament. As such, they were in a position to steer key government policies, including foreign policy, given that the foreign minister was one of the leaders of the movement (until 2022). Despite the party's relevance waning over time, especially in the post 2021 period, the analysis presented here sheds important light on the role that populist parties play in relations with China while in government.

The chapter proceeds as follows. The next section outlines the case selection and the methodology used in the analysis. The third section discusses the conceptual framework of strategic narratives that is used in this chapter, by foregrounding the importance of 'system', 'identity', and 'issue' narratives. This section also introduces the main messages that China has been presenting to foreign audiences about its rise and on some of the key issues (for example, Hong Kong and Xinjiang) that are then analysed in the empirical parts. The fourth section looks at China's engagement with Italian political elites, with a specific focus on one of Italy's ruling parties, the Five Star Movement (M5S). The final section dissects the impact that the 2019 Memorandum of Understanding (MoU) signed by Italy on the BRI had on the promotion of China's view on key issues as part of the partnership between Xinhua and ANSA.

Case Selection and Methodology

Italy is an ideal case study to assess China's normative influence in Europe for a number of reasons. First, it became the first G7 country to sign an MoU with China on the BRI during President Xi Jinping's visit to the country in March 2019. Such a move has put Italy under the spotlight and at the centre of the wider Sino-US global competition. In relation to the MoU, *The New York Times* emphatically titled it 'Italy's Deal with China Signals a Shift as US Influence Recedes', and the Trump Administration expressed its concerns about Italy's decision very vocally, with US Secretary of State Mike Pompeo criticizing China's 'debt-trap diplomacy' (Agence France Press, 2019; Horowitz, 2019). In a similar fashion, the then EU's budget commissioner, Günther Oettinger, went as far as to note about the Italy-China deal that 'a European veto right, or a requirement of European consent could be worth considering' (Euractiv, 2019). As such, what happens in Italy can be indicative of wider trends in EU-China and Sino-US relations alike.

Second, between 2000 and 2021 Italy was the third largest recipient of Chinese FDI in Europe, after the UK and Germany (Kratz et al., 2022). In the Italian government's views, the MoU was aimed at providing Italian businesses market access to China, in order to increase bilateral trade between the two countries and boost Italy's exports to China. As the then

Italian Prime Minister, Giuseppe Conte, claimed during a speech in Parliament in 2019, 'our economic and commercial attention [towards the BRI] is entirely legitimate and … in this way we will be able to strengthen our exports towards a market of gigantic proportion' (Camera dei Deputati, Resoconto Stenografico Assemblea n.144, 2019). Italy's desire to increase its economic ties with China, coupled with the latter's attempts at gaining influence in Europe, represent an ideal convergence of interests to assess the extent to which growing economic relations translate into normative influence.

To this end, the chapter has collected and analysed, through critical discourse analysis, a wealth of new empirical material to assess the impact of the signing of the MoU on the BRI on two specific areas: the uptakes of Chinese narratives among Italian elites; and the impact that media partnership agreements have on the way in which key issues are presented to the general public. To explore elite uptakes of narratives, the chapter has analysed the articles published between 2013 and 2020 on the official blog of M5S. To investigate the media partnership, the analysis is based on 219 articles between 2013 and 2020 that were published by Italy's main independent news agency, Agenzia Nazionale Stampa Associata (ANSA), which entered into a partnership with Xinhua as a result of the MoU. This enabled an assessment over time of the changes, if any, that the MoU has brought about for ANSA's coverage on key issues.

Norm Entrepreneurship and Strategic Narratives: A Conceptual Framework to Understand China's Normative Influence

In line with the 'power as influence' approach outlined in the introduction to this volume, this chapter builds on insights from the literature on how rising powers engage with the norms and values underpinning the international order as well as engaging with the scholarly works on strategic narratives. In doing so, it incorporates in the analysis both state as well as previously underexplored sub-state actors (for example, the media), thereby moving beyond the theoretical state-centrism present in much of the literature dealing with China's normative influence in Europe.

In looking at how rising powers engage with the LIO, Bettiza and Lewis (2020) have identified four types of contestation that illiberal powers engage in, namely liberal performance, liberal mimicry, civilizational essentialization, and counter-norm entrepreneurship. In this chapter, the analysis focuses on counter-norm entrepreneurship, namely a form of contestation which involves articulating and advancing globally a set of non-liberal (1) social and political norms and (2) visions of international order. They argue that the deployment of narratives pertaining to new norms and values represents an 'attempt to positively promote a coherent set of "illiberal" ideas, institutions, and practices worldwide that reflect an ideological alternative to liberal forms of domestic and international order' (2020: 11). Along similar lines, Miskimmon, O'Loughlin, and Roselle have provided a framework to understand what they have called 'strategic narratives', defined as 'means for political actors to construct a shared meaning of international politics, and to shape the perceptions, beliefs, and behaviour of domestic and international actors' (2014: 1). Strategic narratives are articulated around three levels: (1) system narratives, looking at the nature and future of the international system; (2) identity narratives, about the actor's identities; and (3) issue narratives, about topical, contextual problems. Building on these works, and looking specifically at Russian narratives in France, Oliver Schmitt presents an analysis of the effectiveness of these narratives, arguing that if a strategic narrative is successful, 'it should be possible to observe the gradual transfer of content of the Chinese strategic narratives within the French political discourse' (2018: 494). This latter point is of particular interest, since it brings into the analysis a discussion of whether local political elites and publics buy into these narratives advanced by foreign powers, a theme that will be assessed in detail in the ensuing parts of the chapter.

Before moving on to the empirical sections, it is important to identify what are Chinese discourses around domestic and international issues, as well as what type of image Beijing seeks to portray abroad. This is key, as the role of discourse and image building in Beijing's approach to foreign policy has become increasingly more important over the years. The 'Communiqué on the Current State of the Ideological Sphere', issued by the central party office in April 2013 and known as 'Document 9', instructed 'all levels of Party and Government, especially key leaders' to 'make work in the ideological sphere a high priority'. The document further specified that the CCP and its leaders and cadres 'must persist in correct guidance of public opinion, insisting that the correct political orientation suffuse every domain and process in political engagement, form, substance, and technology' (Communiqué on the Current State of the Ideological Sphere, 2013). Along similar lines, at the Central Conference on Work Relating to Foreign Affairs in November 2014, Chinese President Xi Jinping noted that China needed to 'give a good Chinese narrative, and better communicate China's message to the world' (Ministry of Foreign Affairs of the People's Republic of China, 2014). As part of his message at the 19th National Congress of the

Communist Party of China in October 2017, President Xi Jinping reinforced this message by noting that one of the priorities was to 'strengthen the penetration, guidance, influence, and credibility of the media' (Xinhua, 2017). As these official pronouncements demonstrate, Beijing's desire to control international narratives has become a key component of the country's public diplomacy. There are some key themes around which China portrays itself on the world stage, some of which pertain to the international system and China's visions for and role within it, while others are related to key domestic issues. Regarding the former, 'peaceful rise', 'community of shared destiny', and 'non-interference' are some of the dominant themes that are primarily aimed at reassuring other countries that China's ascent is not a zero-sum game and that it does not threaten any country or region. On the domestic front, 'one country, two systems' when referring to Hong Kong, the sanctity of 'sovereignty' and 'territorial integrity', as well as a 'Xinjiang model' of managing ethnic diversity are discourses often put forwards by authorities and state media.

Engaging Italian Elites

The way in which Chinese narratives are absorbed among elites is particularly important to investigate, since it provides evidence of how China is progressively relaxing its focus on 'non-interference' while simultaneously aiming to cultivate consent in key states (Zou and Jones, 2020). Among the main Italian political parties, the M5S has been at the forefront of debates about its role in promoting closer Sino-Italian ties and in the signing of the MoU on the BRI. To be sure, under the Democratic Party's centre-left government (2013–2018), then Prime Minister Paolo Gentiloni attended the BRI summit in Beijing in April 2017, and his predecessor from the same party, Matteo Renzi, had repeatedly expressed an interest in tapping the full potential of an economic relationship with China (Fatiguso, 2017). However, it is one thing to eye business opportunities with China, and another to sign an MoU expressing the will to endorse China's global ambitions.

Those who were in favour and facilitated the signing of the MoU often presented an economic rationale behind the decision. Rejecting the controversy that the signing had created, both with Washington and other European partners, the then undersecretary of state for economic development stated that the deal was 'about helping companies do business' (Reuters, 2019). However, in the three years after the MoU was signed, the economic benefits of the partnership were yet to be seen. By looking at official data from the Italian

Trade Agency, there seems to be a limited impact that the MoU has had on Italy-China trade exchanges, as demonstrated by a number of indicators.

First, between 2017 and 2022, Italy's market share in China's imports remained constant at 1.1%. Second, trade balance between the two countries has not changed in a meaningful way, and Rome was not able to rebalance its trade relationship with Beijing, which is still tilted in the latter's favour. While Italy's exports went up from 12.96 billion in 2019 to 16.44 billion in 2022, so have the imports from China, which rose from 31.66 billion in 2019 to 57.50 billion in 2022, with a negative trade deficit at -41 billion in 2022. (Ministero degli Affari Esteri e della Cooperazione Internazionale, 11 August 2023). If we expand the picture to investments from China to Italy, we find that apart from the notable exception of Jetion Solar (China) Co.'s deal with Eni SpA, an Italian firm and one of the major oil companies in the world, to invest about 2.2 billion USD to develop new solar projects, Italy failed to attract many concrete projects in the year following the signing of the MoU (Crawford, 2020). China's engagement has instead started to yield results in the political sphere, and specifically in the uptake of Chinese narratives among some of the key Members of Parliament (MP), bureaucrats, and academics, especially those close to the M5S.

The penetration of Chinese narratives becomes evident when looking at the content of the articles published about China (including its culture, politics, and society) on the website BeppeGrillo.it (now rebranded as 'Il Blog delle Stelle'), the blog of Beppe Grillo, the founding father and political guarantor of the M5S. Here we find examples of both 'system' and 'issue' narratives, as well as of the uptake of alternative visions of the LIO by some of the elites in key countries. In June 2018, only ten days after the self-proclaimed 'Governo del Cambiamento' (Government for Change) was sworn in following the March 2018 elections, the blog published an article penned by the then undersecretary of economic development, which was a sort of manifesto for the relationship that the new government intended to establish with China. Interestingly, some passages of the article advocated for learning the Chinese way of dealing with a number of financial ('Who can help us manage our debt? It is China'), public security ('Which is the country where public security is effective? It is China'), and geopolitical issues alike ('Which is the country which is closely aligned with Russia and which can help us rewrite Asia's geopolitics? It is China').[2] Following this article, between June 2018 and January 2020, there were twelve more articles published on this online

[2] A similar argument was also made in another article, published in May 2018, which outlined the five pillars of China's economic success (Geraci, 2018). The translation of this and the other articles in the chapter was done by the author.

platform, all promoting greater cooperation and understanding between Italy and China. As far as system narratives are concerned, when the US started directing its criticism at the Italian government's decision to sign the MoU on the BRI, one article ironically stated that such a decision had unleashed the reaction of the 'little White House', also reporting the words of China's Ministry of Foreign Affairs which defined the criticism as 'absurd' (Parenti, 2019c). In a similar fashion, China's rise is defined as 'peaceful', and Beijing is praised for 'not judging and for trying to understand before expressing an opinion and advancing proposals', thereby making a not-so-veiled reference to the non-interference principle (Parenti, 2019b). In addition, in another article titled 'BRI: A New Form of International Relations', the author praised China's cooperation with Africa, stating that Beijing's approach to the African continent provides 'evidence of a different cooperation model that can become a point of reference for the entire world' (Parenti, 2019a).

Beyond system narratives, another important example is the way in which the Xinjiang issue has been covered in the blog. In particular, an article published in September 2019, at the height of reports coming out of Xinjiang about the re-education camps for Uighurs, argued that the Italian government, and Western media by and large, have 'raised conjectures and fabrications on Chinese responses to terrorism'. The article was the report of a visit that the author undertook to Xinjiang and whose conclusion was that internment camps did not exist and that it was just a 'label' used by the CNN and the BBC 'to discredit the Chinese government, presented as one repressive of minorities'. In addition, the article mentioned the words of the Director of the Historic Institute in Serbia, who reportedly claimed that 'in Serbia too we should have adopted these measures [i.e. the ones adopted in Xinjiang], and we have instead imprisoned radicalised youngsters, thereby worsening their existential conditions' (Parenti, 2019d).

In order to assess the elites' uptake of narratives, it is also important to see if politicians and organizations 'walk the talk' and implement decisions, or whether they remain silent, on key issues defining a country's political outlook. Developments in Hong Kong during 2019 are a case in point. Anti-Extradition Bill protests significantly mobilized people in the Special Administrative Region (SAR) of China and led to a tightening of Beijing's control over the territory.[3] While the Italian government, including members of the M5S, officially expressed concerns about the worrying developments in Hong Kong, there is evidence that the Chinese narratives on this issue—primarily focusing on the controversial national security law passed in June

[3] For an assessment of the developments in Hong Kong, see Tritto and Abdulkadir (2020: 163–183).

2020—are penetrating among key members of parliament of one of Italy's ruling parties.

When asked about the Italian Government's position on the ongoing Hong Kong protests during a visit to China to attend the China International Import Export in Shanghai, the Italian Foreign Minister claimed that 'Italy does not interfere in other countries' affairs', thereby keeping a neutral stance on the tensions in Hong Kong (ANSA, 2019). On 28 November 2019, Joshua Wong, one of the main leaders of the Hong Kong protests, was invited to give a talk, via Skype, at the press conference 'La posizione di Italia e UE sulle vicende di Hong Kong' (Italy's and the EU's position on recent developments in Hong Kong). This event was organized by most of the major political forces in the Italian parliament, but excluded M5S representatives, and it was criticized by the Chinese Embassy in Rome with unusually strong words. According to the press release, the spokesperson of the Chinese mission argued that it was a 'serious mistake as well as an irresponsible behaviour' and stated that they were 'strongly dissatisfied with it' (Embassy of the People's Republic of China in the Republic of Italy, 2019). This statement sparked reactions by Italian authorities, starting from Italy's Foreign Minister, Mr Di Maio, who stated that 'commercial ties ... cannot undermine the respect for our institutions, our Parliament and our government' (Bechis, 2019). In a similar fashion, the Chair of the Foreign Affairs Committee of the Chamber of Deputies, a M5S MP, defined China's remarks as 'unacceptable'. A few days later, the same committee unanimously approved a resolution on Hong Kong which called for a European approach on the issue, and which clinched one of Italy's core foreign policy principles, namely the 'defence of individuals' liberty and rights', as one of the members of the committee declared on Twitter. At the time, though, a M5S MP published on the Movement's blog an article calling for a radical change in the framing of the resolution on Hong Kong, as well as for Italy's non-interference to continue. In his appeal for reconsidering the statement coming from the Italian Parliament, he called for looking at human rights 'from the angle of humanity, not that of CNN', and defined the 'West' and the 'exporters of democracy' as exports primarily of 'chaos, great conflicts, urban guerrillas and a dramatic worsening of human rights' (Cabras, 2019), thereby echoing some of the criticism that China often directs against the US.

The developments discussed in this section are indicative of two trends. First, claims that Italy is shifting strategically from the US and Europe towards China are clearly misplaced. As Mr Di Maio claimed in an interview in 2020, 'Italy is in the Euro Atlantic alliance, in NATO and in the European Union', adding that 'Italy has always been a country with friendly ties with a lot of states in the world, and a bridge between East and West' (SkyTg24, 2020: 3:20–3:29). There are also a wide range of parties across the left-right political spectrum, including the Partito Democratico, Fratelli d'Italia, Lega, and +Europa, that have warned of the potential implications of Beijing's growing clout in Italy. Second, the analysis presented in this section shows how Chinese narratives, whether system- or issue-based, were taken on board by some intellectuals and MPs of one of Italy's ruling parties between 2018 and 2022. An explanation for this uptake can be found in Olivier Schmitt's work looking at why narratives succeed. He argues that 'the degree to which an external strategic narrative resonates with local political myths determines the effectiveness and impact of the strategic narrative' (2018: 488). The 'political myth' of anti-Americanism has been one of the core values of the M5S from the very inception and, in this context, China's revisionist narratives have found a fertile ground in a party that already held some of the views advanced by Beijing.

'Telling the China Story': An Assessment of the ANSA-Xinhua Partnership

Another important, yet under-studied, area of Sino-Italian relations under the BRI is the media cooperation between the two countries (for exceptions see Ghiretti and Mariani, 2021; Boni, 2022). The MoU on the BRI signed in March 2019 included the important content-sharing agreement between ANSA, Italy's main independent news agency, and Xinhua, as well as the MoU between RAI, Italy's State Television, and China Media Group.[4] These agreements were part of a wider web of media engagements, including: (1) the partnership between Italian media company Class Editori, which publishes a business paper, with Xinhua and China Media Group; and (2) il Sole 24 Ore, Italy's main business daily newspaper, signing a partnership with *Economic Daily*, a Chinese state-sponsored paper (Han and Harth, 2022). Beyond the Italian case, media cooperation is one of the key areas in which China has invested in its public diplomacy outreach. In an editorial published on 25 November 2019, the Chinese newspaper *Global Times* stated that 'China needs to counter Western public opinion war' (*Global Times*, 2019). This article, as well as a few others in the following days, aimed at

[4] The full texts of both agreements are available at: 'Firmato accordo di collaborazione ANSA-Xinhua', ANSA, 23 March 2019, http://www.ansa.it/sito/notizie/politica/2019/03/22/firmato-accordo-di-collaborazione-ansa-xinhua-_ff9868d9-050d-4747-b0ab-5a7a3fa44206.html; 'Memorandum di Intesa tra RAI–Radiotelevisione italiana S.p.a. e China Media Group', http://www.governo.it/sites/governo.it/files/Intese_istituzionali_Italia-Cina.pdf.

pushing back against Western reports on Xinjiang, especially in the wake of the International Consortium of Investigative Journalists (ICIJ)'s release of leaked documents about detention camps in China's Westernmost region. Chinese economic activities, growing political clout, and, by and large, its going global policy have been accompanied by systematic media efforts that helped frame BRI-related issues and to present Chinese views to the domestic audiences in the countries where political and economic ties were being developed. According to a 2018 Reporters Without Borders report, China has adopted the strategy to present China Watch supplements as 'reasonably enjoyable reads' which are 'nonetheless Trojan horses that enable Beijing to insinuate its propaganda into the living rooms of elites' (Reporters Without Borders, 2018).[5] The report ended with some fifteen recommendations for governments to push back and limit China's growing influence over the media. However, a study of Chinese media in Africa focusing on Kenya and South Africa suggested a limited impact of China's media activities, but noted that 'an indirect effect might be occurring: some students, both in Kenya and South Africa, were receptive toward some of the news values and journalistic norms that characterize Chinese news reporting in Africa' (Wassermann and Morales, 2018). It is therefore important to assess the media strategy deployed in China's relations with Italy.

To this end, the analysis focused on the media coverage on ANSA's website of the Xinjiang issue between 1 October 2013 to 31 January 2020. Xinjiang has been selected in order to ensure methodological rigour, as it is suitable to be analysed over time, given that it has been a regular staple in discussions and allegations, especially from the US and the West, about alleged abuses of Uighurs for a long time. For this reason, it is possible to gauge the variations, if any, that the partnership between ANSA and Xinhua has brought about. The search was performed using the search engine on ANSA's website. The keyword inserted was 'Xinjiang', and the search returned 260 articles overall.

Figure 4.1 below presents the types of narratives that are being put forwards, drawing on the classification of 'system', 'identity', and 'issue' narratives that was introduced in the conceptual framework.

The analysis in the ensuing section focuses on the articles (140) that were published after the MoU was signed. After filtering for articles that were not relevant, the total number of articles included here is sixty-five; these

[5] China Watch supplements are four- to eight-page inserts, sponsored by Chinese media outlets (most notably China Daily), aimed at promoting China's views on key issues. These supplements have appeared in *The Washington Post*, *The New York Times*, and the *Wall Street Journal*, as well as in newspapers in the UK, Spain, and Australia.

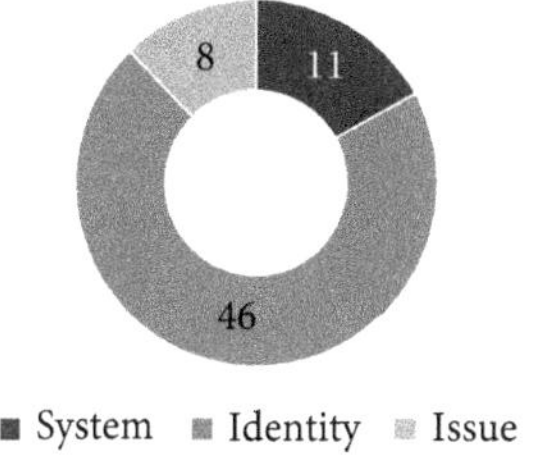

Figure 4.1 Chinese narratives on Xinjiang, as part of the ANSA-Xinhua partnership
Source: Data analysed by the author, from the website ANSA.it

were then coded following the 'system', 'identity', and 'issue' classification introduced in the analytical framework.

Among the pool of articles analysed, eleven articles dealt with system narratives, namely aimed at promoting China's vision and the values underpinning inter-state relations and how the latter should be approached by countries. One article titled 'Common Destiny: How the BRI changes people's lives' was promoting a documentary on the BRI, while others were more directly aimed at punishing or rewarding China-focused policies from the US and other organizations. One article, for instance, said that 'China has warned the United States that if they continue having double standards on anti-terrorism, or if they try to violate the sovereignty and security of other countries, they will end up swallowing a bitter fruit and their own interests will be damaged' (Xinhua, 2019a). Along similar lines, another article titled 'China condemns the law approved in the US on Xinjiang' claimed that the US were 'launching unfounded allegations against the Chinese government's policies in the region' and that the US were therefore 'seriously interfering in China's internal affairs' (Xinhua, 2019b). While the US were criticized, countries that complied with China's non-interference policy were instead praised. An example of this are the remarks reported about Foreign Minister Wang Yi's meeting with the Arab League, in which China's top diplomat stated that his country 'appreciated the Arab Leagues' support on Xinjiang-related matters', adding that China 'favourably welcomes Arab functionaries who would visit Xinjiang to testify the results of China's efforts against terrorism and radicalisation' (Xinhua, 2020).

The bulk (forty-six in total) of the articles analysed contained 'identity' narratives, namely those types of messages aimed at promoting an actor's identity to international audiences. In particular, the identity that China has been trying to promote on Xinjiang revolves around a number of themes. First, Xinjiang is portrayed as a success story in building social housing and in lifting people out of poverty; in this context, one article stated that 645,000 people were brought out of poverty in 2019, as a result of the 13th Five-Year Plan for 2016–2020, also adding that Chinese authorities were aiming to eradicate absolute poverty in the region. Second, Xinjiang is portrayed as a key commercial hub as part of the BRI, between China and Europe; while highlighting a 31.1% increase in Xinjiang's trade with the world, two articles mentioned that the bulk of such trade was with countries and regions that were part of the BRI. A third theme that emerges from the articles analysed in relation to the identity of Xinjiang is the region's rich natural resources alongside the ability to generate energy from renewables, with articles mentioning oil exports from Xinjiang to Kazakhstan as well as the completion of a solar power plant. Finally, Xinjiang is promoted as a tourist destination, with a rich cultural, natural, and historical heritage.

The third type of narrative is issue narratives, namely those that are aimed at promoting Chinese views on a given issue—in this case internment camps and human rights violations in Xinjiang. There are eight articles falling into this category, and they are rebuttals of the US's criticism over Xinjiang and of the *New York Times*'s reporting on the issue, as well as of the 'Uyghur Human Rights Policy Act 2019' passed by the US Congress, which is defined by one Xinhua article as an act moving 'unfounded allegations against the Chinese government's actions in Xinjiang' and a 'serious interference' in China's internal affairs.

The empirical evidence presented here demonstrates how China's vision on key issues pertaining to some of its core interests are being promoted as part of the media partnership agreements that come attached with the BRI. In addition to the content that is presented, it is also important to look at the frequency with which these articles are posted. By analysing the dataset used in this chapter, a pattern emerged that for every article that ANSA independently published on the issue (that is, outside of the partnership with Xinhua), there were eight from Xinhua promoting China's narratives, whether system, identity, or issue, on Xinjiang.

By way of providing an assessment of the content analysed in the dataset presented above, two points are worth emphasizing. First, the flooding of Xinhua information on the website did not translate into ANSA reporting less independently than before on Xinjiang, as there were five items (including videos and a picture gallery) that mentioned internment camps and human rights abuses in the region. As such, on this particular aspect the impact of Chinese narratives has been very limited. The second point, and an area that it would be important for future research to assess systematically and over time, is the extent to which the availability of China-backed content has an impact on the way in which the wider public interprets international issues.

Conclusions

This chapter was a first attempt at assessing the normative implications of China's growing ties with Italy. Here the analysis has focused on two sets of actors, namely state (that is, the main government party between 2018 and 2022) and sub-state (that is, the media). Against such a backdrop, the chapter has demonstrated how, as a result of the MoU on the BRI, China's core narratives on key international issues have been progressively absorbed by some of the elites among one of Italy's ruling parties. At the same time, the chapter has also shown that claims that Italy's Euro Atlantic posture was changing following the MoU were inaccurate. More generally, it is important to note that the M5S' openness towards China is not shared by many of the other parties. When interviewed in May 2020, Emma Bonino, former Italian Foreign Minister and leader of the 'Più Europa' party, warned that 'with regards to China's ambitions there is a need to be very cautious, including on Beijing's investments in critical infrastructures', adding that Italy 'should remain strictly anchored to the Western liberal democracies' (LA7, 2020). In addition, politicians from both centre-right and centre-left parties have, since 2019, joined the 'Inter-Parliamentary Alliance on China', an international cross-party group of legislators working towards reform on how democracies approach China. In order to comprehensively assess how Sino-Italian relations have evolved in recent years, there is a need for future research to scrutinize, along the lines traced in this chapter, the full spectrum of political parties, and whether there was an uptake of Chinese narratives among them. Similarly, future research should explore the multi-scalar nature of China's public diplomacy in Italy, including at the regional and local levels. This would enable a better appreciation of the full spectrum of bilateral engagements occurring under the aegis of the BRI, and what implications these have for the Liberal International Order.

Bibliography

Agence France Press. 2019. 'US Secretary of State Mike Pompeo "Saddened" as Italy Signs Up for China's Belt and Road Project'. 28 March. Available at: https://www.scmp.com/news/china/diplomacy/article/3003610/us-secretary-state-mike-pompeo-saddened-italy-signs-chinas.

Ansa. 2019. 'Di Maio: non interferiamo su Hong Kong'. 5 November. Available at: http://www.ansa.it/sito/notizie/mondo/asia/2019/11/05/di-maio-non-interferiamo-su-hong-kong_49b44bb5-8747-4e17-8cb4-a8d4f6094811.html.

Bechis, F. 2019. 'Di Maio risponde (bene) all'ambasciata cinese. Ora serve un passo in più'. *Formiche.net*, 29 November. Available at: https://formiche.net/2019/11/di-maio-risponde-bene-ambasciata-cinese-ora-serve-passo-in-piu/.

Bechis, F., and G. Carrer. 2020. 'How China Unleashed Twitter Bots to Spread COVID-19 Propaganda in Italy'. *Formiche.net*, 31 March. Available at: https://formiche.net/2020/03/china-unleashed-twitter-bots-covid19-propaganda-italy/.

Benabdallah, L. 2019. 'Contesting the International Order by Integrating it: The Case of China's Belt and Road Initiative'. *Third World Quarterly* 40 (1): pp. 92–108.

Bettiza, G., and D. Lewis. 2020. 'Authoritarian Powers and Norm Contestation in the Liberal International Order: Theorizing the Power Politics of Ideas and Identity'. *Journal of Global Security Studies* 5 (4): pp. 559–577.

Boni, F. 2022. 'Strategic Partnerships and China's Diplomacy in Europe: Insights from Italy'. *The British Journal of Politics and International Relations* [Online]. https://doi.org/10.1177/13691481221127571.

Cabras, P. 2019. 'Hong Kong. Dalla parte della libertà e della pace'. Il Blog delle Stelle, 28 November. Available at: https://www.ilblogdellestelle.it/2019/11/dalla-parte-della-liberta-e-della-pace.html.

Callahan, W. A. 2016. China's "Asia Dream": The Belt Road Initiative and the new regional order. *Asian Journal of Comparative Politics*, 1(3), 226–243. https://doi.org/10.1177/2057891116647806

Camera dei Deputati. 2019. 'XVIII LEGISLATURA, Resoconto stenografico dell'Assemblea'. Seduta n. 144 di martedì 19 marzo. Available at: https://www.camera.it/leg18/410?idSeduta=0144&tipo=alfabetico_stenografico.

Chryssogelos A. 2017. 'Populism in Foreign Policy'. In *The Oxford Encyclopedia of Foreign Policy Analysis*, edited by C. Thies. Oxford: Oxford University Press.

Communiqué on the Current State of the Ideological Sphere. 2013. 'A Notice from the Central Committee of the Communist Party of China's General Office'. 22 April. Available at: https://www.chinafile.com/document-9-chinafile-translation.

Coticchia, F., and V. Vignoli. 2020. 'Populist Parties and Foreign Policy: The Case of Italy's Five Star Movement'. *The British Journal of Politics and International Relations* 22(3): pp. 523–541.

Crawford, A. 2020. 'Italy's China Chill Runs Deeper Than Fears Over the Coronavirus'. *Bloomberg*, 27 February. Available at: https://www.bloomberg.com/news/articles/2020-02-27/italy-s-china-chill-runs-deeper-than-fears-over-the-coronavirus.

de Graaff, N., T. ten Brink, and I. Parmar. 2020. 'China's Rise in a Liberal World Order in Transition—Introduction to the FORUM'. *Review of International Political Economy* 27 (2): pp. 191–207.

Destradi, S., and J. Plagemann. 2019. 'Populism and International Relations: (Un)Predictability, Personalisation, and the Reinforcement of Existing Trends in World Politics'. *Review of International Studies* 45 (5): pp. 711–730.

Economy, E. 2022. 'Xi Jinping's New World Order: Can China Remake the International System?'. *Foreign Affairs* 101: p. 52.

Embassy of the People's Republic of China in the Republic of Italy. 2019. 'Il portavoce dell'Ambasciata Cinese in Italia chiarisce la posizione in merito alla videoconferenza di Joshua Wong con alcuni politici italiani'. 29 November. Available at: http://it.china-embassy.org/ita/xwdt/t1720040.htm.

Euractiv. 2019. 'Oettinger Calls for EU Veto on Italy-China deal'. 25 March. Available at: https://www.euractiv.com/section/eu-china/news/oettinger-calls-for-eu-veto-on-italy-china-deal/.

Fatiguso, R. 2017. 'Italia-Cina, un percorso che punta a chiudere i dossier'. *Il Sole 24 Ore*, 14 May. Available at: https://www.ilsole24ore.com/art/italia-cina-percorso-che-punta-chiudere-dossier-AE2GGJMB?refresh_ce=1.

Geraci, M. 2018. 'I 5 pilastri del successo economico cinese'. BeppeGrillo.it, 5 May. Available at: http://www.beppegrillo.it/i-5-pilastri-del-successo-economico-cinese/.

Geraci, M. 2018. 'La Cina e il governo del cambiamento'. 11 June. Available at: http://www.beppegrillo.it/la-cina-e-il-governo-del-cambiamento/.

Ghiretti, F., and L. Mariani. 2021. 'One Belt One Voice: Chinese Media in Italy'. *IAI Papers*, 21/43. Available at: https://www.iai.it/en/pubblicazioni/one-belt-one-voice-chinese-media-italy.

Glaser, B. 2019. 'China as a Selective Revisionist Power in the International Order'. *ISEAS Perspective* 21: pp. 1–9.

Global Times. 2019. 'China Needs to Counter Western Public Opinion War'. 25 November. Available at: http://www.globaltimes.cn/content/1171174.shtml.

Han, B. C., and L. Harth. 2022. 'Italy'. In 'Beijing's Global Media Influence 2022', edited by S. Cook, A. Datt, E. Young, and B. C. Han. *Freedom House*, September 2022. Available at: https://freedomhouse.org/report/beijing-global-media-influence/2022/authoritarian-expansion-power-democratic-resilience.

Horowitz, J. 2019. 'Italy's Deal with China Signals a Shift as US Influence Recedes'. *New York Times*, 30 March.

Hurrell, A. 2006. 'Hegemony, Liberalism and Global Order: What Space for Would-Be Great Powers?'. *International Affairs* 82: pp. 1–19.

Ikenberry, G. J., I. Parmar, and D. Stokes. 2018. 'Introduction: Ordering the World? Liberal Internationalism in Theory and Practice'. *International Affairs* 94 (1): pp. 1–5.

Kratz, A., M. J. Zenglein, G. Sebastian, and M. Witzke. 2022. Chinese FDI In Europe

LA7. 2020. 'Cina, la stoccata di Emma Bonino: "Di Maio confonde i rapporti commerciali con quelli politici"'. 19 May. Available at: https://www.la7.it/omnibus/video/cina-la-stoccata-di-emma-bonino-di-maio-confonde-i-rapporti-commerciali-con-quelli-politici-19-05-2020-325707.

Lee, P. K., A. Heritage, and Z. Mao. 2020. 'Contesting Liberal Internationalism: China's Renegotiation of World Order'. *Cambridge Review of International Affairs* 33 (1): pp. 52–60.

'Luigi Di Maio. Intervista a SkyTg24 22/04/2020'. 2020. Available at: https://www.youtube.com/watch?v=mlYMEO6C3qQ&t=359s [Accessed ...]

Meacci, L. 2021. 'Italy Has Learned a Tough Lesson on China'. *Foreign Policy*, 24 June. Available at: https://foreignpolicy.com/2021/06/24/italy-china-policy-belt-road/.

Miskimmon, A., O'loughlin, B., & Roselle, L. 2014. *Strategic narratives: Communication power and the new world order*. Routledge.

Ministero degli Affari Esteri e della Cooperazione Internazionale, Osservatorio Economico, 'Scheda di sintesi: Cina'. 2023. Last updated 11 August. Available at: https://www.infomercatiesteri.it/public/osservatorio/schede-sintesi/repubblica-popolare-cinese_122.pdf.

Ministry of Foreign Affairs of the People's Republic of China. 2014. 'The Central Conference on Work Relating to Foreign Affairs was Held in Beijing'. 29 November. Available at: https://www.fmprc.gov.cn/mfa_eng/zxxx_662805/t1215680.shtml.

NATO. 2022. 'NATO 2022 Strategic Concept'. 29 June. Available at: https://www.nato.int/strategic-concept/

Parenti, F. M. 2019a. 'Belt and Road Initiative: una nuova forma di relazioni internazionali'. 31 January. Available at: http://www.beppegrillo.it/belt-and-road-initiative-una-nuova-forma-di-relazioni-internazionali/.

Parenti, F. M. 2019b. 'Italia-Cina: costruire relazioni pacifiche'. 23 March. Available at: http://www.beppegrillo.it/italia-cina-costruire-relazioni-pacifiche/

Parenti, F. M. 2019c. 'L'Italia nella via della seta? Si scatena l'irritazione della 'casetta bianca'!'. 10 March. Available at: http://www.beppegrillo.it/litalia-nella-via-della-seta-si-scatena-lirritazione-della-casetta-bianca/.

Parenti, F. M. 2019d. 'Il nostro silenzio sulla piaga del terrorismo in Xinjiang'. 13 September. Available at: http://www.beppegrillo.it/il-nostro-silenzio-ha-oscurato-la-piaga-del-terrorismo-in-xinjiang-cina-resoconto-da-una-visita-sul-campo/.

Reporters Without Borders. 2019. 'China's Pursuit of a New World Media Order'. March 22. Available at: https://rsf.org/en/reports/rsf-report-chinas-pursuit-new-world-media-order.

Reuters. 2019. 'Italy Mulls Preliminary Belt and Road Deal with China'. 6 March. Available at: https://www.reuters.com/article/us-china-italy-belt-and-road/italy-aims-to-sign-preliminary-belt-and-road-deal-with-china-idUSKCN1QN0D4.

Rhodium Group and the Mercator Institute for China Studies (MERICS). 2022. '2021 Update'. April. Available at: https://rhg.com/wp-content/uploads/2022/04/MERICS-Rhodium-Group-COFDI-Update-2022-2.pdf.

Rolland, N. 2020. 'China's Vision for A New World Order'. NBR special report #83, January 2020.

Tritto, A., and A. Abdulkadir. 2020. 'Hong Kong 2019: Anatomy of a Social Mobilisation through the Lenses of Identity and Values'. *Asia Maior*, 30: pp. 163–183.

Yizheng, Z., and L. Jones. 2020. 'China's Response to Threats to Its Overseas Economic Interests: Softening Non-Interference and Cultivating Hegemony'. *Journal of Contemporary China* 29 (121): pp. 92–108.

Xinhua. 2017. 'Full Text of Xi Jinping's Report at 19th CPC National Congress'. 18 October. Available at: https://www.chinadaily.com.cn/china/19thcpcnationalcongress/2017-11/04/content_34115212.htm.

Xinhua. 2019a. 'Cina a Usa, basta doppio standard su antiterrorismo'. 5 December. Available at: https://www.ansa.it/sito/notizie/mondo/notiziario_xinhua/2019/12/05/cina-a-usa-basta-doppio-standard-su-antiterrorismo_e7943813-6c1b-411e-b974-159abada8d96.html.

Xinhua. 2019b. 'Cina condanna legge approvata negli Usa su Xinjiang'. 4 December. Available at: https://www.ansa.it/sito/notizie/mondo/notiziario_xinhua/2019/12/04/cina-condanna-legge-approvata-negli-usa-su-xinjiang_2c79736f-a795-4462-bfaf-95e10c85d79a.html.

Xinhua. 2020. 'Cina-Lega araba: Wang chiede maggiore collaborazione'. 8 January. Available at: https://www.ansa.it/sito/notizie/mondo/notiziario_xinhua/2020/01/08/cina-lega-araba-wang-chiede-maggiore-collaborazione-2_d7f71958-283d-450d-a3a4-7fe490a24dab.html.

Xuetong, Y. 2019. 'The Age of Uneasy Peace. Chinese Power in a Divided World'. *Foreign Affairs*, 11 December. Available at: https://www.foreignaffairs.com/china/age-uneasy-peace.

Wassermann, H., and D. Madrid-Morales. 2018. 'How Influential Are Chinese Media in Africa? An Audience Analysis in Kenya and South Africa'. *International Journal of Communication* 12: pp. 2212–2231.

Zakaria, F. 2019. 'The New China Scare'. *Foreign Affairs*, 6 December. Available at: https://www.foreignaffairs.com/articles/china/2019-12-06/new-china-scare.

5

China's Engagement with Greece under the BRI

Economics, Politics, and International Imperatives

Dimitrios Stroikos

Introduction

This volume is concerned with the political aspects of Chinese investments in Europe. The principal question is how far and in what ways China's growing economic clout in Europe poses a challenge to the Liberal International Order, with a particular focus on the importance of recent developments associated with the Belt and Road Initiative (BRI). In this regard, this chapter considers China-Greece relations as a case that serves to illustrate China's increasing engagement with small countries in Southern Europe. Greece's dependence on China largely as a result of Chinese investments in the port of Piraeus is frequently noted by policymakers, pundits, and the media, rendering Athens a sort of a quintessential example of how Beijing has ostensibly converted its accumulated economic power into political influence over Greece as a vulnerable small state, especially as a consequence of the Eurozone crisis, with implications for the liberal values and practices that undergird the EU as a political entity and a distinct liberal order. Therefore, a focus on the case of China's presence in Greece is helpful in the broader discussion of the politics of Chinese investments in Europe.

Building on the conceptual framework set out in the introduction of this volume that calls for the treatment of power as influence rather than power as resources, this chapter examines the extent to which China's influence has given rise to the formation of new preferences or the consolidation of existing preferences within Greece and its implications for the Liberal International Order. In doing so, this chapter highlights the role of domestic actors and domestic political considerations. It also suggests that we need

Dimitrios Stroikos, *China's Engagement with Greece under the BRI*. In: *Rising Power, Limited Influence*.
Edited by: Indrajit Roy, Jappe Eckhardt, Dimitrios Stroikos, and Simona Davidescu, Oxford University Press.
 DOI: 10.1093/oso/9780192887115.003.0006

to take into account the wider systemic context and its impact on the ways in which Athens attempts to manage Beijing's influence, which involves moving beyond an analysis that centres merely on the dyadic relationship. Striking as the strengthening of Sino-Greek relations has been, this chapter argues that there are significant constraints on the nature of this bilateral relationship, as well as on the options available to Chinese and Greek policymakers, that are becoming clearer as a result of international imperatives, such as the recent shift in the EU's China policy and the emergence of US-China strategic rivalry.

To develop this argument, this chapter is organized as follows. The first section offers an analysis of the factors that led to the strengthening of China-Greece relations from 2006 to 2016 as a background by stressing the role of sub-state actors and contingent circumstances that created the preconditions for a remarkable shift in their relationship. Next, it provides a more extensive consideration of Sino-Greek relations from 2016 to today, considering the economic and political aspects of their partnership, as well as the promotion of social and cultural exchanges. The analysis shows that the period from 2016 to 2019 witnessed increased bilateral interactions not only in the economic, but also in the foreign policy sphere. But after 2019, there is a degree of both continuity and change, as the rationale for the bilateral relationship is increasingly constrained by a range of political and strategic imperatives. Taking stock of the above, the third section provides an evaluation of China's influence over Greece. In the last section, the chapter concludes with reflections on its findings.

Background: A Growing Partnership, 2006–2016

In recent years, both Beijing and Athens have made an attempt to put their bilateral relationship into high gear. This is largely the result of China's booming economy that has made the Asian country an attractive source of investments in Europe and elsewhere in the world. Even though Athens established diplomatic relations with Beijing in 1972, interactions remained surprisingly limited until the mid-2000s. But bilateral ties have gone a long way since 2006, when the then Greek Prime Minister Kostas Karamanlis paid a three-day state visit to Beijing that led to the signing of a 'Comprehensive Strategic Partnership'. High-level political interactions included meeting Chinese President Hu at the Great Hall of People and Cosco's president, Captain Wei Jiafu, who would play a key role in the Piraeus deal, as I shall explain below.

One of the main reasons for this upgrade of China-Greece relations was cooperation in the areas of trade and investment, with a particular focus on ship-building and shipping. In fact, the Comprehensive Strategic Partnership envisaged that the two sides would facilitate 'cooperation between the ports and shipping enterprises' as well as bring about 'direct waterway and transit transportation via each other's ports to neighbouring countries and regions' (Ministry of Foreign Affairs of the People's Republic of China, 2006). The intended goal at the time was to encourage the establishment of Greece as a principal gateway that would enable the entry of Chinese products into the markets of Central and South-Eastern Europe (Skordeli, 2015: 61)

What merits emphasis is that the Comprehensive Strategic Partnership paved the way towards a steady strengthening of bilateral relations, especially in the field of maritime transport, which resulted in the concession deal between the port of Piraeus, Greece's largest port, and China Overseas Shipping Group Co. (Cosco) during the visit of Chinese President Hu to Athens in 2008. More specifically, even though there were plans for the privatization of the Greek ports, including the Piraeus port, as early as 1999, such attempts were confronted with domestic pressures, the opposition of trade unions, and concerns that a public monopoly would merely be replaced by a private one that could potentially break EU competition rules. Yet, by 2007, the decision was made that the concession of the Pier 2 and the future Pier 3 of the Piraeus port could proceed through an international tender, while Pier 1 would remain under the control of the Greek authorities. In 2008, having made the higher offer, Cosco won the concession to operate the two of the port's piers for a period of thirty-five years. According to the Greek government, the port authority would receive the amount of 4.3 billion euros, with roughly 123 million euros per year during the thirty-five-year concession. Another key dimension of the deal was that the Chinese company had committed to contribute further investments with the goal of expanding the container capacity of Pier 2 and completing the construction of Pier 3. Still, it has been estimated that the actual amount is lower than the one that was formally announced (Psaraftis and Pallis, 2012).

Nevertheless, the point to make here is that different interpretations have been provided about the rationale for the breakthrough in China-Greece relations since the mid-2000s. At one level, it is reasonable to assume that as China's relative standing in the international system was increasing, so was its quest to possess strategic assets abroad by utilizing economic diplomacy as a way to maximize its power (Sklias, Roukanas, and Pistikou, 2012).[1] At another

[1] However, according to a recent study, it is still difficult to jump to the conclusion that China's presence in Greece is part of a grand strategy (Doga, Lioumpas, and Petropoulos, 2021).

level, however, the significance of economic interests and the role of sub-state actors cannot be understated. Indeed, we do know now that Captain Wei was instrumental in promoting the port deal. Wei's role as CEO of China's largest state-owned shipping company gave him access to the highest echelons of the Chinese government, allowing him to garner crucial political support to pursue the company's international agenda. At the same time, Wei was cognizant that the port of Piraeus presented a unique opportunity to operate a European port of potentially great commercial and strategic value by connecting the markets of Asia, Africa, and Europe. Consequently, Wei's involvement in the port deal was largely driven by organizational and commercial interests. In reality, it seems unlikely that the port deal and the transformation of China-Greece relations would have come to much were it not for Wei's participation in key meetings and his personal interest in moving on with the deal (Ma and Peverelli, 2019). What should be emphasized here is that Wei's impact on the port deal is in line with recent studies that demonstrate how the implementation of BRI projects is driven mainly by SOEs on the basis of a 'bottom-up' process (Yu, 2018).

As far as the Greek side is concerned, Asteris Huliaras and Sotiris Petropoulos (2014) show how powerful business interests wedded to the Greek shipping industry have influenced the Greek government's decision to pursue closer ties with China. Historically, given that Greece has been one of the world's leading shipping powers, with the shipping industry occupying a central position in the Greek economy, shipowners have significant potential leverage in the country's political system. Exerting this sort of influence is exacerbated by the fact that the foreign policy decision-making process in Greece is largely shaped by the Prime Minister on the basis of a centralized approach that leaves little room for other actors. As Spyros Economides (2020: 607) observes, 'foreign policy decision-making is normally very "personality driven" and more often than not concentrated within the narrow environment of the prime minister's office'. An important consequence of this process is that Greek shipowners, as a powerful interest group, usually gain direct access to prime ministers. This was especially the case regarding this earlier phase of China-Greece relations under consideration. In particular, Vassilis Constantakopoulos, founder of the Costamare group that had business dealings with Cosco, exerted an important influence on Greece's engagement with China from the outset. A telling illustration of his influence is the fact that seven months before Prime Minister Karamanlis paid a visit to Beijing in 2006, which included meeting with Wei, Constantakopoulos had held a personal meeting with the Greek Prime Minister. It has also been suggested that Constantakopoulos was a key factor in promoting the 2008 port deal (Huliaras and Petropoulos, 2014).

Economic interactions between China and Greece continued unabated since then. The Eurozone crisis was undoubtedly a major reason for the furthering of bilateral relations. By then, Greece's economic partnership with China had assumed more significance, as it was facing a time of great financial and political turmoil due to the economic crisis. In September 2015, Greece's left-wing Syriza government led by Prime Minister Alexis Tsipras, in coalition with the right-wing Independent Greeks (ANEL), was elected. Notably, the newly elected government was initially opposed to the possibility of Cosco extending its hold on Piraeus. Yet, under pressure from the European Union to meet the requirements of Greece's third bailout in tandem with a remarkable degree of uncertainty about the possibility of Grexit, the Tsipras government saw China as a potential alternative partner that could offer valuable and much-needed economic and political support. In this respect, for some analysts China's involvement in the Piraeus port can be seen as contributing to Athens' effort 'to balance the European Union's dominance over Greece's economy and politics' (Calinoff and Gordon, 2020: 69). Similarly, according to Tonchev and Davarinou (2017: 6), Greece appeared 'to count on political dividends in its tense relations with the international creditors'.

To be sure, Chinese investments in the Piraeus port raised legitimate concerns about the increasingly precarious labour conditions in the port that were facilitated by successive Greek governments as a result of the harsh austerity measures imposed on Greece (Neilson, 2019). But the pressure placed on Greece by its EU creditors to open up and privatize the public sector, along with Beijing's constructive engagement, meant that the Greek reaction to Chinese investments in the Piraeus port and elsewhere was largely positive (Kokoromytis and Chryssogelos, 2021: 194).

Against this backdrop, in April 2016 Greece eventually agreed to sell 51% of the Piraeus Port Authority (OLP) to Cosco for 280.5 million euros. As part of the deal, Cosco was also expected to make further investments of up to 300 million euros over the next five years that would lead to the eventual acquisition of a 67% stake in OLP (Georgiopoulos, 2016). Importantly, acquiring a controlling stake in the Piraeus port not only provided a good opportunity for China on financial grounds, but it also dovetailed nicely with Xi Jinping's BRI in the context of the Maritime Silk Road. Since 2014, Chinese analysts and officials have associated the Piraeus port with the so-called China-Europe Land-Sea Express Line. This aims at connecting a land transportation route from the Piraeus port to Budapest—via a railway line—to a maritime transportation route from the Chinese costal ports to the Piraeus port. When the project is completed, it is estimated that the transit time for delivering goods from China to central Europe will be reduced by seven to eleven days (Liu, 2016: 64; Xue, 2022: 498).

In this regard, some observers have illustrated the ways in which the strategic significance of the Eastern Mediterranean routes has increased for China, especially as a consequence of the centrality of the BRI under Xi. Thus, expanding a firm foothold in the Mediterranean with a majority stake in the Greek port would help China to reconfigure its position in the region by turning the Piraeus into a gateway to the EU. Equally, thanks to its proximity to the Suez Canal, the port has the potential to be transformed into a major hub in the Eastern Mediterranean (van der Putten, 2016).

Key Developments in China-Greece Relations, 2016–2022

The economic aspects of the partnership

The 2016 port deal marked a new period in Sino-Greek relations that was not only characterized by growing economic interactions, but also by steps towards further expanding the relationship in terms of foreign policy and cultural exchanges, discussed in some detail later. Economically, the port deal is considered one of the largest foreign investments ever made in Greece, hailed as successful by Athens and Beijing. By 2019, the Piraeus port had turned into the sixth largest container handler in Europe and the top port in the Mediterranean, ranking as one of the world's best-connected ports (Glass, 2019).

What is noteworthy, however, is that the Piraeus port deal also acted as a sort of 'anchor investment' in the sense that it played a role in alluring Chinese follow-up investments in sectors of the Greek economy other than ports and shipping (Tonchev and Davarinou, 2017: 24). For example, in the energy sector, the State Grid International Development, a subsidiary of State Grid Corporation of China, acquired a 24% stake in Greece's Independent Power Transmission Operator (IPTO/ADMIE) by investing 320 million euros in 2016. Concurrently, there has been Chinese interest in the field of renewable energy, exemplified by Shenhua Group's decision to purchase a 75% stake in four wind parks developed by the Greek Copelouzos Group in November 2017. With regards to the telecommunications sector, Chinese companies, including Huawei, the Zhongxing Telecommunication Equipment Corporation (ZTE), and the Pacific Century CyberWorks (PCCW Global), have been active in Greece (Tonchev and Davarinou, 2017: 18–19). In the real estate sector, it should be mentioned that investing in Greek property has been encouraged by the introduction of a 'golden visa' programme in 2013, which has attracted roughly 7,800 visa byers generating approximately 2.6 billion euros, with the Chinese investors making up at least 70% (Seferiadis, 2020). As far as tourism is concerned, in September 2017 Air China started direct flights connecting Beijing with Athens, while the number of Chinese tourists visiting had been in a steady increase before the major disruptive effects of the pandemic on this sector (Georgakopoulos, 2019; Xinhua, 2023).

But although it is clear that Chinese investments in Greece have increased in recent years, assessing their precise total volume, not to mention their impact on the Greek economy in terms of revenues and social benefits, is no easy task. In fact, there have been varying estimates from different sources.[2] For example, according to the China Global Investment Tracker (CGIT) of the American Enterprise Institute, the total volume of Chinese investments in Greece from 2005 to 2021 is placed at 9.46 billion USD,[3] while a recent study from the Rhodium Group and the Mercator Institute for China Studies estimates that Chinese investments from 2000 to 2021 amount to approximately 4.5 billion euros (Kratz et al., 2022). On the other hand, other estimates place the actual volume of Chinese investments at a lower figure (Tonchev and Davarinou, 2017: 13–14). In any case, based on Bank of Greece data from 2011–2021, China (including Hong Kong) has emerged as the sixth top source of investment activity in Greece, after Switzerland, Cyprus, Germany, France, and the Netherlands.[4]

At the same time, the trade relationship between China and Greece has also strengthened. According to Bank of Greece data, in 2021 China became Greece's third most important trade partner with a share of roughly 7.7%, following Germany and Italy, with imports reaching 3,743 billion euros. However, Greek exports to China amounted to 854 million euros in 2020, with China listed as the eleventh major destination for Greek exports, showing that bilateral trade remains unbalanced.[5]

Notwithstanding this overall direction, some Chinese investment plans in Greece have not been realized because of rigid bureaucratic procedures, political instability, and incompatibility with EU competition rules (Tonchev and Davarinou, 2017: 6). For example, in 2016 Cosco was reported to be interested in making an offer for the Greek national rail network as part of a plan to connect the Piraeus port with South-Eastern Europe through

[2] For a useful discussion of some estimates and the reasons why it is difficult to offer precise assessments of Chinese investments in Greece, see Tonchev and Davarinou (2017).

[3] https://www.aei.org/china-global-investment-tracker/.

[4] https://www.enterprisegreece.gov.gr/en/greece-today/why-greece/foreign-direct-investment.

[5] https://www.enterprisegreece.gov.gr/en/greece-today/why-greece/trade.

rail links (Koutantou and Goh, 2016). But eventually the Chinese company did not participate in the tender. In fact, this trend has been reinforced since the election of the centre-right government under Prime Minister Kyriakos Mitsotakis in July 2019. In 2020, for example, two Chinese state-owned enterprises (SOEs) did not reach the final stage of the bid process for the privatization of the Natural Gas Distribution Networks (DEPA Infrastructure), while one year later three Chinese SOEs were eased out from the public tender concerning the sale of a 49% stake in the Hellenic Electricity Distribution Network Operator (HEDNO/DEDDIE). These recent developments are driven, at least in part, by the gradual recovery of the Greek economy that has resulted in the country's ability to attract investment opportunities from countries other than China (Tonchev, 2022: 103–104). But, in part, these are indicative of political considerations at a time when the Greek government is facing pressure from the EU and the United States to adjust its China policy, as discussed below.

The political aspects of the partnership

One of the most noteworthy features of China-Greece relations has been the strengthening of the partnership politically since 2016. This was especially the case from 2016 to 2019, when the Greek government under Prime Minister Tsipras promoted the deepening of political ties with China that transformed the context of the bilateral relationship in significant ways, reinforcing claims about China's ability to translate its economic significance into political influence over smaller European states. As we shall see, such claims look less plausible now, though China was successful in attaining some political gains during this period, at least at the symbolic level (Stroikos, 2022). Indeed, on few occasions the foreign policy stance of the Greek government diverged significantly from EU positions on issues pertaining to liberal values and norms, which was seen as stemming from Athens' closer partnership with Beijing.

More specifically, in July 2016 Greece was among a few small European states that supported the adoption of a softer tone in an EU statement concerning the ruling of the Permanent Court of Arbitration over China's maritime disputes with its Asian neighbours in the South China Sea. China rejected the ruling of the international tribunal that had repudiated much of its claims to the South China Sea, but there were disagreements among EU member states about how to react by reaching a common stance. After seventy-two hours of negotiations, the issued statement on behalf of the bloc stressed the need for maintaining international law and settling disputes through peaceful means, underscoring the importance of the freedoms of navigation and overflight in line with the United Nations Convention on the Law of the Sea (UNCLOS), but it fell short of criticizing China. In a similar fashion, the following year Greece blocked an EU statement in the United Nations Human Rights Council (UNHRC) that was intended to criticize human rights abuses in China, making this the first time that the EU did not issue a statement at the UNHRC (Cumming-Bruce and Sengupta, 2017).

Meanwhile, Beijing and Athens advanced their political ties through the latter's participation in China-led multilateral initiatives. In May 2017, Greece was accepted as a new member of the Asian Infrastructure Investment Bank (AIIB), a day before the first BRI Forum, a big diplomatic event that served as a showcase for the Chinese project, attended by Tsipras (Reuters, 2017). One year later, Greece became the first EU member to formally join the BRI framework (Mo, 2018). Subsequently, in April 2019 Greece joined the '16+1' group of China and Central and Eastern European Countries (CECC), which was renamed '17+1', marking another milestone in China-Greece relations on the diplomatic front.[6]

Typifying these increasing interactions, China and Greece maintained mutual high-level visits between political leaders over the period under consideration. For example, in July 2016, Prime Minister Tsipras paid a five-day visit to China during which he met with President Xi at the Great Hall of People in Beijing. Coinciding with the tenth anniversary of the establishment of the comprehensive strategic partnership, Tsipras' visit provided a good opportunity for the two leaders to reinstate the priority of implementing the Piraeus port project as the cornerstone of Sino-Greek relations under the BRI, with Xi stressing that 'China regards Greece as a strategic partner in the European Union (EU)' (Ministry of the Foreign Affairs of the People's Republic of China, 2016).

It is significant that high-profile visits have continued, even after the election of the new Greek government in July 2019. In November 2019, Xi made a landmark three-day trip to Greece that included visiting the port of Piraeus with Prime Minister Mitsotakis. During his talks with Mitsotakis, Xi pointed out that the two sides should focus on turning 'the Piraeus Port into a key container transit hub in the Mediterranean region, fully give

[6] The Greek decision, which came soon after the European Commission had described China as a 'systemic rival' for the first time, raised eyebrows in Brussels and in large EU member states where the 16+1 mechanism was seen as a vehicle for Beijing to challenge European unity within the bloc (Hopkins and Hope, 2019).

play to its role as a sea-rail transportation hub and improve the capacity of China-Europe Land-Sea Express Line' (Ministry of the Foreign Affairs of the People's Republic of China, 2019). Tellingly enough, Xi's visit took place just a week after Mitsotakis had returned from Shanghai, where he had met with the Chinese President, reflecting the good climate of China-Greece relations (Prime Minister's Office, 2019). Apart from Xi, in September 2020 China's top diplomat, Yang Jiechi, travelled to Greece, which was followed by a meeting between China's State Councillor and Foreign Minister Wang Yi with Mitsotakis in Athens in October 2021, illustrating the importance that the Chinese side still ascribes to its partnership with Greece at a time when its relations with the United States and Europe have deteriorated (Stroikos, 2022: 615-616).

Having said that, politically the picture of Sino-Greek relations is now mixed, with elements of both continuity and change. On the one hand, for instance, in October 2021 Cosco raised its stake in the Piraeus Port Authority to 67%. Then, in February 2022, a trial of activists, who had been arrested in Greece after briefly disrupting the lighting ceremony of the Olympic flame for the Beijing 2022 Winter Olympics by unfurling a banner reading 'No Genocide Games' and waving a Tibetan flag, was postponed apparently in order not to upset China in the run-up to the Games (Smith, 2022). On the other hand, there are signs that the Greek side attempts to keep some distance from Beijing under pressure from the United States and its European allies, which also has an impact on the economic dimension of the partnership. As we have seen, this is evident in the fact that some Chinese SOEs have been gradually eased out of important public bids. Similarly, in 2020 the largest Greek mobile network operator selected the Swedish Ericsson for its 5G network over Huawei. In the foreign policy realm, Greece has aligned with the EU sanctions over human rights abuses in China, while it did not proceed with hosting the gathering of the 17+1 cooperative framework in 2022 (Stroikos, 2022: 618).

Cultural and social aspects

In addition to economic and political cooperation, China-Greece relations have been characterized by increasing cultural and social exchanges. It should be recognized from the outset that these exchanges are usually underpinned by the notion that China and Greece are poised to foster a mutually beneficial partnership as the two great ancient civilizations of the East and the West, a key trope reproduced by both Chinese and Greek elites as well as the media.[7] While it is easy to dismiss this civilizational discourse as mere rhetoric, the impact of its symbolic significance on facilitating Sino-Greek relations should not been downplayed. Indeed, it becomes easier to understand the appeal of such a civilizational discourse, at least for the Greek elites and the public, when we consider the social construction of Greece as the EU/Eurozone's 'financially uncivilised Other' during the economic crisis that rendered Beijing a valuable non-Western partner willing to support Athens amid much economic and political uncertainty, as well as diplomatic isolation (Stroikos, 2022: 614).[8]

Emblematic of this narrative concerning their shared identity as two great ancient civilizations has been the Ancient Civilizations Forum (ACF), a joint initiative developed by China and Greece related to the BRI that led to the First Ministerial Conference of the ACF, which was held successfully in Athens in April 2017, with the participation of ministers and high-level officials from ten countries representing heirs of ancient civilizations: China, Greece, Egypt, Iran, Iraq, Italy, India, Mexico, Peru, and Bolivia (Bian, 2022: 472).[9]

The importance of increasing interactions on the cultural and social front has also been reflected in a series of cultural activities and high-profile events. Typical of such activities in recent years has been the establishment of Confucius Institutes in Greek educational institutions, including the Athens Business Confucius Institute (ABCI) at the Athens University of Economics and Business (AUEB) and the Confucius Institute at the Aristotle University of Thessaloniki (AUTH). In terms of high-profile events, these include the 2017 Thessaloniki International Fair, the country's most significant business event, with the participation of China as the 'Country of Honour' (Stroikos, 2022: 608-609). More recently, Chinese and Greek officials inaugurated the 'Greece-China Year of Culture and Tourism', which ran from May 2021 until May 2022 (Xinhua, 2021).

Whatever one thinks about the impact of cultural and social exchanges on Sino-Greek relations, the Greek public appears to share a favourable image towards China, at least for now. This becomes clearer when compared with the views of other European countries. For example, a 2021 Pew Research Center survey revealed that Greece was the only country out of the nine European countries surveyed where the public held positive views of China,

[7] See, for example, Ministry of the Foreign Affairs of the People's Republic of China (2016); Ministry of the Foreign Affairs of the People's Republic of China (2019); Prime Minister's Office (2019); and Ren (2019).

[8] On Greece as the EU/Eurozone's 'financially uncivilised Other', see Mikelis and Stroikos (2017).

[9] For a brief but useful overview of the rationale and activities of the ACF, see Bian (2022).

with 52% favourable and 42% unfavourable. Still, in the same survey, in Greece 75% of respondents answered that 'China does not respect the personal freedoms of its people' (Silver, Devlin, and Huang, 2021). However, another Pew Research Center study conducted one year later indicated that 44% of Greeks view China favourably and 50% unfavourably (Silver, Huang, and Clancy, 2022). Therefore, whether overall favourable opinions can be sustained in the future remains to be seen.

Evaluating China's Influence over Greece

Having examined the economic and political dimensions of Sino-Greek relations as well as the promotion of social and cultural exchanges, this section now turns to evaluate China's influence over Greece by building on the conceptual framework set out in the introduction of this volume. Limited space precludes a recapitulation of the framework discussed in the introductory chapter but what merits re-emphasizing here is that the principal goal of the following discussion is to evaluate whether China has been successful in converting its growing power resources into effective influence by shaping Greece's preferences or behaviour in a way in which the latter otherwise would not have done (Goh, 2014, 2016). On this basis, it is useful to concentrate on the Piraeus port and Greece's foreign policy, with a particular focus on the 2016 EU statement on the China South China and the 2017 EU statement on human rights discussed earlier and what these can tell us about China's impact on Greece's policy preferences.[10] This is important, given that these two instances of normative divergence from European values are usually seen as a result of China's growing economic power in Greece and its ability to translate it into political influence over a smaller European state, challenging the unity and the interests of the EU and, by extension, the liberal order.

As far as the acquisition of the port of Piraeus by Cosco is concerned, it is useful to recognize from the outset that it is a less straightforward case than it seems. Three aspects of the Piraeus port are worth highlighting. First, despite the asymmetry of power, Greek shipowners with vested interests in China played a key part in facilitating the Piraeus port deal, while Greek plans for the privatization of the port were underway since the late 1990s, as we saw earlier. Second, although there was a converge of preferences on the Piraeus

[10] Although Greece continues to engage with the China-CEEC (17+1) mechanism, the future of this China-led initiative is now uncertain after Lithuania's withdrawal in 2021, hence, it is not discussed here.

port from the mid-2000s and onwards, the Eurozone crisis was a turning point in the sense that the lack of support from its European partners combined with political turmoil and the harsh measures enforced by the 'Troika' made Greece particularly vulnerable to Chinese pressure. This was especially evident in 2016, when the Greek government and Cosco agreed on the 67% stake in the port. Under such circumstances, Greece was in great need of Chinese investments, which culminated in selling the additional stake at a significantly lower price (Freymann, 2021: 186).[11] As already mentioned, the Greek government was also trying to play the 'China card' to counter European pressure associated with the bailouts and economic reforms.

Third, even the most successful case of Chinese investments in Greece has been mired in controversy, characterized by resistance at the domestic and local level. More concretely, in 2019, as part of the 2016 port deal, Cosco announced a new investment plan that included the development of a shopping mall, hotels, an additional cruise ship terminal, and a new logistics centre, but local authorities have opposed the plan, concerned about the potential impact on local businesses and the environment. In the same year, a powerful Greek archaeological council put a halt to the plan when it proposed declaring a large part of the port as area of 'archaeological interest' that requires protection by objecting to some projects (Stamouli, 2019). Regardless of the local and bureaucratic opposition, in 2021 the Greek parliament approved the sale of the additional 16% stake in the port to Cosco. But things took a new turn in March 2022, when the Council of State, Greece's highest administrative court, deemed that the plan had disregarded carrying out an environmental assessment as required by EU and national regulations, adding further delays to the Chinese investments in the port (Kathimerini, 2022).

As per the foreign policy sphere, it is apparent that Greece's move to block the EU from issuing a statement with a direct reference to China in 2016 was driven by an effort not to antagonize Beijing over what Athens perceived not to be a vital issue for its core national interests, although it involved some reputational costs for the Greek side.[12] It seems that the same logic was applied to the decision to block the EU statement on human rights in 2017. However, there is no evidence to suggest that Greece's stance on both occasions was dictated by Beijing. Rather, it is plausible to argue that these two instances

[11] For a useful account of China's pressure on Greece during the Eurozone crisis, see Freymann (2021: 167–188).

[12] From a Greek perspective, however, it was important that the final statement stressed the role of the UN Convention on the Law of the Sea (UNCLOS), as the then Foreign Minister Kotzias explained after the issuing of the EU statement (Kotzias, 2016). It should be noted that international law and the UNCLOS are a key facet of Greece's foreign policy in its maritime disputes with Turkey.

can be seen as an effort on the part of Greece to pre-align its preferences with China. For some observers, these instances of divergence from EU policies towards China during the Eurozone crisis were an expression of a process of de-Europeanization of Greek foreign policy steered largely by domestic political considerations, as the Syriza-led government was utilizing Greece's improved relations with China to offset the additional demands of the EU, while simultaneously appealing to the most radical supporters of its party (Raimundo, Stavridis, and Tsardanidis, 2021).

Beyond domestic politics, this sort of pre-emptive preference alignment was in line with the worldview of the then Foreign Minister Nikos Kotzias, who frequently referred to the need for Greece to adopt a multidimensional foreign policy that rests on an active engagement with rising powers and established ones, and not just on its traditional allies. Accordingly, for the foreign minister the promotion of human rights should be conducted through dialogue and not criticism (Tzogopoulos, 2018; 8–9). Echoing this view soon after Athens' decision to block the 2017 proposed EU statement on human rights, a Greek foreign ministry spokesperson noted that 'Greece's position is that unproductive and in many cases, selective criticism against specific countries does not facilitate the promotion of human rights in these states, nor the development of their relation with the EU' (Denyer, 2017). Since then, it has transpired that the Greek decision in 2017 was made with reference not only to China, but also Egypt. Thus, this suggests that other factors apart from China were also at play in shaping Greece's move to forestall the EU statement.[13]

In assessing the extent of China's influence and its impact on Greece's behaviour, it is also essential to go beyond the dyadic partnership and consider the impact of the target state's interaction with its allies. This is a particularly relevant consideration in the case of Greece as a member of the EU and NATO. For example, the Piraeus port deal is frequently evoked by EU officials as the proverbial wake-up call for better protecting EU's critical infrastructure and forming a coordinated and unified EU response to China (Varvitsioti, 2022). Likewise, the United States has been closely watching the growing presence of China in Greece. Indeed, the remarkable strengthening of ties between Washington and Athens over the last years, which involves US access to additional ports and bases in Greece, can partly be explained by the overall geopolitical context of Sino-American relations. This process began under the Tsipras government and has evolved ever since. For Greece,

[13] Greece's relations with Egypt have assumed more importance over the last years in part due to intensified tensions with Turkey over natural energy sources in the Eastern Mediterranean. For a useful account of these developments, see Proedrou (2021).

the support from traditional allies, such as the United States, France, and the EU, remains critical amid responding to regional challenges such as Turkey's assertiveness under President Recep Tayyip Erdogan and the migrant crisis. Despite its undoubted economic power and unlike Washington, Beijing simply lacks the strategic weight in Greece's neighbourhood associated with the provision of security goods, at least for now (Stroikos, 2022). As well, there has been a growing interest among US high-profile companies in investing in Greece across a wide range of sectors as a result of the closer partnership between Washington and Athens, which means that China's role as a source of investment has diminished (Tonchev and Bentis, 2021: 46).

Therefore, if we want to understand China's influence over Greece, it is necessary to take into account the importance of domestic actors and resistance. But this also requires us to move beyond the dyadic partnership by considering the wider systemic context determining Sino-Greek relations at a time when Athens is adjusting its China policy as part of an effort to confront the dilemma of how to reconcile the economic benefits that can accrue from its partnership with Beijing without endangering the ties with its traditional allies (Stroikos, 2022). This is an especially important observation, given that most analyses evaluate China's economic and political impact on Greece merely at the dyadic level by neglecting Greece's broader foreign policy orientation.[14]

Conclusion

In recent years, there has been a growing debate about China and its ability to translate its economic power into political influence over smaller powers. In many ways, as far as Europe is concerned, Greece has emerged as a quintessential example of how Beijing has been successful in exerting political influence over smaller countries as a result of its economic power and investments in strategic sectors, such as ports. Typifying such claims, most analysts have paid attention to the Chinese investments in the Piraeus port and their impact on Greece's foreign policy, especially with regards to instances of divergence from EU norms and policies that suggest a challenge to the unity of the EU and the Liberal International Order. Yet, less attention has been paid to the constrains on China's influence on Greece due to the fact that influence is usually conflated with material power and resources.

[14] For a few exceptions, see Economy (2022); Brattberg et al. (2021); and Stroikos (2022).

This chapter has shown that a focus on treating power as influence rather than power as resources has the merits of revealing a more mixed and evolving picture of China's influence over Greece. Although it is clear that China has emerged as a significant partner of Greece in economic terms, it was able to achieve limited political gains at the symbolic level when Athens was more vulnerable and susceptible to Chinese pressure during the Eurozone crisis. In evaluating China's exercise of influence over Greece, this chapter has also suggested that it is necessary to highlight the constraints China faces in terms of its ability to attain its goals, which involves paying attention to the ways in which Beijing's policies and activities trigger local and domestic resistance, exemplified by recent developments concerning the Piraeus port. This also entails considering the agency of the small target state and how China's growing clout elicits responses from other great powers, as we have seen. In this respect, the exercise of China's influence in Greece is entangled in and affected by domestic actors with conflicting interests, such as certain Greek shipowners and local communities, contingent factors and specific decision-makers, such as the Eurozone crisis and the agency of Foreign Minister Kotzias, domestic political considerations, and the wider strategic context within which Greece operates that informs national interest calculations and the role of other great powers. Consequently, such an analysis is more pertinent in light of changes in the EU's China policy and the unfolding US-China strategic rivalry.

Bibliography

Alden, C., and A. Aran. 2017. *Foreign Policy Analysis: New Approaches*. 2nd edn. Abington: Routledge.

ANA-MPA. 2018. 'Cosco Unveils Ambitious Development Plan for Pireaus Port'. 23 January. Available at: https://www.amna.gr/en/article/223785/Cosco-unveils-ambitious-development-plan-for-Pireaus-port.

Bian, Y. 2022. 'Ancient Civilizations Forum and The Belt and Road Initiative'. In *The Routledge Handbook of The Belt and Road*, edited by Cai Fang, Peter Nolan, and Wang Linggui, pp. 472–476. 2nd edn. Abingdon: Routledge.

Brattberg, E., P. Le Corre, P. Stronski, and T. de Waal. 2021. *China's Influence in Southeastern, Central, and Eastern Europe: Vulnerabilities and Resilience in Four Countries*. October. Washington, D.C.: Carnegie Endowment for International Peace.

Calinoff, J., and D. Gordon. 2020. 'Port Investments in the Belt and Road Initiative: Is Beijing Grabbing Strategic Assets?'. *Survival* 62 (4): pp. 59–80.

Chryssogelos, A. 2021. 'The Dog That Barked but Did Not Bite: Greek Foreign Policy under the Populist Coalition of SYRIZA-Independent Greeks, 2015–2019'. *Comparative European Politics* 19: pp. 722–738.

Cumming-Bruce, N. and S. Sengupta. 2017. 'In Greece, China Finds an Ally Against Human Rights Criticism'. *New York Times*, 19 June. Available at: https://www.nytimes.com/2017/06/19/world/europe/china-human-rights-greece-united-nations.html.

Denyer, S. 2017. 'Europe Divided, China Gratified as Greece Blocks E.U. Statement Over Human Rights'. *Washington Post*, 19 June. Available at: https://www.washingtonpost.com/news/worldviews/wp/2017/06/19/europe-divided-china-gratified-as-greece-blocks-e-u-statement-over-human-rights/.

Deudney, D., and G. J. Ikenberry. 1999. 'The Nature and Sources of Liberal International Order'. *Review of International Studies* 25 (2): pp. 179–196

Doga, A., A. Lioumpas, and S. Petropoulos. 2021. 'Grand Strategy and the (Re)Shaping of Greece–China Relations'. *Chinese Journal of International Review* 3 (2): 2150009.

Economides, Spyros. 2020. 'Greek Foreign Policy Since the Metapolitefsi'. In *The Oxford Handbook of Modern Greek Politics*, edited by Kevin Featherstone and Dimitri A. Sotiropoulos, pp. 598–612. Oxford: Oxford University Press.

Economy, E. C. 2022. *The World According to China*. Cambridge: Polity.

Freymann, E. 2021. *One Belt One Road: Chinese Power Meets the Word*. Cambridge, MA: Harvard University Press.

Georgiopoulos, G. 2016. 'China's Cosco Acquires 51 pct Stake in Greece's Piraeus Port'. *Reuters*, 10 August. Available at: https://www.reuters.com/article/greece-privatisation-port-idUSL8N1AR252.

Georgakopoulos, G. 2019. 'Spotlight: Greece Sees Increasing Chinese Visitors amid Closer Ties'. *Xinhua*, 13 November. Available at: https://en.imsilkroad.com/p/309352.html.

Glass, D. 2019. 'Cosco Plans New Pier to Expand Piraeus Capacity to Over 10m Teu'. Seatrade-Maritime News, 15 August. Available at: https://www.seatrade-maritime.com/europe/cosco-plans-new-pier-expand-piraeus-capacity-over-10m-teu.

Goh, E. 2014. 'The Modes of China's Influence: Cases from Southeast Asia'. *Asian Survey* 54 (5): pp. 825–848.

Goh, E., ed. 2016. *Rising China's Influence in Developing Asia*. Oxford: Oxford University Press.

Hopkins, V., and K. Hope. 2019. 'Greece Eyes 16+1 Group of China and Eastern European States'. *Financial Times*, 11 April. Available at: https://www.ft.com/content/c098e654-5bfc-11e9-9dde-7aedca0a081a.

Huliaras, A., and S. Petropoulos. 2014. 'Shipowners, Ports and Diplomats: The Political Economy of Greece's Relations with China'. *Asia Europe Journal* 12 (3): pp. 215–230.

Kathimerini. 2022. 'Cosco's Piraeus Masterplan Stopped for Want of Environmental Report'. 16 March. Available at: https://www.ekathimerini.com/economy/1179834/coscos-piraeus-masterplan-stopped-for-want-of-environmental-report/.

Kokoromytis, D., and C. Angelos. 2022. 'Greece between Crisis, Opportunity and Risk as a Key BRI Node'. In *The European Union and China's Belt and Road: Impact, Engagement and Competition*, edited by Vassilis Ntousas and Stephen Minas, pp. 188–201. Abingdon: Routledge.

Kotzias, N. 2016. 'Foreign Minister Kotzias' Statement on the EU Announcement Regarding the Ruling of the Court of Arbitration on the South China Sea'. Ministry of Foreign Affairs of the Hellenic Republic, 15 July. Available at: https://www.mfa.gr/en/current-affairs/top-story/foreign-minister-kotzias-statement-on-the-eu-announcement-regarding-the-ruling-of-the-court-of-arbitration-on-the-south-china-sea.html.

Koutantou, A. and B. Goh. 2016. 'After Piraeus Port, China's COSCO eyes Greek trains to build Europe hub – sources'. *Reuters*, 5 February. Available at: https://www.reuters.com/article/uk-greece-china-port-idUKKCN0VE0VL.

Kratz, A., M. J. Zenglein, G. Sebastian, and M. Witzke. 2022. 'Chinese FDI In Europe 2021 Update'. A report by Rhodium Group and the Mercator Institute for China Studies (MERICS), April. Available at: https://rhg.com/research/chinese-fdi-in-europe-2021-update/.

Liu, Z. 2016. *Europe and the 'Belt and Road' Initiative: Responses and Risks*. Beijing: China Social Sciences Press.

Ma, Y., and P. J. Peverelli. 2019. 'Strategic Decisions in Chinese State-Owned Enterprises as Outcome of the Sensemaking of the CEO: The Case of COSCO's Emerging Involvement in the Port of Piraeus'. *Transnational Corporations Review* 11 (1): pp. 50–64.

Mikelis, K., and D. Stroikos. 2017. 'Hierarchies, Civilization and the Eurozone Crisis: The Greek Financial Crisis'. In *The Internal Impact and External Influence of the Greek Financial Crisis*, edited by John Marangos, pp. 125–142. Cham: Palgrave Macmillan.

Ministry of Foreign Affairs of the People's Republic of China. 2006. 'The Joint Communiqué between the People's Republic of China and the Republic of Greece on the Establishment of Comprehensive Strategic Partnership'. 19 January. Available at: https://www.fmprc.gov.cn/mfa_eng/wjdt_665385/2649_665393/200601/t20060119_679141.html.

Ministry of the Foreign Affairs of the People's Republic of China. 2016. 'Xi Jinping Meets with Prime Minister Alexis Tsipras of Greece'. 6 July. Available at: https://www.fmprc.gov.cn/ce/cegr/eng/zgyw/t1378515.htm.

Ministry of the Foreign Affairs of the People's Republic of China. 2019. 'Xi Jinping Holds Talks with Prime Minister Kyriakos Mitsotakis of Greece'. 11 November. Available at: https://www.mfa.gov.cn/ce/cevu//eng/zgdt/t1715369.htm.

Mo, J. 2018. 'China, Greece ink BRI Memorandum'. *China Daily*, 28 August. Available at: http://english.www.gov.cn/state_council/state_councilors/2018/08/28/content_281476278845176.htm.

Neilson, B. 2019. 'Precarious in Piraeus: On the Making of Labour Insecurity in a Port Concession'. *Globalizations* 16 (4): pp. 559–574.

Prime Minister's Office. 2019. 'Meeting of Prime Minister Kyriakos Mitsotakis with the President of China Xi Jinping in Shanghai'. *Hellenic Republic*, 4 November. Available at: https://primeminister.gr/en/2019/11/04/23061.

Proedrou, F. 2021. 'A Geopolitical Account of the Eastern Mediterranean Conundrum: Sovereignty, Balance of Power and Energy Security Considerations'. *Cambridge Review of International Affairs*: DOI: 10.1080/09557571.2021.1897088.

Psaraftis, H. N., and A. A. Pallis. 2012. 'Concession of the Piraeus Container Terminal: Turbulent Times and the Quest for Competitiveness'. *Maritime Policy & Management* 39 (1): pp. 27–43.

Raimundo, A., S. Stavridis, and C. Tsardanidis. 2021. 'The Eurozone Crisis' Impact: A De-Europeanization of Greek and Portuguese Foreign Policies?'. *Journal of European Integration* 43 (5): pp. 535–550.

Ren, H. 2019. 'China, Greece Promote Wisdom, Responsibility of Ancient Civilizations'. *People's Daily*, 15 November. Available at: http://en.people.cn/n3/2019/1115/c90000-9632540.html.

Reuters. 2017. 'China-Led AIIB Approves Seven New Members Ahead of New Silk Road Summit'. Reuters, 13 May. Available at: https://www.reuters.com/article/us-china-silkroad-aiib-idUSKBN1890B9.

Seferiadis, G. 2020. 'Silk Road Redux: Greece Courts China Money in Crisis Revival Bid'. *Nikkei Asian Review*, 18 August. Available at: https://asia.nikkei.com/Spotlight/Asia-Insight/Silk-Road-Redux-Greece-courts-China-money-in-crisis-revival-bid.

Shams, A. 2022. 'Egypt: Greek Diplomats Worked with Cairo to Block EU Criticism of Sisi'. Middle East Eye, 7 March. Available at: https://www.middleeasteye.net/news/egypt-eu-criticism-sisi-blocked-greece-diplomats-worked.

Silver, L., K. Devlin, and C. Huang. 2021. 'Large Majorities Say China Does Not Respect the Personal Freedoms of Its People'. *Pew Research Center*, 30 June. Available at: https://www.pewresearch.org/global/2021/06/30/large-majorities-say-china-does-not-respect-the-personal-freedoms-of-its-people/

Silver, L., C. Huang, and L. Clancy. 2022. 'Negative Views of China Tied to Critical Views of Its Policies on Human Rights'. *Pew Research Center*, 29 June. Available at: https://www.pewresearch.org/global/2022/06/29/negative-views-of-china-tied-to-critical-views-of-its-policies-on-human-rights/.

Skordeli, M. 2015. 'New Horizons in Greek-Chinese Relations: Prospects for the Eastern Mediterranean'. *Mediterranean Quarterly* 26 (1): pp. 59–76.

Sklias, P., S. Roukanas and V. Pistikou. 2012. 'China's Economic Diplomacy: A Comparative Approach to Sino-Greek and Sino- Turkish relations'. *International Journal of Business and Social Science* 3 (10): pp. 286–29.

Smith, H. 2022. 'Trial of Protesters against Beijing Olympics Postponed in Greece'. *The Guardian*, 5 February. Available at: https://www.theguardian.com/world/2022/feb/05/trial-of-protesters-against-beijing-olympics-postponed-in-greece.

Stamouli, N. 2019. 'China's Biggest Investment in Greece Blocked by Archaeological Authority'. *Wall Street Journal*, 3 April. Available at: https://www.wsj.com/articles/chinas-biggest-investment-in-greece-blocked-by-archaeological-authority-11554317046.

Stroikos, D. 2022. 'Head of the Dragon' or 'Trojan Horse'?: Reassessing China–Greece Relations'. *Journal of Contemporary China* 32 (142): pp. 602-619, DOI: 10.1080/10670564.2022.2067743.

Tonchev, P. 2022. 'Greece: No Meaningful Debate on Dependence on China'. In *Dependence in Europe's Relations with China: Weighing Perceptions and Reality*, edited by John Seaman, Francesca Ghiretti, Lucas Erlbacher, Xiaoxue Martin, and Miguel Otero-Iglesias, pp. 103–108. A Report by the European Think-tank Network on China (ETNC), April. Available at: https://merics.org/sites/default/files/2022-04/etnc_2022_report.pdf.

Tonchev, P., and B. Angelos. 2021. 'The Thrill is Gone: China's Diminishing Appeal in Greece'. In *China's Soft Power in Europe: Falling on Hard Times*, edited by Ties Dams, Xiaoxue Martin, and Vera Kranenburg, pp. 43–47. A Report by the European Think-tank Network on China (ETNC), April. Available at: https://www.clingendael.org/sites/default/files/2021-04/Report_ETNC_Chinas_Soft_Power_in_Europe_Falling_on_Hard_Times_2021.pdf.

Tonchev, P., and P. Davarinou. 2017. 'Chinese Investment in Greece and the Big Picture of Sino-Greek Relations'. Institute of International Economic Relations, Athens, December. Available at: https://idos.gr/wp-content/uploads/2017/12/Chinese-Investment-in-Greece_4-12-2017.pdf.

Tzogopoulos, G. N. 2018. 'Whither Sino-Greek Relations? The Bilateral and Regional Context and International Implications'. China-CEE Institute, Budapest, June. Available at: https://china-cee.eu/working_papers/whither-sino-greek-relations-the-bilateral-and-regional-context-and-international-implications/.

van der Putten, F. P. 2016. 'Infrastructure and Geopolitics: China's Emerging Presence in the Eastern Mediterranean'. *Journal of Balkan and Near Eastern Studies* 18 (4): pp. 337–351.

Varvitsioti, E. 2022. 'Piraeus Port Deal Intensifies Greece's Unease over China Links'. *Financial Times*, 19 October. Available at: https://www.ft.com/content/3e91c6d2-c3ff-496a-91e8-b9c81aed6eb8.

Xinhua. 2021. 'Greece-China Year of Culture and Tourism 2021 to be Inaugurated in May'. 28 January. Available at: http://www.xinhuanet.com/english/2021-01/28/c_139702402.htm.

Xinhua. 2023. 'Greece counts on direct air links to boost Chinese arrivals'. 11 January. Available at: https://english.news.cn/20230111/ec834b7b7bbd4f699be19ecf2f403932/c.html.

Xue, L. 2022. 'China–Europe Land–Sea Express Route with the Belt and Road Initiative'. In *The Routledge Handbook of The Belt and Road*, edited by Cai Fang, Peter Nolan, and Wang Linggui, pp. 496–499. 2nd edn. Abingdon: Routledge.

Yu, J. 2018. 'The Belt and Road Initiative: Domestic Interests, Bureaucratic Politics and the EU-China Relations'. *Asia Europe Journal* 16: pp. 223–236.

6
Between Normative Influence and Securitization Dynamic
China's Engagement in the Visegrád Group

Małgorzata Jakimów

Introduction

China's engagement in Central and Eastern Europe (CEE) in the last decade, both economic and political, has been unprecedented. This engagement was perhaps most boldly signified by the formation of the 16+1 (later relabelled as 17+1 and 14+1) platform in 2012 to facilitate the implementation of China's flagship Belt and Road Initiative (BRI). China's entry was welcomed for its promise of economic investments, especially for those economies in the region which looked for extra-EU sources of investments due to the 2008 global financial crisis. However, despite the proclaimed 'no political strings attached' rhetoric, the BRI investments came with less or more direct political, and, in consequence, normative influences: from the rise of Chinese advisers' influence in local politics, to adoption of China-promoted language and behaviours within the diplomatic conduct, to the rise of pro-China narratives among the prominent politicians in the region. The normative convergence between the nationalistic, populist, and illiberal trends and the values represented by the so-called China model can also be noted. However, this tide started to shift visibly in 2018, when some CEE countries started to approach China's presence in the CEE region with growing scepticism and suspicion. From failed Chinese infrastructure projects to the controversy over the influence of Huawei 5G technology on national security, to mixed responses to China's COVID-19 'mask diplomacy', China's European 'enter the dragon' moment has been stalled by a growing resistance at both the EU and CEE regional level.

Focusing on the Visegrád Four (V4) group of states (Czechia, Hungary, Poland, and Slovakia), this chapter seeks to capture these changing trends

Małgorzata Jakimów, *Between Normative Influence and Securitization Dynamic*. In: *Rising Power, Limited Influence*. Edited by: Indrajit Roy, Jappe Eckhardt, Dimitrios Stroikos, and Simona Davidescu, Oxford University Press.
 DOI: 10.1093/oso/9780192887115.003.0007

and unpack the nexus between normative and securitization dynamic in the region. To what extent are we facing normative convergence between China and the regional illiberal trends? Do Chinese investments result in China's normative influence in the region? What is the impact of the changing approach to China as a 'security threat' in the region on China's ability to wield normative power? This chapter will analyse the impact of the changing securitization dynamic around Chinese investments in the region on China's ability to exert normative influence in the V4 states. To this end, the chapter is not concerned with the soft power influence which is often measured by the spread of Confucius Institutes, China-friendly think tanks or the promotion of Chinese culture via the media, but rather with the ways in which political elites bend accepted norms, or, indeed, adopt new ones, as a result of China's political influence exerted through its economic prowess.

Although China-V4 states relations and the attending possibility of normative influence remain deeply embedded in the 'state-society complexes' (see the introduction to this volume), this paper focuses specifically on political elites as the target actors of such influence for two interlinked reasons. First, there has been a long-standing disconnect between the political elites and popular approaches to China in the V4 countries. According to the recent survey conducted by the Sinophone project, the voters of the ruling parties in V4 countries all hold negative views of China (Turcsányi et al., 2020: 11), and this trend has been largely unchanged throughout the 2010s, despite heavy Chinese investments into improving its image in the region (Song, 2013: 12). However, the negative image of China among the voters has not impacted the ruling elites' preferences towards ever-closer engagement with China over most of the last decade. This disconnect indicates that while the assessment of China's ability to influence the wider public opinion as opposed to the political elites in these countries is important, it merits a separate study. Second, there is a clear preference towards high-level political (or other elite) channels in the conduct of China-V4 countries international relations, with limited role given to the grassroots social exchanges. While the role of non-state actors, particularly the media, in spreading Chinese influence in the region is important,[1] political elites are the primary actors who shape normative outlooks and the resultant policy preferences of the country, deserving a focused study of how normative influence might be exerted upon them specifically.

The first section of this chapter highlights the current discussions on the relationship between China's normative power and securitization and

[1] See, for instance, many publications of the Mapinfluence project. Available at: https://mapinfluence.eu/en/our-projects/.

formulates the study's theoretical framework. The second section highlights the tendency towards China-friendly and even China-admiring narrative among the V4 states in the initial 'honeymoon' phase of China's engagement in the region (in years 2012–2017), spurred by the enthusiastic perception of China's potential investments, and accompanied by the desecuritization of China's image in the region. The third section presents how, with the growing disappointment over the BRI's unfulfilled promises, and the accompanying international securitization of China since 2018, some countries within the region have adopted a more China-sceptic, if not outright securitized view, with the pro-Chinese voices becoming less dominant. However, this section shows that this shift, particularly visible in Poland and Czechia, has not been universal across the region, with Hungary remaining on a strong pro-China course and Slovakia maintaining careful diversification politics. The fourth section highlights how the contrasting trends between China's securitization and desecuritization within the V4 countries came into stark conflict under the COVID-19 emergency. In the early stages of the emergency, China succeeded in projecting a positive image of its governance model and engagement in the region. Those states which embarked on securitization pathways have faced a conflict of interest in the face of shortages of medical equipment and the need to rely on China for the supplies, with normative consequences. However, with the fading of COVID-19 reliance on China, it becomes more apparent that the underlying security concerns in the region largely limit the ability of China to exert long-term political and normative influence.

Theorizing Normative Influence of Chinese Investments

The potential for China to exert normative influence globally through its economic and other soft power tools has attracted much scholarly attention in the past years, and various concepts have been coined to describe it. The concepts of soft power (Callahan, 2015; Nye, 1990), normative power (Kavalski, 2013; Kerr, 2015), sharp power (NED, 2017), and symbolic power (Vangeli, 2018) are but a few which have been used so far to describe the various elements of this impact. In this chapter I mainly rely on two interlinked concepts from this toolkit: normative power and normative influence.

'Normative power' was first defined by Ian Manner with reference to the Normative Power Europe (NPE) model, and it depicts the ability of an actor to determine what passes as '"normal" in international relations' through 'power of ideas and norms' (Manners, 2002: 239, 253). Against clearly defined European values spread by NPE, which are democracy, liberty, human rights, rule of law, anti-discrimination, social solidarity, sustainable development, and good governance (Manners, 2002: 243), the exact norms which are supposed to be diffused by China have been more elusive. Officially, China rejects the idea of norm-spreading, insisting on the Five Principles of Peaceful Co-existence[2] as the foundation of its international conduct. These five principles are: 'mutual respect for sovereignty and territorial integrity', 'mutual non-aggression', 'non-interference in each other's internal affairs', 'equality and mutual benefit', and 'peaceful coexistence' (Ministry of Foreign Affairs of the PRC, 2014). However, these principles are certainly normative and tend to overlap with those professed by the EU (it can hardly be imagined that the EU would not share the norms of 'peaceful coexistence' or 'mutual non-aggression', since its very creation was built on the idea of future war-prevention and peace). Therefore, despite its official declarations of norm-neutrality, China diffuses the norms embedded in the Five Principles, and, arguably, others, which are less explicitly verbalized. Indeed, most scholars see China's normative impact not as exerted through the official rhetoric, which claims that China has no interest in spreading its norms, but rather in the kind of 'new normal' that China builds in international relations (Bryant and Chou, 2016; Kavalski, 2013; Nathan, 2015; Vangeli, 2018). Some scholars point to the 'incidental' spread of Chinese norms and values, as the result of the unintended consequences of its investments (Jones, 2020), diffused by 'the power of example' rather than by direct promotion of its governance model (Bryant and Chou 2016; Nathan, 2015). Others point to the production of new modes of interactions, behaviour, thinking, and language in international relations: China sets new language which establishes what is permissible (Goh, 2014; Vangeli, 2018), and it creates new institutional tools that define power asymmetries between itself and other countries (Goh, 2016; Jakóbowski, 2018). Finally, China's attractiveness relies on its unique approach to IR as 'relational', rather than 'rules-based', which reshapes the rules of international diplomatic conduct (Kavalski 2013: 254; Kavalski and Cho, 2018; Qin, 2016).

An important set of norms, spread by both sides, which do not figure in the official definition of NPE proposed by Manners or in the Chinese legal documents, relate to how both actors approach the established Liberal International Order (LIO). This non-verbalization of the respective approaches to political economy as norms is somehow puzzling, as the disputes over the rules governing the international economic order between the two powers

[2] Herewith referred to as 'Five Principles'.

are long-standing and contentious, and fundamental to the idea of normative power shift, as the articles in this volume attest. Some of these norms relate to global competition over the governance of finance (Peng and Tok, 2016), while others boil down to the contention over what constitutes the permissible extent of a state's intervention in the economy, and which, in the case of EU and China, has long been known as a dispute over China's market economy status (MES). In this respect, China seeks to exert normative pressure on countries it interacts with, seeking for them to align with its interests: Hungary is an example of an EU country which has long lobbied for granting China an MES status as a consequence of Chinese engagement in the country (see Wu, 2016).

Other norms, which spin out of the 'non-interference in domestic affairs' principle, include the 'regime-type-neutral' definition of human rights, which while being heavily emphasized in diplomatic relations and supported by China's propaganda machine (Nathan, 2015) is not portrayed as norm-diffusion at all, but rather as norms-neutrality. The proponents of the 'sharp power' concept argue that these are examples of how China has been diffusing norms internationally in recent years. They argue that China's strategy centres on 'manipulation and distraction' and involves 'suppression of political pluralism and free expression' abroad (Walker and Ludwig, 2017: 10), making China's norms-diffusion obscured, if not insidious.

Whereas the above studies discuss how China projects its normative power, it is equally important to assert the extent to which such projections actually translate into tangible normative influence, that is, the extent to which the target recipient of norms-transfer actually adopts the norms. In this article, I follow the multidimensional understanding of normative influence (or impact) presented by Dandashly and Noutcheva (2022: 422), where normative influence is not simply understood as norm acceptance or rejection, but also as modification, which is particularly common among the cases presented in the article. Modification means that in between accepting or refusing Chinese norms in the V4 region, there is a large variation of how these norms are modified and moulded to suit domestic interests of governments and other actors within the state. Also, as the above discussions on soft, normative, sharp, and symbolic power reveal, China's normative influence can be seen as either intentional (for example, sharp power) or unintentional (for example, symbolic power). This chapter adopts the 'agnostic' approach to the intentionality of China's normative influence (see Roy and Hu's introduction to this volume), by revealing the extent to which normative influence can be unintended or even misrepresented by the recipient political elites.

In order to shed some further light on China's ability to exert normative influence, this chapter pays particular attention to instances of securitization and desecuritization of China as important variables in such a process. Following the seminal study of the Copenhagen School of critical security studies (CSS) (Buzan et al., 1998), 'securitization' is understood as instances of framing an issue as an 'existential threat, requiring emergency measures', and therefore 'as special kind of politics or as above politics' (Buzan et al., 1998: 23, 24), while 'desecuritization' is seen as returning the objects to 'the ordinary public sphere', and has been predominantly viewed in a positive light (Buzan et al., 1998: 4, 29). However, 'resecuritization' of a previously desecuritized actor is seen by some as always inevitable (Floyd, 2015: 137), making desecuritization itself impossible in a long term (Behnke, 2006: 65). However, what has been largely missing from the literature, and is relevant for the cases discussed in this chapter, is the lack of adequate attention to the political and normative implications of securitization and desecuritization (Aradau, 2004; Floyd, 2015; Hansen, 2012: 527–528), including how they might facilitate normative influence. The CSS literature on China, similarly, focuses on investigating the ways in which China engages in 'desecuritization', that is, how it presents itself as non-threatening (Biba, 2014; Danner, 2014; Vuori, 2018: 127), rather than on the impact of securitization or desecuritization on norms-diffusion.

However, it is important to more closely assess the relationship between the two processes. Desecuritization can exert normative impact because it changes the target audience's perception of an actor in line with this actor's soft power projections, and therefore should not be seen as a 'neutral' or apolitical process (Jakimów, 2019). For instance, China presents its economic investments in V4 in desecuritized language such as 'win-win' and 'politically neutral', denying any normative influence of such engagement. However, the very act of presenting the investments in an apolitical and norm-neutral manner (desecuritization) is meant to soften China's image, presenting it as an unthreatening state—therefore it is a tool of its soft power strategy. The new non-threatening image opens the space to accept the norms China promotes, such as 'regime-neutral definition of human rights', or the recognition of China's MES. In this article, I delve into the process of both the desecuritization and resecuritization of China and how these processes influence its investments in the region and the ability to exert normative influence. As the region which relatively recently engaged with China, and which in the span of the last decade has gone through phases of de-/resecuritization of China, the V4 group provides relevant context for the discussion of the relationship between such trends and the possibility of China's normative influence. In the light of the growing discussion of democratic backsliding and the growth of authoritarian regimes, for which V4 appears to be a particularly relevant battleground, the study of China's engagement in this region can shed light on the extent to which China's normative influence can withstand cycles of resecuritization.

The Extent of China's Normative Influence in the 'Honeymoon' Phase (2012–2017)

China's engagement with the V4 region entered a new phase in 2012 with the formation of the 16(17)+1 platform, which led to intensification of both region-wide and bilateral relations with China. At the time, spurred by the promise of economic investments via the BRI, the political elites in the region engaged in intensive political relations with Chinese officials and, as a result, opened doors to Chinese companies. However, to what extent did this economically motivated political opening result in China's normative influence? And how does China's possible normative influence relate to the already present 'illiberal' transformation in the region? Is the 'normative convergence' between China's and some V4 countries' models of governance merely accidental? In order to establish the relationship between these overlapping processes, it is necessary to first analyse the extent and nature of China's normative influence in the region.

One way in which such political opening to China can translate into normative influence can be observed in the phenomenon of personal relationship-building between V4 main political figures and Chinese high officials. Polish president Andrzej Duda, Czech president Miloš Zeman, and Hungarian Prime Minister Victor Órban are but a few such highest-ranking politicians who have been key figures in securing China's investment projects in the region, promoting closer ties with China and participating actively in desecuritizing China (Jakimów, 2019). Their personal engagement with Chinese elite politicians, particularly Xi Jinping, has been noted to abide by the Chinese logic of 'relationships before rules' in international relations (Kavalski and Cho, 2018; Kowalski, 2020), creating an important normative divergence from the way international relations had been handled by the V4 states in the past.

The Chinese investments, which were enabled by such 'relational' engagement, have resulted in various further forms of Chinese political influence in the region, in particular the rise of Chinese advisors to local politicians, as well as the intermingling of V4 countries' political circles with Chinese business circles. This phenomenon is signified perhaps most prominently by the case of Ye Jianming, the CCP member and the now defamed former CEO of CEFC China Energy, a Chinese private energy company now overtaken by a Chinese state-owned enterprise (SOE), CITIC. Before his detention in China on bribery charges in 2018, Ye had been hovering in high circles of the Chinese political elite, and became an economic advisor of President Zeman in 2015 (Dębiec and Jakóbowski, 2018). Their relationship was largely seen as opaque and beyond the scrutiny of taxpayers, once again highlighting the growing normative impact of Chinese-style networking. CEFC's practices of grooming the China-friendly political elite in Czechia illustrate how Chinese political/business elites exert political influence in the region. For instance, Jaroslav Tvrdík, a former defence minister, an advisor to former Prime Minister Bohuslav Sobotka, and a long-term China lobbyist, became the head of the CEFC European division, a favour which further allowed for Chinese interests to be represented among the Czech political elite. Such opaque intermingling between the Czech-Chinese political and business circles, as seen in the examples of Tvrdík and Ye, has resulted in 'repurposing of [democratic] state institutions' to serve the interest of personal relationships between political and business elites so that 'they no longer can fully perform their intended functions' (Hála, 2020: 8). These relationships are, therefore, yet another example of how political-economic engagement can translate into normative influence on the transparency and democratic accountability of politicians in the region.

Another set of examples of how the political opening to China in the 'honeymoon' phase resulted in normative impact can be observed in China's influence on the shaping of foreign policy choices of the V4 states. This pertains in particular to the issue of so-called Chinese core interest (*hexin liyi*), encapsulated in the principle of 'non-interference in countries' domestic affairs'. In practice, China acts on this principle by exerting diplomatic and economic pressure on other states to retreat from any political relations with Taiwan, and to refrain from criticizing China's domestic policies towards Tibet and Xinjiang. Since 2012, a trend of adopting China-promoted language and conduct in this respect has become prominent among the V4 political elites, as discussed below. This, in turn, has resulted in subverting the established EU norms on human rights and multilateral commitments.

For instance, the reversal of the long-standing criticism of the human rights record in China, paired with the retreat from the EU-wide approach in this regard, is visible in Poland, Czechia, and Hungary. In Poland, an example of this drift can be found in the case of the 2016 Polish former Foreign Affairs vice-minister Jan Parys's speech given during the Asia-Pacific Day in front of some Chinese delegates, criticizing 'Western' states' insistence on bringing up China's human rights record (Trybuna, 2016). Similarly, President Zeman, in an interview for Chinese television (CCTV) given in the same year, labelled his country's former critical policy on human rights in China as submissive 'to the pressure from the US and EU'. He posited it against his new policy, which he saw as enabling Czechia to be 'independent again', and 'not intefer[ing] with the internal affairs of any other country' (Zeman quoted in CCTV, 2016). Finally, in the speech given at the 2016 'China-CEE Political Parties Dialogue' event, Hungarian Prime Minister Órban subsumed criticism of the human rights record in China under a 'Western way of thinking', which 'expects other regions of the world to embrace its international doctrines', while Hungary prefers to take a road of 'mutual respect' (Órban, 2016). Clearly, the major political figures in each of these instances parroted Chinese exact wording of the norms embedded in the 'Five Principles', which demonstrates the uptake of Chinese norms by political elites in the region.

China has also exerted direct pressure on the conduct of foreign policy with regard to what it perceives as its 'renegade provinces'. When in 2016 Slovak President Andrei Kiska met with the Dalai Lama, he was criticized by Slovak Prime Minister Robert Fico, as well as by many non-Slovak politicians, including Czech president Zeman (Šebok, 2016). This incident demonstrated the effectiveness of the China-promoted approach to human rights issues, which relies on the deflection of the potential criticism of China's human rights abuses by other states, by expressing official outrage at the meeting of Tibetan government-in-exile representatives, and therefore labelling these issues exclusively as 'internal Chinese affairs', outside of the legitimate purview of international criticism. Another prominent example of an attempt to exert this kind of political influence was the 2016 signing of the Prague-Beijing twin city agreement. Prague was lured by the promise of Chinese investments and agreed to sign the agreement, which, quite unusually, contained a phrase of 'Taiwan being an inalienable part of Chinese territory', going even further than the usual 'One China' remarks that the Chinese governments includes in strategic partnership documents at national level (Kowalski 2020: 15). This unusual politicization of a regular sub-national agreement illustrates how V4 states became the primary battleground in China's struggle to change the European approach to China's human rights record and the conduct of cross-strait relations.

As the examples above indicate, China's political engagement, which follows in the footsteps of its economic engagement, has pushed for recalibration of V4 states' normative outlook. The normative impact of such engagement is particularly visible in the ability of China to influence the change in interstate diplomatic conduct from rule-based to relational interactions. This new relationship-based conduct can lead to the instances of 'repurposing of democracy' (Hála, 2020). Paired with the adoption of China-promoted language, it can also reshape norms around human rights and multilateralism. As I argued elsewhere (Jakimów, 2019), while these countries' political and normative engagement with China is ultimately pragmatic, it nevertheless promotes the process of China's desecuritization in the region, which aids the adoption of China-promoted language and norms. However, these trends started to substantially shift in 2018, when the US-China trade war resulted in the growing securitization of China in the US, which spilled over into the V4 region. This was accompanied by the growing disappointment over the unfulfilled investment expectation. The following years revealed with greater clarity the domestic struggles over the role of China and the political approach to China in some countries of the region.

Resecuritizing China and the Loss of Normative Influence (2018–2020)

While the pompous overtures between the CEE countries and China might have dominated the initial relation-building period after the formation of the 16(17)+1 platform, since 2018 the deeply rooted idea of a 'China threat' in the region (see, for instance, Godement et al., 2011) has resurfaced. This resecuritization shift, just like the earlier desecuritization of China, has been the V4 political elites' response to the domestic and close neighbourhood challenges, and their own domestic position. Among these, the earlier securitization of China at the EU level (see Jakimów, 2019 for more detail), and particularly the sharp turn to curb Chinese telecommunication companies' market presence due to the alleged cyber-security threat they pose, on both European and US levels, have played an important role. This resecuritization trend is most visible in the case of the recent Czech and Polish securitization moves against the Chinese telecommunication giant Huawei, but also in the growing Czech and Slovak resistance to China's attempts at political influence, particularly the attempts to exert leverage over normative choices in foreign policy. So far, only Hungary has remained on its previous course of complete acceptance and appraisal of China's engagement in the CEE.

The purported cyber-espionage, and particularly the Huawei case, deserves deeper analysis, as it is linked to the politics of the V4 countries towards their closest neighbourhood and the transatlantic alliance. In the case of Poland, the salience of the transatlantic alliance has been driven by the long-standing security concerns over Russia's behaviour in the region. China-perceived threats, such as this of cyber-espionage, have also been growing in recent years, but Poland has subsumed these under wider strategic interests vis-à-vis Russia, as the main international threat, and the US, as the main security guarantor. When a Chinese Huawei executive, Wang Weijing, was arrested in Warsaw in January 2019 on spying charges, this was quickly interpreted as part of the US-led anti-Huawei offensive (Šimalčík et al., 2019: 40). Indeed, soon after the 2018 arrest of Huawei executive Meng Wangzhou in Canada, the Polish Ministry of Foreign Affairs expressed its concerns over the alleged Chinese cyber-espionage (Ministry of Foreign Affairs of Poland, 2018). This convergence of interests was later confirmed in the September 2019 signing of the US-Poland Joint Declaration on 5G, the move which has been further institutionalized by the proposed legislative changes, which make Polish cyber-security law compliant with US's anti-Huawei strategy (Kasonta, 2020). All these closely timed events clearly show a strategic aligning of Poland's response to the US's anti-Huawei offensive. However, while pragmatically aimed, this revaluation of the Polish approach to China clearly contains genuine security concerns regarding China itself, which the Polish Interior Minister Mariusz Kamiński expressed in his December 2019 US Wilson Centre address: 'Poland, like the United States, speaks clearly about the China threat' (Kamiński, quoted in Kasonta, 2020).

A similar resecuritization move towards China has been taking place in Czechia. Here, the US is also regarded as a security guarantor, and therefore an important power to look up to for support (Fürst, 2020a: 43). In late 2018, the Czech National Cyber Security Agency warned against the security threat of Chinese telecommunication companies Huawei and ZTE, over their legal obligation to cooperate with Chinese intelligence agencies (Bachulska and Turcsányi, 2019). This was followed by the immediate decision of the Czech government under Prime Minister Andrej Babiš to ban Huawei technologies and develop screening procedures alongside new public information networks guidelines. The high-level visits between US and Czechia followed in early 2019, allegedly propelled by Czechia's anti-Huawei turn (Fürst, 2020a). Under the Babiš's more China-sceptic government and highly China-critical media, Czechia was clearly steering away from the wholesale partnership with China, as had been the case under the Zeman-Sobotka leadership.

However, to what degree has this resecuritization played a role in the weakening of China's normative influence? This is perhaps more visible in the case of the Czechia-China spat over the issue of Taiwan, which epitomizes a growing pushback against what is perceived as a threat of China's normative influence. In Czechia this change started with the reversal of the

Prague-Beijing partnership agreement, when the new Prague mayor, Zdeněk Hřib, insisted on removal of the controversial quote on 'Taiwan being an inalienable part of Chinese territory' from the city partnership document (Kowalski, 2020: 15). This resulted in Beijing abandoning the partner city agreement, followed by Prague signing a new one with Taipei. Hřib has also been pushing a pro-human rights agenda in relation to China, by hosting Tibetan government-in-exile head Lobsang Sangay, hanging the Tibetan flag over the City Hall, and officially visiting Taipei (Šimalčík et al., 2019: 23–24). This change was soon followed on the national level by the Czech Senate Speaker Jaroslav Kubera, who in early 2020 announced a trip to Taiwan. In response, the Chinese embassy in Czechia immediately threatened to take retaliation measures, which, in turn, resulted in the opposition parties' sharp response against China's interference and Prime Minister Babiš's call for the replacement of China's ambassador Zhang Jianmin. While Kubera's sudden death interrupted these plans, his replacement, Miloš Vystrčil, did travel to Taiwan in August 2020, where he delivered the speech on a common experience of democratization in both countries and called himself 'a Taiwanese', paraphrasing John Kennedy's words pronounced in West Berlin. This, again, was met with a harsh response from Chinese Foreign Secretary Wang Yi, who threatened that Vystrčil 'will pay a high price for his short-sighted behaviour and political opportunism' (Johnson, 2020). The critical response towards the Chinese ministry's words, perceived as 'a threat', was overwhelming in Czechia and soon supported by Germany, France, and Slovakia (Zachová, 2020). Such reversal back to the traditional pro-democratic and pro-human rights normative stance in the region is also visible, perhaps on a less vocal level, in Slovakia, where new president, Zuzanna Caputova, famous for a liberal and pro-human rights agenda, confronted PRC Foreign Secretary Wang Yi on the issue of human rights in July 2019. These cases illustrate how the resecuritization trend among both local- and national-level politicians in Czechia and Slovakia has resulted in the pushback against what is being perceived to be Chinese attempts at exerting normative influence, the attempts which are themselves framed as a security threat.

A New Turn in the Tale? COVID-19 and the Future of China's Normative Influence

The period since the onset of the COVID-19 pandemic has brought the contradictions between the desecuritization and resecuritization of China to the fore. At the beginning of the pandemic, in late 2019 and early 2020, China's governance model came under attack in some of the V4 regional media, with the media pointing towards the complicity of the authoritarian system in the mishandling of the initial stages of the pandemic and the spread of the virus outside of China (Fürst, 2020b: 17; Matura, 2020b: 34). However, these voices were quickly subdued in the face of international competition for the Personal Protective Equipment (PPE) supplies, which compelled the governments to continue their overtures towards China. These can be observed in particular in the period from February 2020 onwards, countering the earlier resecuritization moves.

In the initial phase of the COVID-19 emergency in Europe, the personal relationships that earlier played such a crucial role in the facilitation of China's BRI investments were once again invoked to secure mostly commercial deliveries of the PPE, labelled, nevertheless, as 'aid' (Seaman, 2020: 8). For instance, Czech President Zeman's pro-China lobby efforts allowed Czechia to presumably jump the queue, and, in effect, to secure shipment of the PPE in early March (iRozhlas, 2020). However, the press was quick to point out that the 'deal' was an opaque arrangement, accompanied by 'kowtowing' to the Chinese shipment of goods which were purchased, and not even donated (Fürst, 2020b: 18). In Poland, similarly, the initial response to the pandemic relied on securing the delivery of equipment from China via personal connections between presidents Duda and Xi, with simultaneous restraint in criticism over China's responsibility in the evolution of the pandemic (Szczudlik, 2020: 50–51). President Duda's sympathy letter to Xi Jinping, praising the Chinese response to the pandemic, was accompanied by aid deployments from Poland in February 2020, which resulted in the ability to secure some shipments back from China in March, via both private purchases and donations (Szczudlik, 2020: 50–51). In Slovakia, a similar dynamic to that observed in Czechia took place: commercial purchases overtook aid (Turcsányi and Šimalčík, 2020: 60), and a welcoming party headed by the outgoing Prime Minister Peter Pellegrini was organized to receive Chinese transport of the PPE in March 2020. Moreover, the former Prime Minister Robert Fico and Member of Parliament Ľuboš Blaha emphasized the importance of praising China for its 'aid' and refraining from criticism (Turcsányi and Šimalčík, 2020: 61). Hungary had been active in sending aid to China prior to March 2020. In exchange, it received mainly commercially purchased Chinese equipment. However, these shipments were not clearly labelled as 'purchases', and their price was not revealed (Matura, 2020a: 33). Moreover, the COVID-19 emergency allowed the government to classify the details of the EU-investigated Belgrade-Budapest railway tender (Matura, 2020a: 34), which deepened the lack of transparency over Hungary's deals with China. Last but not least, as the teleconference regarding the equipment delivery to the 16(17)+1 region took place one week before the one with the rest of the EU (Seaman, 2020: 7), V4 and other 16(17)+1 countries were given priority in securing 'PPE purchase deals', reflecting the 'gift-bestowing' approach of Chinese authorities to those who proved loyal to China.

Akin to the cases of the pre-2019 coproduction of China's desecuritization narratives by the political elites in the region (Jakimów, 2019), the early months of the European phase of the pandemic saw similar instances of desecuritization. The kowtowing, the kissing of the Chinese flag (Niewenhuis, 2020), thanking China in national speeches (Fürst, 2020b: 19), and praising China's response to the pandemic among the V4 and other 16(17)+1 countries were quickly echoed in China's press and boosted its image-building in the region (see Šebok and Karásková, 2020: 10). The language adopted by the V4 political elites was not accidental either: by portraying China-purchased equipment as 'aid', the political elites in the region subscribed once again to the China-promoted narrative, this time on 'mask diplomacy', helping to boost its desecuritization efforts. The nearly uncritical embrace of China-promoted narratives and conduct, including 'kowtowing' and the adoption of Chinese propaganda around the COVID-19 pandemic and 'mask diplomacy', has translated into a strengthening of Chinese normative influence. This normative impact should be understood, again, not as the wholehearted adoption of authoritarianism or the 'China model', but rather as the subscription to China-promoted relational forms of international relations (in order to secure the PPE shipments), as well as the undermining of due democratic procedures and mechanisms (the lack of transparency around the PPE shipments, and the manipulation of the pandemic 'emergency' status to further obscure the details of Chinese investments in the region).

Additionally, certain normative convergences between China and the V4 countries can also be noted during the pandemic. In Poland and Hungary, in particular, the ruling parties have pushed for various legislative initiatives, which either undermined normal democratic procedures or introduced socially controversial reforms at the time when social protest was officially disallowed. In Hungary, rule-by-decree was introduced in March 2020, which extended Órban's executive power indefinitely. While these special powers were curtailed by the parliament later that year, this move created a dangerous precedence towards potential dictatorial power. As to Poland, the government sought to hold the national elections and to push through a highly controversial anti-abortion law in the midst of the pandemic (European Parliament, 2020). Additionally, regional governments boosted their national images of 'saviours' amidst the COVID-19 pandemic (see Matura, 2020a), by arguing that they dealt more decisively and effectively with the pandemic than Western Europe, a move eerily mirroring that of the Chinese domestic propaganda.

However, while the initial regional responses to the COVID-19 pandemic and to China's role in it point to the continuation of the trend initiated in the 'desecuritization' phase of the relationship with China, after the initial period of competition for the PPE resources, the security concerns once again visibly came to the fore. In Czechia, critical oppositional voices pointed to the lack of transparency and the overt commercial character of China's overpriced 'mask diplomacy' (Valášek, 2020). The opposition also emphasized the institutional impact of Czech-Chinese state collusion brought about by the pandemic, Czech over-reliance on Chinese supplies, and the uncritical embrace of Chinese propaganda by the politicians (Fürst, 2020b: 18). Ultimately, the Czech Senate passed legislation to move away from reliance on China towards the EU-based and domestic suppliers for PPE in April 2020, with Pavel Fischer, the Senate's Foreign Affairs Commission chair, proclaiming that 'self-sufficiency in medical supplies is the first step towards country security' as the basis for the decision (Pavel Fischer, quoted in Kahn and Muller, 2020). This shift clearly continues the 2019 resecuritization trend, this time around health security concerns. Slovakia also followed in Czechia's footsteps, led by the new, more China-sceptic government, sworn in March 2020, with many pro-Western politicians emphasizing China's complicity in early mismanagement of the pandemic, including the Slovak Minister of Foreign Affairs who decried the Chinese 'infodemic' around the COVID-19 pandemic (Turcsányi and Šimalčík, 2020: 62). Poland and Hungary have not witnessed a clear resecuritization of China during the COVID-19 pandemic so far, but Poland's siding with the US over anti-China legislature with regard to 5G and Huawei clearly stayed the course in this period, despite the government's overtures towards China over the PPE shipments.

In summary, the COVID-19 pandemic revealed the ambiguity and fluctuations in the securitization dynamic vis-à-vis China for three countries in the region: Czechia, Poland, and Slovakia. The normative impact that was facilitated via the desecuritization dynamic appears largely erratic. As the later resecuritization moves indicate, the pro-China stands are pragmatic and temporary, and the stretching of rules around democratic institutions paired with the adoption of 'relational' conduct in international relations, which can be associated with China's influence, might not have a lasting effect. Hungary might prove an exception here, as its response to China has been on a steady course of desecuritization and normative convergence and, so far, it has not yet been unnerved by the resecuritization trend. China's normative impact is also not the same as normative convergence in terms of authoritarian tendencies, which increased during the pandemic in the cases of both Poland and Hungary, but which does not appear to be a direct result of relations with China.

Conclusion: Between Securitization Dynamic and China's Normative Influence

Exploring the relationship between the de/resecuritization of China and its normative influence among the V4 countries provides an important facet to understand China's ability to exert normative influence. The cases discussed in this article indicate that a unified, region-wide trend cannot be ascertained, as the study of each country reveals different national strategies vis-à-vis China's engagement. However, some general trends are still worth noting. Overall, the desecuritization of China's economic and political engagement in the region has led to the adoption of some China-promoted norms, such as 'relational' conduct in international relations, a change in the outlook on human rights issues, and the re-emphasis of the 'sovereignty over multilateralism' principle in foreign policy. The reverse also appears true: the normative influence of China seems to falter when V4 states are faced with security concerns over Chinese engagement in the region, and in the case of Czechia and Slovakia, the resecuritization of China has led to the reversal in such normative influence. In the case of Poland, concerns over cyber-security did take precedence over good relations with China, putting limitations on the adoption of China-promoted language, image, and, in effect, norms. In Hungary, which has continued on the desecuritization trajectory, normative influence has not faltered, with Órban's rhetoric remaining strongly supportive of China-desired narratives of itself and the normative consequences that it brings. These subtle yet clear trends point to the limits of China's normative impact, closely tied to its ability to shape desecuritization narratives of itself.

While the normative convergence between the illiberal trends in the region and the China model can also be noted, there is no sufficient evidence to ascertain that this trend is directly influenced by China's normative influence. Indeed, the resecuritization dynamic observed since 2018, though briefly interrupted by the COVID-19 crisis, points to a certain ambiguity in the relationship between China's ability to exert normative influence and the normative convergence between V4 countries and China. Not all the countries in the region follow the normative convergence trend. While Hungary and Poland clearly deepened their illiberal turn during the COVID-19 pandemic, the same cannot be said about Czechia and Slovakia, which both saw a rise of more liberal-minded and Sino-sceptic politicians in this period. This divergence within the region perhaps points to the limited role that China plays in dictating or even shaping these trends. At the same time, the illiberal trends remained apparent in the cases of Poland and Hungary, with both countries simultaneously choosing a different approach towards China: one of securitization, the other of desecuritization. This shows that China-promoted norms are adopted selectively and modified if necessary to meet domestic interests. These findings also suggest that the normative convergence between illiberal regional trends and China-promoted norms is hardly a result of China's intentional norm-transfer, but rather part of a wider global shift, equally signified by Donald Trump's period in office and the rise of populism and right-wing politics in Europe.

Bibliography

Aradau, C. 2004. 'Security and Democratic Scene: Desecuritization and Emancipation'. *Journal of International Relations and Development* 7 (4): pp. 388–413.

Bachulska, A., and R. Turcsányi. 2019. 'Behind the Huawei Backlash in Poland and the Czech Republic'. *The Diplomat*, 6 February. Available at: https://thediplomat.com/2019/02/behind-the-huawei-backlash-in-poland-and-the-czech-republic/?fbclid=IwAR3CacEd5iwOPK12cthr_OElXNaCHmgRRHyfG7CfPoQCyUhuDkl6PrvQAp0.

Behnke, A. 2006. 'No Way Out: Desecuritization, Emancipation and the Eternal Return of the Political. A Reply to Aradau'. *Journal of International Relations and Development* 9 (1): pp. 62–69.

Biba, S. 2014. 'Desecuritization in China's Behavior towards its Transboundary Rivers: The Mekong River, the Brahmaputra River, and the Irtysh and Ili Rivers'. *Journal of Contemporary China* 23 (85): pp. 21–43.

Bryant, O., and M. Chou. 2016. 'China's new Silk Road. Autocracy Promotion in the New Asian Order?'. *Democratic Theory* 3(2), pp. 114–124

Buzan, B., O. Waever, and J. de Wilde. 1998. *Security: A New Framework of Analysis*. Boulder, CO: Lynne Reiner.

Callahan, W. 2015. 'Identity and Security in China: The Negative Soft Power of the China Dream'. *Politics* 35 (3–4): pp. 216–229.

CCTV. 2016. 'Czech President Milos Zeman on China-Czech Ties'. CCTV, 27 March. Available at: http://english.cntv.cn/2016/03/27/VIDErzRMqU3S6DkYaTnLx8es160327.shtml

Dandashly, A., and G. Noutcheva. 2022. 'Conceptualizing Norm Diffusion and Norm Contestation in the European Neighbourhood: Introduction to the Special Issue'. *Democratization* 29 (3): pp. 415–432.

Danner, L. 2014. 'Securitization and De-Securitization in the Diaoyu/Senkaku Islands Territorial Dispute'. *Journal of Alternative Perspectives in Social Sciences* 6 (2): pp. 219–247.

Dębiec, K., and J. Jakóbowski. 2018. 'Chinese Investments in the Czech Republic: Changing the Expansion Model'. 6 June. Available at: https://www.osw.waw.pl/en/publikacje/analyses/2018-06-06/chinese-investments-czech-republic-changing-expansion-model-0.

European Parliament. 2020. 'Rule of Law in Poland: Meps Point to 'Overwhelming Evidence' Of Breaches'. 14 July. Available at: https://www.europarl.europa.eu/news/en/press-room/20200712IPR83209/rule-of-law-in-poland-meps-point-to-overwhelming-evidence-of-breaches.

Floyd, R. 2015. 'Just and Unjust Desecuritization'. in *Contesting Security: Strategies and Logics*, edited by Thierry Balzacq. London and New York: Routledge, pp. 122–138.

Fürst, R. 2020a. 'The Czech Republic's Pragmatic China Policy: Balancing between the EU and the US'. In Europe in the Face of US-China Rivalry, edited by Mario Esteban and Miquel Otera-Iglesias. European Think-Tank Network on China (ETNC) Report. Available at: https://www.ifri.org/sites/default/files/atoms/files/etnc_report_us-china-europe_january_2020_complete.pdf.

Fürst, R. 2020b. 'Czechia: Covid-19 Puts China at Centre of Increasingly Divisive National Debate'. In *Covid-19 and Europe-China Relations. A Country-Level Analysis*, edited by John Seaman. European Think-tank Network on China (ETNC) Special report, 29 April. Available at: https://www.ifri.org/sites/default/files/atoms/files/etnc_special_report_covid-19_china_europe_2020.pdf.

Godement, F., J. Parello-Plesner, and A. Richard. 2011. 'The Scramble for Europe'. *European Council on Foreign Relations* report, July. Available at: http://www.ecfr.eu/page/-/ECFR37_Scramble_For_Europe_AW_v4.pdf.

Goh, E. 2014. 'The Modes of China's Influence: Cases from Southeast Asia'. *Asian Survey* 54 (5): pp. 825–848.

Goh, E. 2016. 'Introduction'. In *Rising China's Influence in Developing Asia*, edited by Evelyne Goh, pp. 1–23. Oxford: Oxford University Press.

Hála, M. 2020. 'A New Invisible Hand. Authoritarian Corrosive Capitalism and the Repurposing of Democracy'. National Endowment for Democracy Report. Available at: https://www.ned.org/wp-content/uploads/2020/03/New-Invisible-Hand-Authoritarian-Corrosive-Capital-Repurposing-Democracy-Hala.pdf.

Hansen, L. 2012. 'Reconstructing Desecuritisation: The Normative-Political in the Copenhagen School and Directions for How to Apply It'. *Review of International Studies* 38: pp. 525–546.

iRozhlas. 2020. 'We Ironed Babiš's Statement, Says Mynář. According to Him, the Trip to China and Symbolic Help Kept Us in the Game' [original in Czech]. 19 March. Available at: https://www.irozhlas.cz/zpravy-domov/vratislav-mynar-cina-delegace-vyprava-diplomacie-vztahy-rousky-andrej-babis_2003191024_tzr.

Jakimów, M. 2019. 'De-Securitisation as a Soft Power Strategy: Belt & Road Initiative, European Fragmentation and China's Normative Impact in Central-Eastern Europe'. *Asia Europe Journal* 17 (4): pp. 369–385.

Jakóbowski, J. 2018. 'Chinese-Led Regional Multilateralism in Central and Eastern Europe, Africa and Latin America: 16+1, FOCAC, and CCF'. *Journal of Contemporary China 27 (113)* [Online, 11 April], pp. 659–673.

Johnson, D. 2020. 'The Czechs and Germans Are Standing Up to China Over Taiwan. Why?'. *The Article*. Available at: https://www.thearticle.com/the-czechs-and-germans-are-standing-up-to-china-over-taiwan-why.

Jones, L. 2020. 'Does China's Belt and Road Initiative Challenge the Liberal, Rules-Based Order?'. *Fudan Journal of the Humanities and Social Sciences* 13: pp. 113–133.

Kahn, M., and R. Muller. 2020. 'Czech Lawmakers Call on Government to Look Beyond China for Coronavirus Supplies'. *Reuters*, 17 April. Available at: https://mobile.reuters.com/article/amp/idUSKBN21Z37P?

Kasonta, A. 2020. 'Poland Officially Joins US-Led Tech War Against China'. *Asia Times*, 16 September. Available at: https://asiatimes.com/2020/09/poland-officially-joins-us-led-tech-war-against-china/.

Kavalski, E. 2013. 'The Struggle for Recognition of Normative Powers: Normative Power Europe and Normative Power China in Context'. *Cooperation and Conflict* 48 (2): pp. 247–267.

Kavalski, E., and Y. C. Cho. 2018. 'Worlding the Study of Normative Power'. *International Relations* 15 (57), pp. 49–65

Kerr, D. 2015. 'China's Search for Normative Power and the Possibilities of the Asian Century'. In *China, India and the Future of International Society*, edited by Jamie Gaskarth, pp. 105–128. Lanham, MD: Rowman & Littlefield.

Kowalski, B. 2020. 'Central and Eastern Europe, China's Core Interests, and the Limits of Relational Politics: Lessons from the Czech Republic in the 2010s'. *East European Politics and Societies and Cultures* 20 (10): pp. 1–24.

Manners, I. 2002. 'Normative Power Europe: A Contradiction in Terms?'. *Journal of Common Market Studies* 40 (2): pp. 235–258.

Matura, T. 2020a. 'The Chinese COVID-19 Information Campaign in Hungary: Keeping a Low Profile'. In Ivana Karásková, Alicja Bachulska, Tamás Matura, Filip Šebok, and Matej Šimalčík. 'China's Propaganda and Disinformation Campaigns in Central Europe'. MapInfluence Briefing Paper.

Available at: https://www.amo.cz/en/mapinfluence-en/chinas-propaganda-and-disinformation-campaigns-in-central-europe/.

Matura, T. 2020b. 'Hungary: Business as Usual with China amid Covid–19'. In *Covid-19 and Europe-China Relations. A Country-Level Analysis*, edited by John Seaman. European Think-tank Network on China (ETNC) Special report, 29 April. Available at: https://www.ifri.org/sites/default/files/atoms/files/etnc_special_report_covid-19_china_europe_2020.pdf.

Ministry of Foreign Affairs of Poland. 2018. 'Poland's MFA Statement on Commercial Cyber-Espionage'. *Twitter*, 21 December. Available at: https://twitter.com/PolandMFA/status/1076115014816317441.

Ministry of Foreign Affairs of the PRC. 2014. 'The Five Principles of Peaceful Coexistance—The Time-Tested Guideline of China's Policy With Neighbours'. 30 July. Available at: https://www.fmprc.gov.cn/mfa_eng/wjb_663304/zwjg_665342/zwbd_665378/t1179045.shtml.

Nathan, A. J. 2015. 'China's Challenge'. *Journal of Democracy* 26 (1): pp. 156–170.

NED (National Endowment for Democracy). 2017. 'Sharp Power. Rising Authoritarian Influence'. National Endowment for Democracy. Available at: https://www.ned.org/sharp-power-rising-authoritarian-influence-forum-report/.

Niewenhuis, L. 2020. 'Serbian President Kisses PRC Flag: Updates On "Mask Diplomacy"'. *SupChina*, 23 March. Available at: https://supchina.com/2020/03/23/serbian-president-kisses-prc-flag-updates-on-mask-diplomacy/.

Nye, J. 1990. 'Soft Power'. *Foreign Policy* 80: pp. 153–171.

Órban, V. 2016. 'Victor Orban's Speech at the Conference "China-CEE Political Parties Dialogue"'. 6 October. Available at: http://www.miniszterelnok.hu/viktor-orbans-speech-at-the-conference-china-cee-political-parties-dialogue/.

Peng, Z., and S. K. Tok. 2016. 'The AIIB and China's Normative Power in International Financial Governance Structure'. *Chinese Political Science Review* 1: pp. 736–753

Qin, Y. 2016. 'A Relational Theory of World Politics'. *International Studies Review* 18: pp. 33–47.

Seaman, J. 2020. 'Introduction: China as Partner, Competitor and Rival amid Covid–19'. In *Covid-19 and Europe-China Relations. A Country-Level Analysis*, edited by John Seaman. European Think-tank Network on China (ETNC) Special report, 29 April. Available at: https://www.ifri.org/sites/default/files/atoms/files/etnc_special_report_covid-19_china_europe_2020.pdf

Šebok, F. 2016. 'Chinese Media Watch: Dalai Lama visits Central Europe'. *Institute of Asian Studies*, 15 November. Available at: http://www.asian.sk/en/chinese-media-watch-dalai-lama-visits-central-europe/.

Šebok, F., and I. Karásková. 2020. 'Chinese Propaganda on Covid-19: Eldorado in Czech Cyberspace'. In Ivana Karásková, Alicja Bachulska, Tamás

Matura, Filip Šebok, and Matej Šimalčík. 'China's Propaganda and Disinformation Campaigns in Central Europe'. MapInfluence Briefing Paper. Available at: https://www.amo.cz/en/mapinfluence-en/chinas-propaganda-and-disinformation-campaigns-in-central-europe/.

Šimalčík, M., A. Bajerová, I. Karásková, T. Matura, A. Ostrowska, and B. Surdel. 2019. 'Perception of China among V4 Political Elites'. Central European Institute of Asian Studies Report. Available at: https://ceias.eu/perception-of-china-among-v4-political-elites/.

Song, L. 2013. 'From Rediscovery to New Cooperation: The Relationship between China and Central and Eastern Europe'. *Europe-China Observer* 5: pp. 8–14.

Szczudlik, J. 2020. 'Poland: Mutual "Charm Offensive" with China amid Covid-19'. In *Covid-19 and Europe-China Relations. A Country-Level Analysis*, edited by John Seaman, pp. 50–53. European Think-tank Network on China (ETNC) Special report, 29 April. Available at: https://www.ifri.org/sites/default/files/atoms/files/etnc_special_report_covid-19_china_europe_2020.pdf.

Trybuna. 2016. 'Poland De-Communised China (Polska zdekomunizowała Chiny)'. *Dziennik Trybuna*, 10 October. Available at: https://trybuna.info/polska/polska-zdekomunizowala-chiny/.

Turcsányi, R. Q., and M. Šimalčík. 2020. 'Slovakia: Changing Views of China during the Covid-19 Pandemic'. In *Covid-19 and Europe-China Relations. A Country-Level Analysis*, edited by John Seaman. European Think-tank Network on China (ETNC) Special report, 29 April. Available at: https://www.ifri.org/sites/default/files/atoms/files/etnc_special_report_covid-19_china_europe_2020.pdf.

Turcsányi, R., M. Šimalčík, K. Kironská, and R. Sedláková. 2020. 'European Public Opinion on China in the age of Covid-19. Differences and Common Ground across the Continent'. Central European Institute of Asian Studies. Available at: http://www.realinstitutoelcano.org/wps/portal/rielcano_en/publication?WCM_GLOBAL_CONTEXT=/elcano/elcano_in/publications/european-public-opinion-on-china-in-the-age-of-covid-19 [Accessed 30 July 2022].

Valášek, L. 2020. 'The Chinese Embassy Bought Respirators in the Czech Republic and Sent Them Home, Warned the BIS'. 24 March. Available at: https://zpravy.aktualne.cz/domaci/cinska-ambasada-skupovala-v-cesku-respiratory-a-posilala-je/r~e9a4e5746ddb11eaa25cac1f6b220ee8/.

Vangeli, A. 2018. 'Global China and Symbolic Power: The Case of 16+1 Cooperation'. *Journal of Contemporary China* 27 (113): pp. 674–687.

Vuori, J. A. 2018. 'Let's Just Say We'd Like to Avoid Any Great Power Entanglements: Desecuritisation in Post-Mao Chinese Foreign Policy towards Major Powers'. *Global Discourse* 8 (1): pp. 118–136.

Walker, C., and J. Ludwig. 2017. 'Introduction. from "Soft Power" to "Sharp Power": Rising Authoritarian Influence in the Democratic World'. In NED (National

Endowment for Democracy), *Sharp Power. Rising Authoritarian Influence*. Available at: https://www.ned.org/sharp-power-rising-authoritarian-influence-forum-report/.

Wu, G. 2016. 'Hungary: EU Should Give China "Market Economy" Status'. CCTV, 10 June. Available at: http://english.cctv.com/2016/06/10/VIDEpCKf294TecatnMQbX9SI160610.shtml.

Zachová, A. 2020. 'Germany and France Stand up for Prague in Light of China's Threats'. *Euractiv*, 2 September. Available at: https://www.euractiv.com/section/all/short_news/germany-and-france-stand-up-for-the-czech-republic-in-light-of-chinas-threats/.

7

China's Economic Diplomacy in the Western Balkans

Limited Strategy, Limited Influence

Nicholas Crawford

Introduction

The countries of the Western Balkans—Albania, Bosnia and Herzegovina, Kosovo, Montenegro, North Macedonia, and Serbia—have longstanding but chequered relations with China. For decades following the establishment of the People's Republic of China, the fate of relations between Beijing and the Western Balkans was tangled up with ideological divisions within the communist movement—between Josep Broz Tito's Yugoslavia and Joseph Stalin's USSR, and then between Enver Hoxha's Albania and the USSR of Nikita Khrushchev and his successors. By the end of the Cold War and of communism in the Western Balkans, the ties were loose between the Western Balkans and China.

A new chapter in China's relations with the Western Balkans began in 2009. That year, Beijing emerged as a prominent supporter of Serbia's efforts to block Kosovo's independence, a development that prompted renewed diplomatic engagement between Beijing and Western Balkan governments, manifest in a series of commercial and economic deals. Over the following decade, Chinese policy banks lent more than 6.9 billion USD to the Western Balkans, Chinese engineering and construction companies built power plants and roads, and various Chinese businesses invested in the region.

China's re-engagement with the Western Balkans roughly coincided with Beijing's establishment in 2011 of a new initiative, the China-Central and Eastern Europe Cooperation Framework ('China-CEEC', also known as the 16+1 or 17+1 according to the number of members at the time). Albania, Bosnia and Herzegovina, Montenegro, North Macedonia, and Serbia were

Nicholas Crawford, *China's Economic Diplomacy in the Western Balkans*. In: *Rising Power, Limited Influence*.
Edited by: Indrajit Roy, Jappe Eckhardt, Dimitrios Stroikos, and Simona Davidescu, Oxford University Press.
 DOI: 10.1093/oso/9780192887115.003.0008

among the initiative's founding members.[1] The establishment of the 17+1 led to the announcement of a 10 billion USD credit line for its European members, and this provided funding for many capital projects in the Western Balkans in the following years. Shortly thereafter, China launched the Belt and Road Initiative (BRI), which the countries of the Western Balkans again quickly joined.

Economic diplomacy has been central to both the BRI and 17+1. However, exactly what China's economic diplomacy involves or what China's ambitions are for its economic diplomacy in the Western Balkans is contentious. So too is the strategic impact of China's economic diplomacy in the region—especially its implications for the Western Balkans' (rather varied) convergence with the European liberal order. These debates about China's economic diplomacy in the Western Balkans are the subject of this chapter.

For China, economic diplomacy 'cannot be compartmentalised into separate economic and political activity or purposes' (Shuxiu, 2016, p.5). It 'concerns both the economic dimension of foreign policy and the strategic dimension of economic policy' (Heath, 2016, p.160). Its economic activities may serve political objectives, and its political activities may serve economic objectives. This is not to say that 'economic diplomacy' is all-encompassing. Firstly, it is concerned primarily with the initiation, cessation, expansion, reduction, and manipulation of economic relations between states, and only 'includes diplomacy, military, and any other type of policy, so long as the policy promotes economic gain' (Heath, 2016, p.163). Secondly, it only involves activity undertaken by the Chinese state itself or on its behalf; it does not include activity by Chinese firms and individuals with no involvement of the state. (It can, however, be difficult to distinguish between state-directed initiatives and the private enterprises of Chinese firms and individuals [Garlick, 2019]).

The first part of this chapter argues that China's economic diplomacy in the Western Balkans resembles organized economic opportunism more closely than the pursuit of a grand economic plan. And its political ambitions for its economic diplomacy in the region are similarly limited. While China makes clear the quid pro quo on issues such as Taiwan, it has not attempted to influence Western Balkan politics now and nor has it established the structural linkages between China and Balkan states that will give it political influence in future.

[1] China has not granted diplomatic recognition to Kosovo, and so the latter is not party to the China-CEEC.

The second part of this chapter argues that China's willingness to lend to the region has presented Western Balkan governments with an opportunity to dispense with some of the liberal norms of good governance and to play China off against other major powers—the European Union and United States—to wrest concessions from them on their compliance with those norms. Not all governments in the region have exploited Chinese economic diplomacy in this way, but some certainly have, with successive Serbian governments foremost among them.

The chapter examines China's economic diplomacy throughout the Western Balkans, but focuses especially on Bosnia and Herzegovina, North Macedonia, and Serbia—three countries at different stages of progress towards membership of the European Union, and of varying importance to the regional economy. The conclusions are based on field research undertaken with the support of my research assistant, Azra Dizdar, in the three focus countries, plus a review of varied literature including legal documents and news media. The field research involved semi-structured (anonymized) interviews with sixty individuals including politicians, diplomats, and other civil servants, researchers, and civil society actors from the three countries, plus diplomats from China, the United States, the United Kingdom, and Germany, and officials from development banks based in the region.

China's Strategy for Economic Diplomacy in the Western Balkans

It has been popular to ascribe grand ambitions to China's economic diplomacy in the Western Balkans—both geo-economic and geopolitical. On the geo-economic side, Vangeli and Pavlićević, for example, have argued that the Western Balkans are central to China's economic plan in Europe. The region sits astride two prospective trade routes set out in China's 2015 document 'Vision and Actions on Jointly Building Silk Road Economic Belt and 21st-Century Maritime Silk Road',[2] and they therefore see the region as critical to Beijing's efforts to facilitate the export of Chinese goods to Europe (Pavlićević, 2014; Vangeli, 2017; Verlare and van der Putten, 2015). Moreover, China allegedly plans to relocate manufacturing bases and establish industrial parks overseas in order to reduce land and labour costs as part of a Chinese scheme to 'advance production capacity cooperation'. The Western

[2] The two trade routes that may link to the Western Balkans are the China-Central Asia-West Asia Economic Corridor and the Maritime Silk Road. See National Development and Reform Commission (2015).

Balkans are an important venue for that (Vangeli, 2017). And by investing in the region now, China will enjoy an economic bridgehead into the European Union in a few years' time, as the Western Balkans are expected to eventually join the EU (although the prospects remain distant) (Levitin, Milatovic, and Sanfey, 2016).

On the geopolitical side, there are widespread fears about Beijing's intentions in the Western Balkans, with worries that its economic diplomacy in the region is part of an effort to divide Europe (Pavlićević, 2018; Vangeli, 2020). One prominent suspicion is that China seeks to gain an economic foothold in Europe to give it future influence in European institutions, with the Western Balkans as 'trojan horses'—an argument made by several scholars (see, for example, Karásková et al., 2020; and Pepermans, 2018), but also by leading policymakers. In 2018, Johannes Hahn, then EU Commissioner for EU Neighbourhood Policy and Enlargement Negotiations, suggested that China sought to use infrastructure projects in the Western Balkans for 'political sway', and remarked on the danger of Chinese influence over Western Balkan countries for unanimous decision-making in the EU, once they become members (Hahn, 2018). Others see China's economic diplomacy in the Western Balkans as a means to export a 'China model' of state capitalism, with the Western Balkans and Central and Eastern Europe perceived as a susceptible audience (Benner et al., year; Fukuyama, 2016; Hala, 2018). The advantage of the Western Balkans is that it is presumably a cheap place to buy influence.

This falls into a category of political influence which Reilly has called 'structural engagement', involving deliberately building 'structural linkages' between China's economy and European economies to alter the balance of political interests in Beijing's favour (Reilly, year). Reilly distinguishes this from two alternative tactics—specific and diffuse reciprocity, which involve the use of economic coercion or economic inducements through a clear quid pro quo.[3] Specific reciprocity is a tactic whereby Beijing promises European governments benefits if they pursue specific preferred policies and threatens harm if they do not. Diffuse reciprocity involves Beijing promising European government beneficial economic outcomes over time in return for compromising on Chinese interests in general.

However, China's economic diplomacy in the Western Balkans resembles organized economic opportunism more closely than a grand economic or political plan specific to the Western Balkans. As Kavalski and Mayer (2019) observe, China is using the tools at its disposal to exploit economic opportunities as they arise. And while China makes clear the quid pro quo on issues

[3] The terms originate from O Keohane (1984).

such as Taiwan, it has made little wider attempt either at political influence now or to establish the structural linkages that will give it political influence in future.

This is not to say there is no strategy behind China's economic diplomacy in the Western Balkans. On the contrary, it is part of China's wider Belt and Road Initiative strategy, whereby Beijing supports Chinese businesses (state-owned and private) to expand overseas, particularly in sectors that are crucial to China's industrial strategy. And as China's industrial strategy has evolved—with Beijing trying to move its economy up the industrial value chain—its economic diplomacy has reflected that change (The International Institute for Strategy Studies, 2022). More broadly, Holslag (2018) describes China's strategy as one of 'offensive mercantilism'—a policy of 'manipulating [the] openness' of other economies in order to gain market share and to generate profits overseas and transfer them back to China (Holslag contrasts offensive mercantilism with China's longstanding policy of *defensive* mercantilism, involving protectionist measures to prevent wealth from *leaving* China.)

According to Holslag, China manipulates European countries' openness primarily through four economic tactics, namely offering credit to European governments; supporting (and subsidizing) select Chinese companies to become national champions that can compete internationally with the largest firms in the world; developing global transportation and communications links to facilitate the export of Chinese goods; and working to set the terms of trade and technical standards for goods and services. In addition, China uses a variety of political tactics, including currying favour with foreign leaders, building support among local interest groups, and persuading other governments of the economic benefits to them of buying cheaper Chinese goods 'to prop up the purchasing power of their citizens' (Holslag, 2018: page).

In terms of geopolitical influence, Beijing's ambitions appear to be more limited to the specific and diffuse reciprocity described by Reilly. In addition, as Pepermans (2018) argues, soft power plays a part, with economic relations cultivating a sense of affinity towards China on the part of European countries—either for China as a nation, for China's strategic influence in the world, or for China's political and economic model.

There are good *prima facie* reasons to think that China is likely to be less economically and politically ambitious in the Western Balkans. After all, the region lacks much of the economic appeal of other regions both in Europe and elsewhere. There are few attractive targets for brownfield investment; most countries in the region are not rich in natural resources (except coal);

and, as discussed in more detail below, there are geographic obstacles to building transport corridors through the Balkans.

Western Balkan countries have little geopolitical influence outside the Balkan region; they have no agenda-setting influence, and the policies they pursue have little knock-on effect on other European governments' policies. In this regard, Western Balkan states are unlike EU member states such as Greece, Italy, and Poland, who have a greater degree of influence, particularly by giving license to other governments in Central and Eastern Europe to follow their lead. Moreover, Western Balkan states are still some way from membership of the EU and influence within it as 'trojan horses'. In fact, their membership is far from a foregone conclusion. And already, concerns about China's influence on European decision-making are prompting discussions about a move away from unanimous voting towards majority voting.

At crunch moments, if forced to choose between Europe and China, the Western Balkans are bound to choose Europe. The EU and its member states are far more important to Western Balkan countries than China in terms of foreign direct investment, trade, and official development assistance. The Western Balkans neighbour the EU and, for those Balkan countries that want it, European institutions offer a security umbrella which China will not provide. Beijing likely recognizes the limits of what it can achieve with economic diplomacy in the Western Balkans.

The reality of China's economic diplomacy reflects this more modest scope of Beijing's geo-economic and geopolitical strategy in the Western Balkans. Despite talk about transport corridors, these are not the priority. Nor is it a Chinese priority to establish a manufacturing hub in the region. Rather than building deep economic linkages with the aim of long-term influence, China's political focus is on shorter-term economic inducements and economic coercion on a limited set of issues relating to China's core interests. At the 17+1 summit in 2015 (then the 16+1, with Greece yet to join), Premier Li Keqiang stated, 'We can secure funds for the [members of the 16+1] in line with our needs. As long as the projects use Chinese products and Chinese equipment, China is ready to secure financial assistance at low cost' (Tanjug, 2015). This neatly summarizes China's prioritization of short-term economic gains for Chinese businesses and the growth of Chinese national champions.

This is borne out in its economic diplomacy in three ways. Firstly, China's economic diplomacy is designed primarily to support the export of Chinese engineering and construction services. Lending for capital projects in the Western Balkans is conditional on the award of those projects to Chinese companies—sometimes as the result of open tender procedures, but more often without any such competitive process. Indeed, China encourages

Western Balkan governments to avoid such competitive processes, and bilateral agreements on projects between Serbia and China, and between North Macedonia and China, have been used to justify circumventing competitive tender processes. Moreover, the overarching pledge by China to 17+1 members that it would fund 10 billion USD in projects has reinforced a sense of confidence that China will fund projects agreed with Chinese companies.

Secondly, China's economic diplomacy is supporting the growth of China's largest (often state-owned) firms. Of the nineteen Chinese capital projects completed or underway in the region, fourteen are implemented by Chinese companies listed in the Fortune Global 500 and all are with companies with an annual turnover of more than 4 billion USD (see Table 7.1). This contradicts one Chinese diplomat's description of the Western Balkans as a destination for smaller Chinese companies' involvement in the Belt and Road Initiative.[4] Although Chinese companies do subcontract significant roles to local contractors, with up to 49% of some projects undertaken by local firms, the use of local contractors is largely determined by the demands of the developers. For example, in the case of the construction of Stanari thermal power plant (TPP Stanari) in Bosnia and Herzegovina, the developer and local stakeholders were concerned about local discontent if Dongfang Electric were to complete all the work themselves and hire only Chinese labourers. As a result, local contractors were given a substantial role on the project, and the contract limited Dongfang Electric to having no more than 350 Chinese workers on site.[5]

Thirdly, Chinese capital projects in the Western Balkans have often come about only because previous attempts to pursue the projects have failed. Chinese firms and Chinese policy banks have been indiscriminate in their choice of projects and have been able to seize on these opportunities. Since 2010, China has provided 6.7 billion USD in loans to the Western Balkans, and the largest of these loans have gone to the region's most ambitious and contentious infrastructure projects: the Serbian sections of the Belgrade-Budapest railway (1.286 billion USD), the Bar-Boljare highway in Montenegro (802 million USD), the Kicevo-Ohrid and Miladinovci-Stip highway in North Macedonia (963 million USD), and coal-fired power plants in Tuzla, Bosnia-Herzegovina (731 million USD) and Kostolac, Serbia (608 million USD).

[4] Author interview with Chinese diplomat, November 2019.

[5] According to an interviewee involved in the construction of the plant, Dongfang Electric complied with this until near the end of the construction, at which point they allowed nearly 800 Chinese workers on site due to the unavailability of appropriately qualified local workers.

Table 7.1 Chinese companies involved in capital projects in the Western Balkans

Company	Fortune Global 500?	Project
China Communications Construction Company	Yes	Surcin-Obrenovac Highway Preljina-Pozega Highway
China Communications Construction Company, and China Railways International	Yes	Belgrade-Stara Pazova Railway Novi Sad-Subotica Railway
China Machinery Engineering Company	Yes	TPP Kostolac B1 and B2 (Rehabilitation) TPP Kostolac B3 (Construction)
China Road and Bridge Corp	Yes	Pupin Bridge Smokovac-Uvač-Mateševo Highway
China State Construction Engineering Corp	Yes	Počitelj-Zvirovići
Power Construction Company	Yes	Heating Pipeline Obrenovac-Novi Beograd
Power Construction Company (in consortium with Azvirt)	Yes	Belgrade Bypass Section B, Ostruznica-Bubanj
Sinohydro	Yes	Miladinovci-Stip Highway Kicevo-Ohrid Highway HPP Ulog
Gezhouba Group, and Guangdong Electric Power Design	Yes[a]	TPP Tuzla Termoblok VII
China Shandong International Economic & Technical Cooperation Group	No	Banja Luka-Prijedor Highway
Dongfang Electric Corporation	No	TPP Stanari TPP Banovici
Shandong Hi-Speed Group	No	Obrenovac-Ub and Lajkovac-Ljig Highways

[a] Gezhouba Group is a subsidiary of China Energy Engineering Corporation, which is listed in the Fortune 500.

The Western Balkans' other official lenders (including the European Bank of Reconstruction and Development, and the European Investment Bank) have warned against these projects. When the Montenegrin and Macedonian governments discussed their ambitious multi-lane highway projects with their main European development partners in the early 2010s, they were told their plans were not economically viable. Likewise, when the state-owned energy company of the Federation of Bosnia and Herzegovina decided to replace the aging, high-polluting coal-fired blocks at Tuzla with a new supercritical generator, European development banks refused financing due to rules preventing them from financing coal-fired plants.

In each case, Western Balkan governments have turned to China for funding, and the China Export-Import Bank has obliged. At least until around 2019, the sole concern has been that these projects present a viable short-term business opportunity. (More recently, this appears to have changed. In 2019, China's Ministry of Finance took on a bigger role in overseeing and scrutinizing China's overseas lending, and it has since imposed stricter standards for both the financial and environmental sustainability of Chinese loan-financed projects. See International Institute for Strategy Studies [2022]. Moreover, Beijing pledged at the United Nations General Assembly in 2021 to no longer fund coal-fired power plants [*The Economist*, 2021].)

The short-term commercial focus of China's economic diplomacy has sometimes been obscured by Chinese announcements and rhetoric about much grander plans for the Western Balkans, especially for transport corridors. Most notably, in 2014 Li Keqiang proposed extending the planned Budapest-Belgrade railway to the port of Piraeus via North Macedonia, and since then there has been repeated mention in regional, Chinese, and Western press of the China-Europe Land-Sea Express Line (or 'Route') (Kynge, Beesley, and Byrne, 2017; *Novinite*, 2014). The proposed line initially received a cautious welcome from the North Macedonian government of Nikola Gruevski, with the proposed project requiring major changes to a railway line that had only recently been renovated (to operate at a lower speed than in China's proposed line). In the following years, some customs cooperation work took place involving China, Hungary, Serbia, and North Macedonia, but plans for a high-speed railway between Belgrade and Piraeus via North Macedonia have not progressed, and China did not push the matter further with Macedonia's successor government.[6]

The remaining impetus for the project comes from the Serbian and Greek governments and from Chinese construction and engineering firms, who have pressed the Macedonian government on the issue, and not from the Chinese state (which has not). Tellingly, the China-Europe Land-Sea Express Route does not appear on any map of the BRI published by the Chinese government or by Chinese state media to date. Instead, the notion of a railway connecting Belgrade and Piraeus is promoted by Chinese companies who see it as a lucrative business opportunity, albeit one that Beijing would likely finance if the North Macedonian government decided to pursue

[6] Author interviews with an adviser in the Macedonian Prime Minister's Office and a high-level official in the Macedonian transport ministry, December 2019.

it.[7] The project looks more like a short-term construction and engineering opportunity for China rather than part of a long-term global connectivity plan.

Chinese foreign direct investment in the Western Balkans is opportunistic as well. Some Chinese companies have set up manufacturing plants in the Western Balkans, mostly in Serbia, to supply customers in Europe. The automotive industry has been a key target, with Chinese firms investing an estimated 1.3 billion USD in new greenfield projects between 2011 and 2021 (with 994 million USD of that accounted for by Shandong Linglong Tyre's investment in Zrenjanin) (*Financial Times*, year). Other important investments have included the acquisitions of struggling companies in the steel and aluminium industries. However, despite some eye-catching investments, China's share of foreign direct investment inflows into the Western Balkans has been small, hardly amounting to a significant transplant or 'nearshoring' of Chinese manufacturing activity to Europe (see Figure 7.1). China's share of Serbia's inward FDI picked up in 2020 and 2021, to above 10%, but it remains to be seen whether this continues.

Serbia is, in some ways, the exception that proves the rule that Beijing has no particular plan for the Western Balkans beyond economic opportunism. China's investments in Serbia are far more extensive than in other

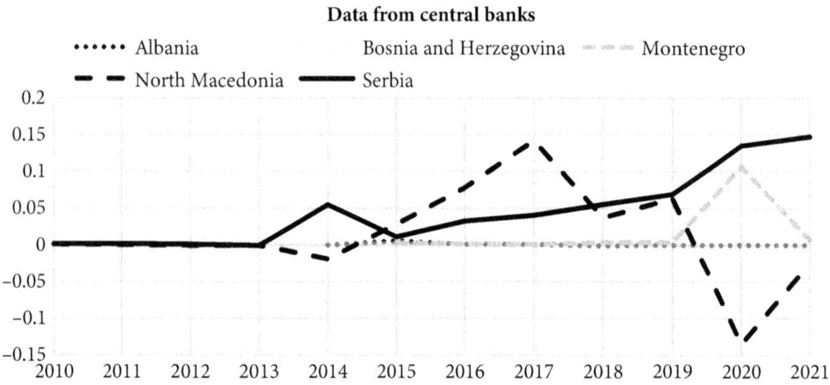

Figure 7.1 Net FDI inflows from China, share of total FDI inflows

[7] The government of North Macedonia may eventually be forced to proceed with the railway. Although it sees limited benefits to the Macedonian economy from the railway, if the railway were instead to run through Bulgaria it would reduce the freight travelling from Thessaloniki and Piraeus by road through North Macedonia. Therefore, despite the limited benefits and a potentially high cost for Macedonian public finances and the Macedonian economy, the government may eventually feel compelled to pursue it.

Western Balkan countries, but it is Belgrade rather than Beijing that has shaped these economic outcomes, by flinging opening Serbia's doors to Chinese investors. It has actively pursued Chinese investments in Serbia's core industries: the automotive industry, steel, aluminium, and coal. For Belgrade, building economic ties to China is a way of demonstrating the government's independence of the European Union, which plays well with its electorate. It has also allowed Serbian President Aleksandar Vučić (now and formerly as Prime Minister) to play the EU and Russia off against China. He has railed against the EU to fire up his domestic, nationalistic support base, and yet remained confident that the EU will not stop providing support. Indeed, Vučić has often exaggerated Serbia's trade linkages with China for political purposes. For example, in Serbia, joint patrols between Serbian and Chinese police were introduced, supposedly to help with increasing tourism from China, and yet Chinese tourism accounted for a mere 1.4% of Serbia's tourism receipts in 2018 (a record year at that time) (National Bank of Serbia, year). Insofar as structural linkages exist between Serbia and China, it is because Belgrade has forged them.

Where China has exercised political influence in the Western Balkans, it has relied not on these structural linkages, but on the 'reciprocity' tools of short-term economic inducements and economic coercion: the promise of further FDI, the promise of future lending for capital projects, the possibility of suspending ongoing Chinese-financed or Chinese-implemented capital projects, and the ability to deprive elites that it has recruited of private or political gain from their relations with China. The significance of these tools should not be understated. After all, China's lending allows Western Balkan governments to pursue projects it would not otherwise be able to pursue, with huge political capital to be made. However, these tools are declining in potency over time as Western Balkan states get closer to EU membership and need to stick closely to EU rules, and once they have actually joined and are legally bound by them.

Strategic Implications of China's Economic Diplomacy in the Western Balkans

Despite the limited geo-economic and geopolitical ambition of China's economic diplomacy in the Western Balkans, the question of its strategic implications remains open. Fears abound that China's economic diplomacy has a countervailing effect on the region's convergence with the European liberal order—whether by design or as a side-effect (Benner et al., year; Hala, 2018).

The liberal order is described by Ikenberry as a 'general and longstanding set of ideas, principles and political agendas for organizing and reforming international order', characterized by five general convictions: support for openness in trade and exchange; a commitment to rules-based relations, especially between states; the pursuit of security cooperation between states; a belief in the possibility of reforming international society; and a determination to see states move in a progressive direction towards liberal democracy (Ikenberry, 2009, 2018). But as Ikenberry observes, the Liberal International Order varies in scope from one geographical domain to another, with either a '"thin" social purpose, providing, for example, only rudimentary rules and institutions for limited cooperation and exchange among liberal democracies ... [or] a "thick" social purpose, with a dense set of agreements and shared commitments aimed at realizing more ambitious goals of cooperation, integration and shared security'.

The European liberal order is the embodiment of a regional order with a thick social purpose. It has exactly such a dense set of institutions, agreements, and ambitions. This is manifested most clearly in the European Union—a community based on what Schimmelfennig calls a 'European and liberal collective identity' (Schimmelfennig, 2001, p.59). These norms of the European liberal community are embodied in the criteria for the European Union's enlargement—respect for the rule of law and human rights, conformity to the principle of an open-market economy with free competition, and acceptance of the Acquis Communautaire and Acquis Politique (Schimmelfennig, 2001). Garton Ash (1998) likewise describes liberal order as the paradigm which best characterizes Europe, with 'the EU, NATO, the Council of Europe, and the Organization for Security and Cooperation in Europe ... all building blocks of such a liberal order'.

Schimmelfennig outlines the principles of the European liberal order in two domains—the domestic sphere and the international sphere: 'In the domestic sphere, the liberal principles of social and political order—social pluralism, the rule of law, democratic political participation and representation, private property, and a market-based economy—are derived from and justified by the liberal human rights. In the international sphere, the liberal order is characterized by the democratic peace and multilateralism' (Schimmelfennig, 2001, p.59.

In the domestic sphere, there have been notable derogations from the European liberal order in the Western Balkans in connection with Chinese economic diplomacy. However, the region's governments have ultimately been responsible for these decisions to set aside the norms and principles expected of them as EU membership candidates, rather than Beijing. This can be seen in relation to two key liberal norms: having an open-market economy with free competition, and commitment to the rule of law.

First, Chinese-financed infrastructure projects have usually seen Western Balkan governments dispense with openness and competition in their procurement procedures. Project financing by China's policy banks (China Export-Import Bank [Exim Bank] and China Development Bank [CDB]) is intended to create opportunities for Chinese contractors, and therefore Chinese officials expect (and require) Western Balkan governments to award Chinese-financed contracts directly to Chinese firms, without opening up the procurement to competition. Clearly, this conflicts with the European liberal norm of an open-market economy with free competition.

There are numerous examples of this in the region. Between 2010 and 2020, Serbia pursued at least eleven infrastructure projects for which it pre-agreed financing with China and then awarded contracts to Chinese companies. The combined value of these projects totalled around 4.5 billion USD. None of them went through open tender procedures. (Among these projects was the construction of the Budapest-Belgrade high-speed railway in Hungary and Serbia. The Hungarian government tried, like the Serbian government, to award construction contracts to Chinese firms without going through an open tender, but the European Commission forced Hungary, as an EU member state, to cancel contracts and go through the proper open tender procedure although, ultimately, this made no difference to who got the contract.) Likewise, in North Macedonia, the Government of Nikola Gruevski passed a *lex specialis* to allow for the Miladinovci-Stip and Kichevo-Ohrid highways to be exempted from normal procurement rules.

This approach is anti-competitive and opaque. In the first place, it excludes local companies and other non-Chinese companies from the infrastructure projects, except as subcontractors. Moreover, there is little competition even among Chinese firms for these projects. For the highway projects in North Macedonia, the government received a shortlist of just two Chinese firms to choose between. Significantly, China's state-owned Assets Supervision and Administration Commission tries to manage competition even between Chinese state-owned enterprises overseas (Xu, 2015). The lack of competition in these BRI projects and the opaque negotiation process risk both inflated costs and grand corruption.

There can be no doubt that China has pushed for this approach to procurement. Under Prime Minister Zoran Zaev, the Macedonian government ruled out non-competitive all-Chinese procurement processes and advised Chinese companies that they would have to compete in open tender procedures in future. Since then, Chinese firms have pressed the Macedonian government to revert to closed or negotiated procedures. And other governments which previously held open, competitive procurement processes have caved in to the approach promoted by China. The Montenegrin government, for example, held a competitive tender for the first section of the Bar-Boljare highway, but for the section second has simply proceeded to sign a Memorandum of Understanding with the China Road and Bridge Corporation.

However, governments in the Western Balkans have dispensed with open and competitive procurement processes for their own reasons too. In some instances, it is merely a matter of expedience—trying to push ahead with projects quickly, whether for economic or political reasons. In other instances, the reasons may be more troubling, and this is where the issue of compliance with open-market, free competition norms overlaps with the issue of compliance with the rule of law. The best (but still only partially) understood example is the process by which the Gruevski government in North Macedonia awarded contracts to Sinohydro to build the Kicevo-Ohrid and Miladinovci-Stip highways. Gruevski's government held a closed tender with participation from two Chinese firms: Sinohydro and China Water and Electric Company, although it seems that only the Sinohydro bid was considered. Recordings of wiretappings resulted in the indictment of Gruevski and three ministers for allegedly extracting bribes from Sinohydro, which saw the cost of the contract inflated by around 155 million euros, with costs of some materials in the contract inflated by around 300% (Vangeli, 2018). Gruevski was also indicted on several other corruption charges, and only this case involved a Chinese contractor. (One case was successfully prosecuted—the others passed North Macedonia's statute of limitations for prosecution. See Radio Free Europe, 2018).

Nevertheless, China is, at the very least, facilitating a divergence from the norms of having an open-market economy with free competition in the Western Balkans. And it appears more likely that China is actively encouraging that divergence, motivated by its commercial interests.

There have also been concerns about state aid in relation to Chinese projects in the Western Balkans, but neither of the two cases—both in Bosnia and Herzegovina—is clear-cut. In the first case, the government of Republika Srspka (one of the two subnational administrations in Bosnia and Herzegovina) changed its laws to provide additional guarantees to CDB, which was financing the construction of Stanari Thermal Power Plant. Specifically, in 2012, CDB required that in return for lending the necessary funds to EFT, the concessionaire, to contract Dongfang Electric to build the power plant, it received the right to 'step in' to the rights and obligations of the concessionaire should EFT go bankrupt and be unable to repay the loan. This required a change to the concession law in Republika Srpska, and so the government amended its legislation accordingly (Center for Investigative Reporting, 2014; Law on Concessions, 2013). Some politicians and civil society actors felt that this amounted to the government giving the company discretionary support, and also that it was a weakening of the country's laws at CDB's behest. However, step-in rights are standard practice,[8] and so CDB's requirement for this legal provision was not unusual. The resulting amendment to the law was not a clear divergence from European norms of governance.

In the second case, the Government of the Federation of Bosnia and Herzegovina (FBiH, the other of the two subnational administrations in Bosnia and Herzegovina) provided a guarantee for an Exim Bank to the Bosnia state-owned electricity company Elektroprivreda BiH to fund the construction of Tuzla Thermal Power Plant Block VII by Gezhouba Group. Civil society groups submitted a complaint to the European Energy Community (EEC), which subsequently adjudged that the guarantee breached state aid rules to which Bosnia and Herzegovina had committed as a party to the Energy Community Treaty. The EEC's stated concern was that providing a loan guarantee artificially reduced the borrowing costs and effectively subsidized the electricity that would, in future, be produced by Tuzla power plant. A failure to resolve the dispute led FBiH to press ahead anyway (Energy Community website, 2019), leading the EEC to demand that the FBiH Government rectify its non-compliance within two months (Energy Community website, 2020). However, the Tuzla case was a marginal case of state aid. As a Bosnian politician involved in negotiations with the EEC said, FBiH could have avoided the problem simply by being a little 'smarter' and negotiating a guarantee for 80% of the loan's value. Other state borrowers had offered 80% guarantees and faced no consequences from the EEC. And, he said, this might easily have satisfied the Chinese lenders. Moreover, even if this was, technically, a derogation from the EEC's state aid rules, some European diplomats and Bosnian stakeholders perceived the EEC's pursuit of the case as politicized and based on vested interests in other European electricity exporting countries. And in Bosnia, officials were convinced that providing the guarantee was a perfectly acceptable course of action, and involved very little pressure from China.

[8] The United Nations Commission on International Trade Law, the European Bank of Reconstruction and Development (EBRD), and the World Bank, for example, advise permitting such step-in rights in concession law, and the EBRD describes step-in rights as '"good standard" bankability provisions in project financing, without which it will be difficult, if not impossible, to arrange for the financing of a project.' See EBRD Legal Transitions Team (2018); 'Law in Transition Online (2012); Pinsent (2011); United Nations Commission on International Trade Law (2001); and World Bank Group (2020).

Certainly, there is not enough evidence to attribute the divergence from state aid rules to China.

In the international sphere, Western Balkan states, except for Serbia, have not obviously weakened their alignment with European liberal norms. Most Western Balkan states have remained committed to membership of key liberal institutions—the European Union and North Atlantic Treaty Organization (NATO)—and although they have not always adopted the same critical stances as Brussels or Washington D.C. on liberal issues that would antagonize Beijing, they have generally remained silent, rather than actively supporting China. By contrast, in Serbia, there has been a marked change in the government's position on liberal institutions through the 2010s, especially the EU, and it has been more supportive on the international stage of China's illiberal policies.

Three episodes illustrate the differences between Serbia and other Western Balkan governments in the international sphere. The first such episode was the 2010 award of the Nobel Peace Prize to the Chinese dissident Liu Xiaobo. Western Balkan governments were faced with a decision on whether to send a representative to the award ceremony. Eventually, all Western Balkan governments did so, but in Serbia this was preceded by a debate on the issue within the Serbian government which was played out in public. At first, then foreign minister Vuk Jeremić announced that Serbia would not send a representative, admitting that this decision was 'not ideal' but was an effort to preserve Chinese support for Serbia (BBC, 2010). (Shortly before, Beijing had supported Jeremić's efforts at the United Nations to prevent international recognition of Kosovo. Also at that time, the first Chinese loans to Serbia for infrastructure projects were under negotiation.) However, the President and Prime Minister, who had not been consulted on the matter, shortly thereafter overturned Jeremić's decision and elected instead to send the national ombudsman Saša Janković (BBC, 2010a).

A second episode took place in 2013–2016. The Philippines brought a case against China before the Permanent Court of Arbitration in The Hague to contest China's claims to certain islands in the South China Sea and to challenge the legality of Chinese activities in the area. The Philippines' decision to refer the case to the Court met with widespread support from Western, liberal nations. However, China refused to participate in the arbitration and rejected the Court's eventual ruling in favour of the Philippines. Albania, Bosnia and Herzegovina, and Montenegro all supported an EU statement criticizing China's actions in the South China Sea (Mogherini, 2016), although Montenegro later rowed back on its support for the EU statement and criticized the Philippines' unilateral referral of the issue to the Court (Government of Montenegro, 2016). It appears that Serbia and North Macedonia decided not to support the EU statement. When the Court ruled in the Philippines' favour, Western Balkan governments did not make clear public statements of support or opposition. Serbia simply called for the issue to be resolved by peaceful means (Government of Serbia, 2016).

A third, more recent episode occurred in 2019 on the issue of China's abuse of the human rights of Uighurs in Xinjiang, China. No Western Balkan state was among the twenty-two states that signed a letter to the United Nations Human Rights Council (UNHRC) condemning the mass detention of Uighurs. Instead, Serbia was among the fifty signatories of a counter-letter to the UNHRC, rejecting Western 'politicization' of the issue (Yellinek and Chen, 2019).

China is not vocal, nor obviously coercive, in influencing Western Balkan states' policies, but behind the scenes China ensures that Western Balkan governments are aware of China's position on its so-called core interests, such as relations between Beijing and Taiwan, the politics of Hong Kong, human rights in Xinjiang, and Chinese domestic politics more generally. Some senior Western Balkan officials report, for example, that they are expected by their Chinese counterparts to restate repeatedly their support for Beijing's 'One China' policy during meetings and in communications, and that if they do not do so, they are reminded of the policy. Anything that might be perceived as interfering in China's internal affairs is to be avoided.

However, with the exception of Serbia, Western Balkan governments have become more aligned in recent years with EU foreign policy (Novaković, Albahari, and Bogosavljevic, 2020). On issues pertaining to China, their general approach is one of equivocation or silence.

By contrast, Serbia has become progressively more supportive of Beijing. Serbia itself has benefitted from China's support on the issue of Kosovo's secession, and it was Kosovo's unilateral declaration of independence in 2008 which reignited close relations between China and Serbia, rather than economic diplomacy. (Chinese lending to Serbia followed thereafter.) In addition, under President Aleksandar Vučić (and previously, during his tenure as Prime Minister), Serbia has become more authoritarian,[9] and just as the Serbian government rejects foreign criticisms of its own democratic backsliding, it opposes criticism of other illiberal governments. And so Serbia's alignment with China is largely driven by its domestic politics. Therefore, it is not only on issues pertaining to China that Serbia derogates from liberal

[9] Freedom House reports in its annual Nations in Transit report that between 2014 and 2020, Serbia's democracy percentage worsened from 56% to 49%. See Damnjanović (2020), and Savic (2015).

European foreign policy positions.[10] It has also been supportive of Russia in the wake of its invasion of Ukraine in 2022, for example.

Likewise, Serbia's interest in joining the European Union has faded. But, again, this is due to Serbia's domestic politics—and the politics of President Alexander Vučić—rather than the pull of China. Vučić's changing stance on the EU reflects a certain political opportunism and a recognition that an important segment of the Serbian electorate is equivocal about the EU and has considerable sympathy instead for Russia (National Democratic Institute, 2018). During his early career to 2008, ascending the ranks of Slobodan Milošević's ultranationalist Serbia Radical Party, Vučić was strongly Eurosceptic. After 2008, as deputy leader of the splinter Serbian Progressive Party, he softened his position on the EU, only to shift position again in a 2011 interview, stating, 'People are not jubilant about the European Union ... But they realize we need to go that way and there is nowhere else to go' (Brunwasser, 2011). In the 2014 General Election, Vučić again adopted a pro-European stance (Economist Intelligence Unit, 2013), but within months of his election began to backslide on his more progressive political positions (*The Economist*, 2014). And Vučić loudly criticized the EU during the COVID-19 pandemic over a perceived lack of support for Serbia from Europe; he declared that 'European solidarity does not exist. That was a fairy tale on paper. I have sent a special letter to the only ones who can help, and that is China' (Simić, 2020).

There is no evidence at all of China seeking deliberately to discourage Western Balkan countries from pursuing membership of European institutions. (Russia, by contrast, does do so. See Bechev, 2019; International Institute for Strategic Studies, 2019). On the contrary, Chinese diplomats state that Beijing is supportive of the Western Balkans' EU path, and this is widely recognized to be the case among political stakeholders in the region.

Conclusion

For all the political attention it has garnered, China's economic diplomacy in the Western Balkans is altogether less ambitious and less influential than is often feared. Beijing has no grand plan to use the Western Balkans either

[10] Since 2014, the Belgrade-based International and Security Affairs Centre (ISAC) has undertaken annual analyses of Serbia's alignment with the European Union's foreign policy declarations and measures which look at the percentage of EU declarations and measure how Serbia and other countries in the EU neighbourhood align. Whereas Albania and Montenegro align almost completely, and North Macedonia mostly aligns, Serbia and Bosnia and Herzegovina diverge from the EU on a large proportion of policy issues. See, most recently, Novaković, Albahari, and Bogosavljevic (2020). Previous reports are available on ISAC's website, www.isac-fund.org.

as a vehicle for political influence in Europe or as a critical cog in China's economic machine. Its ambitions are instead limited to a form of economic opportunism and the ad hoc use of trade and investment deals as a political carrot.

Given the uncertainties of Western Balkan countries' political futures and the indefinite timeframe for their membership of the EU, it makes little sense for China to invest too heavily, however cheap the cost of doing so. Instead, its approach relies on a shorter time horizon—easy economic wins and short-term economic inducements.

The impact of Chinese economic diplomacy in the Western Balkans depends primarily on the region's governments. Those with strong institutions and determined political leaders can force European standards on Chinese lenders and Chinese firms, and uphold open-market rules and the rule of law. Those that prioritize political or personal gain and sacrifice the European liberal rules and norms will find in Chinese firms willing accomplices.

Likewise, Western Balkan leaders who are determined to uphold liberal values in their foreign policy may confront stark choices about economic inducements and economic coercion. But for now, their economies are not deeply connected with China's, and the scale of disruption will be limited.

Bibliography

BBC. 2010. 'Serbia Defends China-Led Boycott of Nobel Ceremony'. 9 December. Available at: https://www.bbc.co.uk/news/world-europe-11957094.

BBC. 2010a. 'Serbia Makes U-Turn over Nobel Prize Ceremony'. 10 December. Available at: https://www.bbc.co.uk/news/world-europe-11968854.

Bechev, D. 2019. 'Russia's Strategic Interests and Tools of Influence in the Western Balkans'. *New Atlanticist*. Available at: https://www.atlanticcouncil.org/blogs/new-atlanticist/russia-strategic-interests-and-tools-of-influence-in-the-western-balkans/.

Benner, et al. 2018. 'Authoritarian Advance: Responding to China's Growing Political Influence in Europe'. Global Public Policy Institute and Mercator Institute for China Studies. Available at: https://www.merics.org/sites/default/files/2020-04/GPPi_MERICS_Authoritarian_Advance_2018_1.pdf.

Brunwasser, M. 2011. 'Nationalism Fading from Serbia's Political Stage'. *New York Times*, 6 June. Available at: https://www.nytimes.com/2011/06/06/world/europe/06serbia.html.

Center for Investigative Reporting. 2014. 'Public Property for Chinese Loan'. Available at: https://www.cin.ba/energopotencijal/en/istrazivacke_price/javno-dobro-za-kineski-kredit.php.

Damnjanović, M. 2020. 'Nations in Transit 2020: Serbia'. Freedom House. Available at: https://freedomhouse.org/country/serbia/nations-transit/2020

EBRD Legal Transitions Team. 2018. 'EBRD Core Principles for a Modern Concessions Law—Selection and Justification of Principles'. Available at: https://www.ebrd.com/cs/Satellite?c=Content&cid=1395239038817&d=&pagename=EBRD%2FContent%2FDownloadDocument.

Economist Intelligence Unit. 2013. 'Aleksandar Vucic: Man on a Mission'. 27 September. Available at: http://country.eiu.com/article.aspx?articleid=764088660&Country=Serbia&topic=Economy&oid=974181481&flid=1841007368.

The Economist. 2014. 'Europe or Russia?'. 18 October. Available at: https://www.economist.com/europe/2014/10/18/europe-or-russia.

The Economist. 2021. 'China Pledges to Stop Financing Coal Plants Abroad'. 22 September. Available at: https://www.economist.com/china/china-promises-to-stop-backing-new-coal-power-projects-overseas/21804956.

Energy Community website. 2019. 'Negotiations about State Guarantee for the Tuzla 7 Project End without Agreement'.

Energy Community website. 2020. 'Case ECS-10/18: Bosnia and Herzegovina / State Aid: Summary of the Case'. Available at: https://www.energy-community.org/legal/cases/2018/case1018BH.html.

Fukuyama, F. 2016. 'One Belt, One Road: Export the Chinese Model to Eurasia'. *The Australian*, 3 January. Available at: https://www.theaustralian.com.au/commentary/one-belt-one-road-exporting-the-chinese-model-to-eurasia/news-story/269016e0dd63ccca4da306b5869b9e1c

Garlick, J. 2019. 'China's Principal–Agent Problem in the Czech Republic: The Curious Case of CEFC'. *Asia Europe Journal* 17 (4): pp. 437–451.

Garton Ash, T. 1998. 'Europe's Endangered Liberal Order'. *Foreign Affairs* 77 (2): pp. 51–65.

Government of Montenegro. 2016. 'Announcement on the Occasion of the Announcement of the Verdict of the Permanent Court of Arbitration in The Hague on the Dispute between China and the Philippines'. 12 July. Available at: http://www.gov.me/naslovna/vijesti-iz-ministarstava/163193/Saopstenje-povodom-objavljivanja-presude-Stalnog-arbitraznog-suda-u-Hagu-o-sporu-izmedu-Kine-i-Filipina.html.

Government of Serbia. 2016. 'Serbia Advocates a Peaceful Resolution of the South China Sea Issue Serbia Advocates a Peaceful Resolution of the South China Sea Issue'. 12 July. Available at: http://www.mfa.gov.rs/en/press-service/statements/15517-serbia-advocates-a-peaceful-resolution-of-the-south-china-sea-issue.

Hahn, J. 2018. 'Interview'. *Politico, EU Confidential Podcast*, July 27. Available at: https://soundcloud.com/politicoeuconfidential/episode-57-johannes-hahn-western-balkans-trump-juncker-love-in.

Hala, M. 2018. 'China in Xi's "New Era": Forging a New "Eastern Bloc"'. *Journal of Democracy* 29 (2): pp. 83–89

Heath, T. R. 2016. 'China's Evolving Approach to Economic Diplomacy'. *Asia Policy* 22: pp. 157–92.

Holslag, J. 2017. 'How China's New Silk Road Threatens European Trade'. *International Spectator* 52 (1): pp. 46–60,

Ikenberry, G. John. 2009. 'Liberal Internationalism 3.0: America and the Dilemmas of Liberal World Order'. *Perspectives on Politics* 7 (1): pp. 71–87.

Ikenberry, G. John. 2018. 'The End of Liberal International Order?'. *International Affairs* 94 (1): pp. 7–23.

The International Institute for Strategic Studies. 2019. 'Russia and the Western Balkans'. *Strategic Comments* 25 (17). Available at: https://www.iiss.org/publications/strategic-comments/2019/russia-and-the-balkans.

The International Institute for Strategy Studies. 2022. *China's Belt and Road Initiative: Geopolitical and Geo-economic Assessment*. IISS Strategic Dossier. Available at: https://www.iiss.org/publications/strategic-dossiers/chinas-belt-and-road-initiative/

Karásková, I. et al. 2020. 'China's Sticks and Carrots in Central Europe: The Logic and Power of Chinese Influence'. Prague, Czech Republic, Association for International Affairs.

Kavalski, E., and M. Mayer. 2019. 'How to Make the Most of China's Accidental Rise as a European Power'. *South China Morning Post*, 4 April. Available at: https://www.scmp.com/comment/insight-opinion/article/3004542/how-make-most-chinas-accidental-rise-european-power.

Kynge, J., A. Beesley, and A. Byrne. 2017. 'EU Sets Collision Course with China over "Silk Road" Rail Project'. *Financial Times*, 20 February. Available at: https://www.ft.com/content/003bad14-f52f-11e6-95ee-f14e55513608.

Law on Concessions. 2013. Article 40. Available at: http://www.investsrpska.net/files/Law_on_Concessions.pdf.

Law in Transition Online. 2012. Funding Public Infrastructure: Challenges and Horizons. Available at: https://www.ebrd.com/cs/Satellite?c=Content&cid=1395238313109&pagename=EBRD%2FContent%2FDownloadDocument

Levitin, O., J. Milatovic, and P. Sanfey. 2016. 'China and South-Eastern Europe: Infrastructure, Trade and Investment Links'. EBRD Paper. Available at: www.ebrd.com/documents/comms-and-bis/see-china-investments.pdf&usg=AOvVaw0Mwft8HJ8n2hhikVAcjCd_.

Mardell, J. 2020. 'China's Economic Footprint in the Western Balkans'. Bertelsmann Stiftung, Asia Policy Brief. Available at: https://www.bertelsmann-stiftung.de/en/our-projects/germany-and-asia/news/asia-policy-brief-chinas-economic-footprint-in-the-western-balkans/.

Pinsent Masons. 2011. 'Key Issues for Lenders in Project Finance Agreements'. Out-Law Guide. Available at: https://www.pinsentmasons.com/out-law/guides/key-issues-for-lenders-in-project-finance-agreements.

Mogherini, F. 2016. 'Declaration by the High Representative on Behalf of the EU on Recent Developments in the South China Sea'. *Press Release by the Council of the EU*, 11 March. Available at: https://www.consilium.europa.eu/en/press/press-releases/2016/03/11/hr-declaration-on-bealf-of-eu-recent-developments-south-china-sea/.

National Bank of Serbia. *Balance of Payments*. Available at: https://www.nbs.rs/internet/english/80/platni_bilans.html.

National Democratic Institute. 2018. 'Western Balkans between East and West: Public Opinion Research in Bosnia and Herzegovina, Macedonia, Montenegro, Serbia'. Available at: https://www.ndi.org/sites/default/files/DownloadReport_1.pdf.

National Development and Reform Commission. 2015. 'Vision and Actions on Jointly Building Silk Road Economic Belt and 21st Century Maritime Silk Road'. March. Available at: http://english.www.gov.cn/archive/publications/2017/06/20/content_281475691873460.htm.

Novaković, I., N. Albahari, and J. Bogosavljevic. 2020. 'CFSP and Serbia's Accession to the European Union: An Analysis of Serbia's Alignment with the European Union's Foreign Policy Declarations and Measures in 2019'. Available at: https://www.isac-fund.org/wp-content/uploads/2020/02/ISAC-CFSP-Analysis-2019-1.pdf.

Novinite. 2014. 'Chinese PM Li Keqiang: China to Propose Land-Sea Express Line to Europe'. Available at: https://www.novinite.com/articles/165437/Chinese+PM+Li+Keqiang%3A+China+to+Propose+Land-Sea+Express+Line+to+Europe.

Keohane, R. O. 1986. 'Reciprocity in International Relations'. *International Organization* 40 (1): pp. 1–27.

Pavlićević, D. 2014. 'China's Railway Diplomacy in the Balkans'. *China Brief* 14 (20): pp. 8–11

Pavlićević, D. 2018. '"China Threat" and "China Opportunity": Politics of Dreams and Fears in China-Central and Eastern European Relations'. *Journal of Contemporary China* 27 (113): pp. 688–702.

Pepe, J. M. 2017. 'China's Inroads into Central, Eastern and South Eastern Europe: Implications for Germany and the EU'. DGAPanalyse, 2017.

Pepermans, A. 2018. 'China's 16+1 and Belt and Road Initiative in Central and Eastern Europe: Economic and Political Influence at a Cheap Price'. *Journal of Contemporary Central and Eastern Europe* 26 (2).

Pepermans, A. 2018. 'China's 16+1 and Belt and Road Initiative in Central and Eastern Europe: Economic and Political Influence at a Cheap Price'. *Journal of Contemporary Central and Eastern Europe* 26 (2–3): pp. 181–203.

Radio Free Europe. 2018. 'Former Macedonian Leader Faces Two Years in Prison After Losing Appeal'. 10 November. Available at: https://www.rferl.org/a/former-macedonian-prime-minister-gruevski-faces-two—years-prison-after-losing-appeal/29592874.html.

Reilly, J. 2019. 'China's Economic Statecraft in Europe'. *Asia Europe Journal* 15 (2): pp.173–185.

Savic, M. 2015. 'Nations in Transit 2015: Serbia'. Freedom House. Available at: https://freedomhouse.org/country/serbia/nations-transit/2015.

Schimmelfennig, F. 2001. 'The Community Trap: Liberal Norms, Rhetorical Action, and the Eastern Enlargement of the European Union'. *International Organization* 55 (1): pp. 47–80

Shuxiu, Zhang. 2016. *Chinese Economic Diplomacy: Decision-Making Actors and Processes*. Routledge.

Simić, J. 2020. 'Serbia Turns to China Due to "Lack of EU Solidarity" on Coronavirus'. *Euractiv*, 18 March. Available at: https://www.euractiv.com/section/china/news/serbia-turns-to-china-due-to-lack-of-eu-solidarity-on-coronavirus/.

Tanjug. 2015. 'China Proposes USD 10bn Investment Fund to Serbian President Addresses'. *Tanjug*, 24 November. Available at: https://www.b92.net/eng/news/politics.php?yyyy=2015&mm=11&dd=24&nav_id=96149.

Vangeli, A. 2017. 'China's Engagement with the Sixteen Countries of Central, East and Southeast Europe under the Belt and Road Initiative'. *China and World Economy* 25 (5): pp. 101–124.

Vangeli, A. 2018. 'Macedonia Economy Briefing: The Controversial Case of the Kichevo-Ohrid Highway'. China CEE-Institute, Weekly Briefing, vol. 11. Available at: https://china-cee.eu/wp-content/uploads/2018/10/2018e1042(2)Macedonia.pdf.

Vangeli, A. 2020. 'China: A New Geo-Economic Approach to the Balkans'. in *The Western Balkans in the World: Linkages and Relations with Non-Western Countries*, edited by Florian Bieber and Nikolaos Tzifakis. Routledge.

Vecer. 2019. 'За Изградба На патиштата „Синохидро 'На Тендер понудил До Четири пати пониски Цени Од Договорените Во Четири Очи [For the Construction of the Roads, "Sinohydro" Offered up to Four Times Lower Prices than the One Agreed in the Tender.]'. 21 May. Available at: https://www.vecer.press/за-изградба-на-патиштата-синохидро/.

United Nations Commission on International Trade Law. 2001. '§IV Construction and Operation of Infrastructure: Legislative Framework and Project Agreement; §§6. Breach and Remedies; §§§(c) Step-in Rights for the Lenders'. In *Legislative Guide on Privately Financed Infrastructure Projects*, pp. 169–70. New York: United Nations.

Verlare, J., and F. P. van der Putten. 2015. '"One Belt, One Road": An Opportunity for the EU's Security Strategy'. Clingendael Policy Brief. Available at: https://www.clingendael.org/sites/default/files/pdfs/One_belt_one_road_vdPutten_Verlare_Clingendael_policy_brief_2015.pdf.

World Bank Group, Public-Private Partnership Legal Resource Center. 2020. 'Key Issues in Developing Project Financed Transactions (§3. Lender Protection, Step-In, Direct Agreement and Taking Security)'. Available at: https://ppp.worldbank.org/public-private-partnership/financing/issues-in-project-financed-transactions#lender.

Xinhua. 2014. 'China, CEE Countries Eye Land-Sea Express Passage'. 18 December. Available at: http://english.www.gov.cn/premier/news/2014/12/18/content_281475025689786.htm

Xu, Cao. 2015. '央企抱团出海已达成国家意志可避免恶性竞争等 [Central Enterprises Have the National Determination to Avoid Vicious Competition in Going Overseas]'. *China News*, 24 June. Available at: chinanews.com/cj/2015/06-24/7361419.shtml.

Yellinek, R., and E. Chen. 2019. 'The '22 vs. 50′ Diplomatic Split Between the West and China Over Xinjiang and Human Rights'. *China Brief* 19 (22): pp. 20–23.

8

Nuclear Dreams or Nightmares?

Chinese Investments in the Energy Sector in the UK and Romania

Simona Davidescu

Introduction

Nuclear energy policy is closely linked to national security and military power, shrouded in secrecy, while at the same time being hailed by supporters as an important part of the solutions to decarbonization. China has emerged in recent decades as a key civil nuclear power and major global investor in this sector, with forty-nine nuclear reactors in operation at the domestic level, third only in terms of capacity to the United States and France (Conca, 2021). Chinese investments in nuclear energy projects outside of China could be seen as a potential direct threat to national sovereignty, and indirectly as a threat to the Liberal International Order (LIO). This is because access to nuclear technology is linked to concerns of industrial espionage, access to military technology, or the ability to control major infrastructure (Thomas, 2017). Following and extending scholarship about Chinese investments in the energy sector (Conrad and Kostka, 2017), this chapter presents a snapshot of how this potential threat plays out in two European countries, the United Kingdom (UK) and Romania, and uncovers a range of domestic and external factors shaping policy decisions and their reversal.

Investment in nuclear power in China and its expansion abroad is consistent with the 'Chinese Dream' under President Xi, with 'the development of nuclear energy on the premise of security' coupled with safety as a top priority and 'win-win cooperation' (Xi, 2014). There is general agreement in the literature that China is now the most significant energy player in large parts of the world, from the Middle East to Eurasia, Africa, and Latin America, with the main aim of gaining privileged access to energy and resources (Gao, 2017), as well as pursuing commercial interests (Zhang, 2019).

Simona Davidescu, *Nuclear Dreams or Nightmares?*. In: *Rising Power, Limited Influence*. Edited by: Indrajit Roy, Jappe Eckhardt, Dimitrios Stroikos, and Simona Davidescu, Oxford University Press. © Oxford University Press (2024). DOI: 10.1093/oso/9780192887115.003.0009

We show in this chapter that the picture of Chinese investments in energy in Europe is far patchier and requires in-depth analysis on a sectoral basis. The key debate in the global energy governance literature is linked to whether China will confront or integrate with the current system, dominated by the United States (US), and some of the literature looks at the extent to which there is evidence that neither integration nor confrontation is taking place in the case of energy governance (Gao, 2017). This research argues in favour of a more nuanced approach that looks at a hybrid picture of 'both conflict and adaptation, differently entangled in different issue areas' (de Graaff et al., 2020: 191).

We look at Chinese nuclear energy investments in Romania and the UK as examples of the most likely Chinese nuclear power investments in Europe over the last decade, but also as exceptional cases of commitment to new nuclear power ambitions in the post-Fukushima disaster period (Johnstone et al., 2017: 154). Romania and the UK have a diverse energy mix and limited dependency on exports, while also having a similar percentage of electricity generated from nuclear power, between 15–20% (World Nuclear Association Romania; World Nuclear Association UK), placing them in a relatively privileged position in the current context of crisis. We engage in an explanation of a policy puzzle, as Chinese investments in UK projects were until very recently more likely to go ahead, while the Romanian project fell through after inaction. This seems counter-intuitive at first glance, given the assumptions in the literature that Eastern European states have been more susceptible to Chinese influence (for a discussion on this see chapters in this volume by Jakimow, Crawford, and Szunomar) and more interested in attracting Chinese funding (Vangeli, 2018), posing a threat to the European Union, as China adopted a 'divide and conquer' strategy (Turcsanyi, 2014).

We argue that the divergent routes seen in our case studies were not linked to domestic politics alone, but are reflective of a wider interplay of international influences in this policy area, especially from the US. External pressures acted as a catalyst for legislative changes in both countries, securing support from all parts of the political spectrum. These resulted in longer-term policy changes such as the National Security and Investment Act (2021) and the Nuclear Energy (Financing) Bill (2022) in the UK, while in Romania they led to a shift in strategy towards small modular nuclear reactors (TVR News, 2022).

In looking at these cases, we uncover the interplay of domestic actors supporting and opposing Chinese investments in the nuclear sector. We also consider the role of private actors, as the strategies for financing the nuclear sector differ in the two countries: the UK has adopted a corporate model of financing, involving partnership with established actors in the field, such as Electricite de France (EDF), while Romania has used the national model of bilateral negotiations. The two countries initially had joint trajectories in terms of nuclear investment from China, based on economic rationale. The signing of an agreement between China Guangdong Nuclear (CGN) and the Romanian state-led Nuclearelectrica had followed the example of the UK, after the letter of intent signed by CGN with EDF in October 2013 over the Hinkley Point C nuclear plant (WNN 2013). In both the UK and Romania, China's key mode of influence was persuasion, which also involved a healthy dose of economic inducement. While we expect to see its impact in altering behaviour in weaker states, more dependent on FDI (Goh 2014: 832), such as Romania, this is more puzzling for the case of the UK and has prompted fierce domestic debates (House of Commons, 2016). After a period of divergence, with Romania abruptly cutting off Chinese investments in the nuclear sector in mid-2020, after years of delays, the UK seems set to gradually follow a similar trajectory, after a range of legislative changes from 2021 onwards.

For Chinese State-Owned Enterprises (SOEs) in the nuclear sector, the European investments in this policy area are strategic, long-term, and involve partnerships with other state-owned and private actors. For China overall these could have the potential to change China's standing in global energy governance, which could reinforce the liberal international regime, if that provides a competitive advantage to China. The strong regulatory oversight in Europe can benefit China, in terms of prestige, and its interest goes beyond financing, with the potential to expand its nuclear fleet and build a reactor of its own design in the UK, at Bradwell, as well as to branch out into other areas such as nuclear fuel reprocessing, while working towards 'harmonizing safety standards' (Reuters, 2019).

This chapter draws on secondary literature and primary documents from the Romanian and UK governments and parliaments, as well as media reports and speeches, focusing on the position of key domestic actors in the nuclear power sector and beyond. We start with a look at the context of nuclear energy policy and cooperation between the EU and China, before engaging with the two case studies in turn. We look at the apparent success of Chinese nuclear energy investments in the UK, in partnership with EDF, and then explain the failure of Chinese nuclear energy investments in Romania and the pivotal role played by the US in this policy reversal. Finally, the chapter concludes with reflections beyond these cases, on the implications for the rest of the energy sector and Europe in the context of crisis.

Early Nuclear Energy Policy Cooperation between the EU and China

The debate on energy security and the relationship with China started in France much earlier than in the rest of the EU, from the 1980s, when the first nuclear powerplants with French technology were inaugurated in China (at Daya Bay and Qinshan I). From 2007 Electricite de France (EDF) and CGN signed a cooperation agreement to build and operate power stations in Guangdong, followed by an agreement with French Areva totalling 8 billion euros (World Nuclear Association, China). This was not smooth sailing at the domestic level, as there was a sustained media campaign in France against this partnership and strong public opinion opposition (Torres, 2015). Despite this, major French companies with global reputation in the field such as EDF, AREVA, Alstom, and PME-PMI have been working closely with the nuclear industry in China (Torres, 2015). In the wake of the global financial crisis of 2008, the French nuclear company Areva collapsed and Chinese companies were able to gain a stake in rescued companies (Thomas, 2017: 687).

China developed its own nuclear reactor designs in partnership with Western companies investing in China, and by 2013 started to target global export markets, with the three Chinese State Council approved companies splitting those amongst themselves (Thomas, 2017). This runs counter to the LIO logic of competition and free trade: CGN developed projects in UK, Romania, and Kenya; the Chinese National Nuclear Corporation (CNNC) in Argentina, Algeria, and Sudan; and the State Nuclear Power Technology Company (SPIC) in Turkey and South Africa (World Nuclear Association, China).

Research looking at the role played by these SOEs in their international expansion towards Europe reveals a much more nuanced picture of divergence from the official Chinese central government strategy, relative autonomy of the SOEs, and divergent strategies linked primarily to maximizing profit, as well as limited coordination between the Chinese actors involved (Zhang, 2019).

The overall attractiveness of this investment drive for other parts of the world is the financial backing behind it, from the China Development Bank and Export, the Import Bank of China, or the Industrial and Commercial Bank of China (Thomas, 2017). This was particularly important at a time when funding for such costly projects was sparse in the post-2008 economic crisis period, and there was a brief window of opportunity in which Western governments were willing to support a 'golden era' of bilateral relations with China.

It is difficult to understand the importance of the CGN-EDF partnership without looking at the scale of national developments in China and the costs of nuclear energy in OECD countries compared to China. For example, over the last sixteen years OECD countries have built only two nuclear reactors of Generation 3 (EPR, AP1000), while facing a tripling of costs and long delays for ongoing builds. China has built six such reactors in only one decade, while also guaranteeing the price of electricity produced (twice as cheap as for the European EPRs). This makes the Chinese nuclear sector highly competitive globally, currently amounting to 'two-thirds of worldwide reactor start-ups—35 out of 59' (Pomper 2019).

China has been keen to show that it can integrate within the Western regulatory framework and the LIO by becoming party to most major treaties and conventions relating to nuclear matters and seeking frequent interaction and cooperation with the International Atomic Energy Agency (Andrews-Speed, 2020). This trajectory has potential implications for global energy governance and US global dominance on several levels, from global nuclear non-proliferation efforts to maintaining high safety standards. China faces very different export regimes in Europe compared to elsewhere, as Europe is subject to a 'traditional competition system ... organised along the OECD guidelines, ECA financing and the EU rules' (Pehuet Lucet, 2015). Elsewhere, Russian and Chinese investments are supposed to be able to reap the advantage of being free from regulations and constraints and offer advantageous financing through bilateral agreements (Pehuet Lucet, 2015). Despite a more permissive context elsewhere, for China investing in the nuclear sector in the UK is a vital strategic move that can provide economic, political, and reputational benefits on a global scale, by signalling its competitiveness and providing 'huge advantage in markets with less experienced regulatory bodies' (Thomas, 2017: 688). In what follows we look at the rationale and framing of Chinese investments in the nuclear sector in the UK and the constellation of stakeholders that have shaped the process.

Chinese Nuclear Energy Investments in the UK

The UK nuclear energy sector has moved from a post-Second World War pro-nuclear consensus to nuclear freeze in the 1980s and a renewal post-2000, while facing key challenges such as an ageing capacity, decommissioning and decarbonization commitments, the financial crisis and lack of private investment, delays, and spiralling costs. Political parties' positions on the issue have changed significantly, from the New Labour governments of 1997 to 2010 initially opposing new nuclear power plants to being in favour and linking this to their ambitious targets of the Climate Change Act 2008.

The following coalition government (Conservative and Liberal Democrats) launched a bilateral process of cooperation in the energy sector in 2010, the UK-China Energy Dialogue, under the leadership of the Department of Energy and Climate Change (DECC). This also had the industry executives on board, showcasing common interests and challenges and an innovation drive spanning a range of subsectors such as civil nuclear, oil, and gas. For China, this forum had not only an economic significance, but also potential for integration into the LIO and the energy governance architecture. According to the Secretary of State of DECC, Edward Davey MP, the UK was willing to 'work closely with the Chinese government to explore global energy governance reform' (DECC 2014).

Chinese investments in the UK in the energy sector and other infrastructure sectors were part of the so-called golden era of Sino-British relations over the last decade, during which the main framing of the relationship was in terms of deepening economic ties. Recent analysis of UK-China relations suggests a move from 'the golden era to the deep freeze' (Ford and Hughes, 2020), in the aftermath of the 5G policy reversal. However, minority Chinese stakes in UK nuclear energy projects (in partnership with EDF) were still in place by early 2022, despite calls for a rethink following Russia's invasion of Ukraine and in the context of an increased commitment, in the 2022 Energy Security Strategy, for eight more nuclear reactors to be built in the UK over the next decade at an accelerated pace. In this section, we look at the rationale for these projects from both the UK and Chinese perspectives.

In the UK, CGN is particularly interested in playing 'the long game', which involves sequential investments: from a minority investment share in Hinckley Point C and Sizewell in partnership with EDF and with French design reactors, to a final stage and the ultimate prize, a reactor of its own design (Hualong One) and a majority share (66.5%) for Bradwell (World Nuclear Association, UK). The EDF-CGN partnership is crucial for understanding developments in the UK. This partnership provides an entry into EU markets and is subject to EU rules. In March 2016, the European Commission gave the green light to the 'Strategic Investment Agreement' signed by EDF and CGN in October 2015 on the Hinkley Point C project. This meant testing against the EU's merger regulations and the concern that this would alter competition in the UK's wholesale electricity market (WNN, 2016). The key rationale offered by the Commission for its approval was the limited market share of CGN in the nuclear market and the existence of other competitors (WNN, 2016). The provision of state aid and the type of contract approval process for Hinkley Point C has created a precedent for other EU member states, such as Hungary's use of this example to justify Russian investment in the Packs nuclear power plant (Lindstrom, 2021).

The nuclear expansion and Chinese investments associated with it had political support at the very top of the UK government: Prime Minister, Treasury, and DECC (later BEIS), as the issue was framed primarily in terms of economic benefits. In a Speech to the House of Commons, the BEIS Secretary of State presented this as a clear economic opportunity: 'Hinkley unleashes a long overdue new wave of investment in nuclear engineering in the UK, creating 26,000 jobs and apprenticeships and providing a huge boost to the economy' (House of Commons, 2016). The emphasis on economic benefits needs to be placed into context, after the 2008 economic crisis. This is a sector for which the UK government already faced withdrawal of investors (such as Centrica for Hinkley Point C and Korea Electric Power Corporation and later Toshiba for the Moorside nuclear plant and Hitachi for the Wylfa nuclear power station), because the costs are huge and the 'pool of investors is quite small' (Morison, 2020).

Research by Zhang (2019: 1464) reveals initial competition between Chinese SOEs—CGN and CNNC—for several UK nuclear projects, and policy divergence from the Chinese central government position, at a time when China was 'freezing' relations with the UK in the aftermath of the UK leadership meeting with the Dalai Lama in 2012.

At the domestic level in the UK there were sharp divisions between supporters and detractors of Chinese investments in infrastructure sectors, cutting across party lines, and involving the private and voluntary sector as well as public opinion. The critics included environmentalists and private actors from other sectors such as renewable energy, which saw their subsidies slashed, but also prominent MPs from all main parties, including backbenchers. Critics framed the issue primarily in energy security terms, asking the government for a clear assessment of the security risks associated with the deal and issues of intellectual property (House of Commons, 2016). In light of this framing linked to energy security, the Labour opposition asked the government during the House of Commons debate to decouple 'the building of the Hualong One reactor at Bradwell from the deal at Hinkley Point C' (House of Commons 2016), to differentiate between the projects with French technology and future projects using Chinese technology.

Security issues were put into new light with developments in the US, where a senior CGN adviser was accused of trying to obtain sensitive US nuclear technology for China, prompting the US government to put CGN on an export blacklist (Watt, 2017). Furthermore, the backdrop of Brexit has provided new constraints, and the exit of the UK from the EURATOM treaty raised 'implications for the freedom of movement of nuclear material and personnel across Europe' (Pollitt and Chyong 2017: 44), as well as the potential weakening of regulatory oversight in this sector.

Another issue signalled by critics is linked to short- and long-term costs, as Hinkley Point C is 'the most expensive power station in the world' (Watt, 2017), with spiralling costs and four years late. Moreover, the UK government had offered the investors a range of subsidies coupled with a 'strike price' guarantee of up to £92.50 per megawatt hour, raising concerns that the costs would be dumped on consumers (Mustoe, 2015). Critics amongst MPs and the voluntary sector have further framed the issue in political terms, by linking it with a stronger stance from the UK on respect for human rights in China and the crackdown on democratic opposition in Hong Kong (*The Guardian*, 2020). In retaliation, China banned nine UK MPs from entry into its country, as well as other vocal critics and four institutions (*Evening Standard*, 2021). Despite this significant level of opposition, the Hinkley Point C project is going ahead, making this a highly politicized decision, despite the government claims that this was based mainly on economic rationale.

The saga of Chinese nuclear investments in the UK might not be over, as the guarantees offered by the UK government have significantly risen the cost of policy reversal and have a lock-in effect, while there is a lack of other credible investment opportunities. In the words of Professor Steve Thomas, in the case of Hinkley Point C 'the issue now is that nobody has a good exit strategy. I think everyone wants out. But there are penalties to pay now, and there is the humiliation of 10 wasted years' (quoted in Watt, 2017).

To enhance political control over the process of financing nuclear energy, the Johnson government promoted two crucial legislative changes: the National Security and Investment Act (2021) and the Nuclear Energy (Financing) Bill (2022). These can help policy reversal and avoid lock-in, while also making the sector more attractive to a wider pool of investors. The Nuclear Energy (Financing) Act, adopted in 2022 with the support of Labour at the second reading, stated its purpose as to:

> ... make provisions for the implementation of a regulated asset base (RAB) model for nuclear energy generation projects ... and a special administration regime for licensees subject to that model; while also clarifying the circumstances in which corporate bodies are not associated with site operators for financing of decommissioning of nuclear sites. (BCIP, 2022)

There was significant debate at the committee stage on amendments proposed by Labour to explicitly refer to companies controlled by foreign powers, but the government was concerned that this could prevent other international partners from investing in the sector[1] and could contravene Article 129 of the trade agreement with the EU (Nuclear Energy Bill, 2021).

The UK government attempted to offload the share of Chinese investment in Hinkley Point C and Sizewell in late 2021, but it has not yet been successful (Collingridge and Ambrose, 2021), while a recent approval by the UK regulator of the Chinese-design reactor is being seen as increasingly unlikely to be built at Bradwell (*The Economist*, 2022). It seems that the window of opportunity when Chinese investments in the nuclear sector were framed primarily as an economic opportunity has now firmly closed. This finding has been recently confirmed by the speech of the UK Prime Minister Rishi Sunak, regarding the evolution of the Chinese-British relations, stating that 'The so-called "golden era" is over, along with the naive idea that trade would lead to social and political reform' (Allegretti, 2022).

Energy Investments in Romania

Although the case of Hinkley Point C has been cited as a justification for Chinese investments in the case of Romania's nuclear reactors 3 and 4 at Cernavodă, the context has been markedly different. There are some similarities with the UK, in the way supporters at the top of the political establishment in Romania framed the issue in terms of economic benefits, in the early years of negotiations. The main differences were linked to the level of politicization of the project in Romania from the start, and the less influential opposition to the project. There has been a lack of transparency and significant delays in negotiations between CGN and state-controlled Nuclearelectrica, in an energy sector described in the literature as a case of 'state capture' (Buzogány and Davidescu, 2022). This made the project more exposed to reversal on political and security grounds, when the governing political coalition changed in 2020. This was prompted by separate negotiations with the US, which in 2020 emerged as a credible alternative to Chinese investments.

Romania's relationship with China in the post-communist period has fluctuated greatly, with the initial period of 1989–2006 considered to be dominated by high-level political contacts and sustained support at the highest

[1] The announcement of the French government that it intends to nationalize EDF in order to restructure its debt seems to have justified the government's concern on the wording of the amendments (Aloisi and Rosemain, 2022).

level from the social democrat governing party, PSD, but not matched by economic developments (Popescu and Brinza, 2018; see also Szunomar, this volume). The trade relationship between Romania and China has known several stages, with the initial two waves being very limited and small scale and the third wave of Chinese ODI being mainly focused on large infrastructure projects with significant levels of funding, but still very slow, with most projects in the negotiations stage for several years (Pencea, 2017). There were four investment memoranda with China signed in 2013 by the PSD-led Ponta government: the nuclear reactors 3 and 4 at Cernavodă Nuclear Plant, the Tarnița-Lăpuștești Hydropower Plant, the Rovinari Thermal Power Plant, and the Mintia-Deva Thermal Power Plant, all of these coinciding with the occasion of Li Keqiang's visit to the 16+1 Bucharest Summit, but none has been implemented (Popescu and Brinza, 2018: 31). Surprisingly, the CGN-led investment in nuclear power reactors at Cernavodă was considered the most advanced and ambitious (Pencea, 2017), as it was designed to double capacity at Cernavodă within one decade (WNN, 2021). This followed the failure of the previous investment projects associated with Cernavodă 3 and 4, in the context of economic crisis. A large consortium set up in 2008 included the Romanian state-owned nuclear power company Nuclearelectrica and a range of companies such as ArcelorMittal, CEZ, GDF SUEZ, Enel, Iberdrola, and RWE. One by one, the partners have withdrawn, citing costs and unfeasibility of the project (Pirvoiu, 2013), so having CGN as a single partner that was able to provide the entire financing through Exim-Bank and ICBC promised to simplify and speed up the process (Pirvoiu, 2013).

The process was incremental, but several key stages were completed, and formal documents were signed. In 2015, China Nuclear Power Engineering Co (CNPEC) signed a 'binding and exclusive' cooperation agreement with Candu Energy for the construction of two more reactors at the Cernavodă plant in Romania. CGN is CNPEC's parent company (WNN 2020). Romanian national nuclear company Nuclearelectrica signed a preliminary investors' agreement with CGN in May 2019 to build two 700 MWe Candu 6 pressurized heavy water reactors at the Cernavodă plant. During this 'golden' decade, many Chinese companies were interested in investing in Romania in infrastructure projects, but both sides blamed delays on bureaucracy, corruption, non-transparent negotiations, and frequent policy reversals (Buzogány and Davidescu, 2022). This was coupled with high levels of political instability in Romania: in a 'period of two and a half years, five prime ministers have led the Romanian Government and the negotiations at Cernavodă' (Popescu and Brinza, 2018: 32). Moreover, reports of frustrating delays seemed to be related to CGN's excessive demands of a 15% internal rate of return compared with industry standards, and a mismatch between CGN's position of maximizing profits and China's official foreign policy of deeper cooperation under the 16+1 framework (Zhang, 2019: 1469).

By June 2020, a new coalition government (PNL, UDMR, USL-PLUS) made a sudden policy reversal and suspended negotiations with CGN, invoking building tensions between China and the US, while stating that Romania needs to find investment partners from the EU or US in order to strengthen its strategic partnership with the US and its NATO alliance ties (Digi 24, 2020). Only a few months later, in October 2020, Romania and the US signed an intergovernmental agreement of cooperation in key sectors, including the Cernavodă nuclear reactors 3 and 4, re-technologization of Cernavodă 1, and cooperation in other areas of civil nuclear power (Nuclearelectrica, 2020). This is consistent with findings from the literature that show how other CEE countries have been open to sacrificing relations with Beijing for other objectives, in particular security and political ones (Stec, 2020). Countries in the region engaged in leveraging the Sino-American rivalry to help ensure the US administration's continued commitment to NATO (Stec, 2020), which was perceived as being under threat during the Trump presidency.

The constellation of domestic actors supporting the CGN investment at Cernavodă included the leadership of the Social Democratic Party (PSD) governments and Nuclearelectrica, which prioritized nuclear in the energy mix, according to Romania's energy strategy for 2018–2030. There has been little contestation in Parliament of this project and more widely within society. Some limited opposition from environmental groups was not influential in policy circles, and their position was against the expansion of nuclear power in general, citing the danger for human health and the environment, in relation to the heating of water in the Danube and tritium liquid discharges (Fairlie, 2007).

The recent deal between Romania and the US on the Cernavodă 3 and 4 reactors seemed to silence critics and, despite the slow progress since, as well as a change in the US government in the meantime, there is high hope from the government that this project will go ahead with more urgency in the wake of the war in Ukraine. Romania's Ministry of Economy, Energy and Business Climate also signed in 2020 a Memorandum of Understanding with the Export-Import Bank of the USA covering the energy and infrastructure industries, and Romania and France signed a declaration of intent on cooperation in the civil nuclear field (WNN 2021). Despite all these agreements, energy experts consider this type of costly and lengthy project as unrealistic, with limited impact on Romania's energy transition (Pirvoiu, 2021; see also Buzogány and Davidescu, 2022).

Conclusions

Overall this chapter exposed the limits of looking at power as resources even at a time when the context and framing was favourable. There is limited evidence that China set out to challenge the LIO on investments in nuclear energy policy, while its own position lacked coherence (Zhang, 2019). Also, it did not seem to have the effect of undermining the LIO in terms of power as influence, as investments stalled and were seen as not credible even in the apparently most likely case, such as Romania, where there was no significant domestic opposition. The nuclear energy investment projects in Europe were delayed or reversed from 2020 onwards, in the aftermath of the deterioration in US-China strategic relations. European governments initially framed Chinese investments in nuclear power as an economic opportunity. But since 2020 this position shifted to a security framing of the issue that made these investment decisions politically costly both domestically and internationally and led to a policy reversal in Romania. The UK has also indicated it would follow suit, but this would need to be accompanied by the existence of credible alternatives and sources of funding, given the high level of ambition of current strategies. Within this context the UK seems to be an outlier, as we find higher levels of political and societal opposition than in Romania, as well as significant contestation of the economic benefits of the projects. Overall, in both countries it seems increasingly difficult for political elites to make a case for pursuing Chinese investments in nuclear energy on either economic or political grounds.

The global context of continuous crisis since 2008 has proved to be highly beneficial to Chinese investments in the energy sector, as Chinese SOEs have emerged as key investors, willing and able to play the long game in a sector that requires state guarantees. Rather than a strategy of contestation, China does not seem to adopt a concerted push strategy and has varied approaches in different parts of Europe. Moreover, the different strategies pursued by CGN in Romania and the UK, as well as the lack of coherence and consistency between their commercial interests and the Chinese foreign policy agenda (Zhang, 2019), suggests that there was limited scope and no coherent plan to undermine the LIO, even at a time when the economic framing and the governing elites in both the UK and Romania were favourable to these investments.

While Chinese SOEs have more extensive projects for nuclear power elsewhere in the world, being able to complete projects in Europe (with its strong regulatory framework) was a matter of prestige that could have further boosted China's credentials worldwide. These seem now unlikely under the current security framing of the issue and Russia's ongoing war in Ukraine.

As long as European nations are hung up on nuclear dreams for which they seem increasingly ill equipped to provide financing in the immediate future, these investment decisions could prove extremely costly for future generations. Meanwhile Chinese SOEs will continue to play an increasing role in this sector globally, as investors of last resort for 'white elephants' type of projects. Further debate on the role of nuclear energy in the energy transition in Europe is needed, given the difficulty of securing investments and spiralling costs. A shift of focus might help, from nuclear dreams for a distant future, towards more sustainable, cheaper, and shorter-term investments in renewable energy, another sector in which China is catching up fast.

Bibliography

Allegretti, A. 2022. 'Rishi Sunak Signals End of "Golden Era" of Relations between Britain and China'. *The Guardian*, 28 November. Available at: https://www.theguardian.com/politics/2022/nov/28/rishi-sunak-signals-end-of-golden-era-of-relations-between-britain-and-china.

Aloisi, S., and M. Rosemain. 2022. 'France to Announce Details of EDF Nationalisation'. *Reuters*, 18 July. Available at: https://www.reuters.com/business/energy/france-announce-details-edf-nationalisation-2022-07-18/#:~:text=PARIS%2C%20July%2019%20(Reuters),grapples%20with%20an%20energy%20crisis.

Andrews-Speed, P. 2020. 'The Governance of Nuclear Power in China'. *The Journal of World Energy Law & Business* 13 (1): pp. 23–46.

BCIP. 2022. 'Is Nuclear Energy (Financing) Act 2022 an Answer to UK's Energy Security?'. Bryan Cave Leighton Paisner, 28 April. Available at: https://www.bclplaw.com/en-GB/insights/is-nuclear-energy-financing-act-2022-an-answer-to-uks-energy-security.html

Buzogány, A., and S. Davidescu. 2022. 'Energy Governance in Romania'. In *Handbook of Energy Governance in Europe*, Springer Link. pp. 993–1018. https://doi.org/10.1007/978-3-319-73526-9

Cecil, N. 2021. 'China Sanctions: Boris Johnson Praises MPs Censured by Beijing for "Shining A Light" on Human Rights Abuses'. *Evening Standard*, 26 March. Available at: https://www.standard.co.uk/news/politics/china-sanctions-mps-iain-duncan-smith-xinjiang-uyghurs-b926373.html [Accessed 10 July 2021].

Collingridge, J., and J. Ambrose. 2021. 'Ministers Close to Deal That Could End China's Role in UK Nuclear Power Stations'. *The Guardian*, 25 September.

Available at: https://www.theguardian.com/environment/2021/sep/25/ministers-close-to-deal-that-could-end-chinas-role-in-uk-nuclear-power-station.

Conca, J. 2021. 'China Will Lead the World in Nuclear Energy, along with All Other Energy Sources, Sooner Than You Think'. *Forbes*, 23 April. Available at: www.forbes.com.

Conrad, B., and G. Kostka. 2017. 'Chinese Investments in Europe's Energy Sector: Risks and Opportunities?'. *Energy Policy* 101: pp. 644–648.

de Graaff, N., T. ten Brink, and I. Parmar. 2020. 'China's Rise in a Liberal World Order in Transition—Introduction to The FORUM'. *Review of International Political Economy* 27 (2): pp. 191–207.

DECC. 2014. 'Speech. UK-China Energy Dialogue'. Edward Davey's opening speech, 7 July. Available at: https://www.gov.uk/government/speeches/uk-china-energy-dialogue.

Digi 24. 2020. 'Cum s-a spulberat mirajul investitiilor Chineze pentru reactoarele de la Cernavoda' [How the Mirage of Chinese Investments for Cernavoda Nuclear Reactors Dissipated Away]'. 29 May. Available at: https://www.digi24.ro/stiri/economie/cum-s-a-spulberat-mirajul-investitiilor-chineze-pentru-reactoarele-de-la-cernavoda-1314992?__grsc=cookieIsUndef0&__grts=54218041&__grua=365ff76f15f5e9dae3ba7736e2f90a23&__grrn=1.

Fairlie, I. 2007. 'Cernavoda 3&4: Environmental Impact Assessment'. Report for Greenpeace. Available at: https://www.banktrack.org/download/cernavoda_3_and_4_environment_impact_analysis_report_for_greenpeace/200709_cernavoda_report_for_gp_central_europe_final.pdf.

Ford, J., and L. Hughes. 2020. 'UK-China Relations: From "Golden Era" to the Deep Freeze'. *Financial Times*, 14 July, The Big Read China. Available at: https://www.ft.com/content/804175d0-8b47-4427-9853-2aded76f48e4.

Gao, S. 2017. 'China and Global Energy Governance: Integration or Confrontation?'. *Global Governance: A Review of Multilateralism and International Organizations* 23 (2): pp. 307–325

Goh, E. 2014. 'The Modes of China's Influence. Cases from Southeast Asia'. *Asian Survey* 54 (5): pp. 825–848.

House of Commons. 2016. 'Hinkley Point C Debate'. HC Deb, c1066, 15 September. Available at: https://www.theyworkforyou.com/debates/?id=2016-09-15c.1065.11https://www.world-nuclear.org/information-library/country-profiles/countries-t-z/united-kingdom.aspx.

Johnstone, P., A. Stirling, and B. Sovacool. 2017. 'Policy Mixes for Incumbency: Exploring the Destructive Recreation of Renewable Energy, Shale Gas "Fracking," and Nuclear Power in The United Kingdom'. *Energy Research & Social Science*, 33: pp. 147–162.

Lindstrom, N. 2021. 'Aiding the State: Administrative Capacity and Creative Compliance with European State Aid Rules in New Member States'. *Journal of European Public Policy* 28 (11): pp. 1789–1806.

Morison, R. 2020. 'U.K. Nuclear's Future Left in Limbo as Investors Walk Away'. *Bloomberg Green*, 17 September. Available at: https://www.bloomberg.com/news/articles/2020-09-17/clouds-gather-over-u-k-nuclear-as-another-project-fails [Accessed 11 May 2021].

Mustoe, H. 2015. 'What Does the Nuclear Deal with China Mean?'. BBC News, 21 October. Available at: https://www.bbc.co.uk/news/business-34585219

National Security and Investment Act. 2021. Chapter 25. Available at https://www.legislation.gov.uk/ukpga/2021/25/introduction/enacted

Nuclear Energy Bill. 2021. *Nuclear Energy (Financing) Bill Third Sitting*. Hansard, Public Bill Committees.

Nuclearelectrica. 2020. 'Parafarea Acordului între Guvernul României și Guvernul Statelor Unite ale Americii privind cooperarea în legătură cu proiectele nuclearo-energetice de la Cernavodă si în sectorul energiei nucleare civile din România'. Available at: https://www.nuclearelectrica.ro/2020/10/09/parafarea-acordului-intre-guvernul-romaniei-si-guvernul-statelor-unite-ale-americii-privind-cooperarea-in-legatura-cu-proiectele-nuclearo-energetice-de-la-cernavoda-si-in-sectorul-energiei-nucleare-c/ [Accessed 10 June 2021].

Pehuet Lucet, F. 2015. 'Financing Nuclear Power Plant Projects a New Paradigm?' (INIS-FR–16-0009). France.

Pencea, S. 2017. 'Romania-China Trade and Investment Relations against the Backdrop of "One Belt, One Road" Strategy'. *Romanian Economic and Business Review* 12 (2): pp. 17–29.

Pirvoiu, C. 2021 'Dezbatere: Cat este de pregatita Romania pentru tranzitia energetica? [Debate: How Well Prepared is Romania for the Energy Transition?]'. Guest speakers Razvan Nicolescu and Dumitru Chisalita, *Hotnews*, 23 May. Available at: https://www.hotnews.ro/stiri-romania_in_europa-24814854-dezbatere-cat-este-pregatita-romania-pentru-tranzitia-energetica-razvan-nicolescu-dumitru-chisalita-interviurile-hotnews-live-luni-11-45.htm.

Pirvoiu, C. 2013. 'Enel and ArcelorMittal are Leaving the Cernavoda 3&4 Nuclear Reactor Project [Enel si ArcelorMittal parasesc proiectul reactoarelor 3 si 4 de la Cernavoda]'. 23 December. Available at: https://economie.hotnews.ro/stiri-energie-16268804-enel-arcelormittal-parasesc-proiectul-reactoarelor-3-4-cernavoda.htm [Accessed 17 May 2021].

Pollitt, M. G., and C. Kong. 2017. 'Brexit and Its Implications for British and EU Energy and Climate Policy'. Centre on Regulation in Europe, Project Report. Available at: https://cerre.eu/publications/brexit-and-its-implications-british-and-eu-energy-and-climate-policy/.

Pomper, M. 2019. 'China Has Big Plans for Its Nuclear Energy Industry. But Will They Pan Out?'. World Politics Review, 29 April. Available at: https://www.worldpoliticsreview.com/insights/27799/china-has-big-plans-for-its-nuclear-energy-industry-but-will-they-pan-out.

Popescu, L., and A. Brinza. 2018. 'Romania-China Relations. Political and Economic Challenges in the BRI Era'. *Romanian Journal of European Affairs* 18 (2): pp. 20–38.

Reuters. 2019. 'China Still Pursuing Nuclear Fuel Reprocessing Plant with France'. 3 September. Available at: https://www.reuters.com/article/china-nuclear-idAFL3N25U0WV [Accessed 1 May 2021].

Stec, G. 2020. 'Central and Eastern Europe and Joint European China Policy: Threat or Opportunity?'. *MERICS*. Available at: https://merics.org/en/analysis/central-and-eastern-europe-and-joint-european-china-policy-threat-or-opportunity.

The Economist. 2022. 'British Regulators Have Approved a Chinese Reactor Design. It is Unlikely to be Built'. Britain Section: Hualong, farewell, 12 February. Available at: https://www.economist.com/britain/2022/02/12/british-regulators-have-approved-a-chinese-reactor-design.

The Guardian. 2020. 'Ian Duncan Smith Calls for Review of Chinese Investment in UK'. Interview by Dan Sabbagh. 11 October. Available at: https://www.theguardian.com/politics/2020/oct/11/iain-duncan-smith-calls-for-review-of-chinese-investment-in-uk-bpl-huawei [Accessed 10 May 2021].

Thomas, S. 2017. 'China's Nuclear Export Drive: Trojan Horse or Marshall Plan?'. *Energy Policy* 101: pp. 683–691.

Torres, F. 2015. 'La coopération nucléaire franco-chinoise : histoire d'un modèle de développement partagé [The Nuclear Cooperation Franco-Chinese: The History Of A Joint Development Model]'. *La Revue de l'Energie* 624: pp. 144–163.

Turksanyi, R. 2014. 'Central and Eastern Europe's Courtship with China: Trojan Horse Within the EU?'. *EU-Asia at a Glance*. Brussels: European Institute for Asian Studies. Available at: http://www.eias.org/wp-content/uploads/2016/02/EU-Asia-at-a-glance-Richard-Turcsányi-China-CEE.pdf [Accessed 15 January 2019].

TVR News. 2022. 'The New York Times: The War in Ukraine, Romania's Chance to Become an Energy Power in Europe'. *Economie*, 15 June. Available at: http://stiri.tvr.ro/the-ny-times-razboiul-din-ucraina-ansa-romaniei-de-a-deveni-o-putere-energetica-in-europa_907386.html#view.

Vangeli, A. 2018. 'Global China and Symbolic Power: The Case Of 16+1 Cooperation'. *Journal of Contemporary China* 27: pp. 1–14.

Watt, H. 2017. 'Hinkley Point: The "Dreadful Deal" Behind the World's Most Expensive Power Plant'. *The Guardian*, The Long Read, 21 December. Available at: https://www.theguardian.com/news/2017/dec/21/hinkley-point-c-dreadful-deal-behind-worlds-most-expensive-power-plant.

WNN. 2013. 'Romania Signals Intent with China'. World Nuclear News, 26 November. Available at: https://www.world-nuclear-news.org/Articles/Romania-signals-intent-with-China [Accessed 7 November 2020].

WNN. 2016. 'European Commission Clears EDF, CGN Partnership'. World Nuclear News, 11 March. Available at: https://www.world-nuclear-news.org/Articles/European-Commission-clears-EDF,-CGN-partnership [Accessed 7 November 2020].

WNN. 2020. 'Romania Restarts Approach to New Cernavoda Units'. World Nuclear News, 16 July. Available at: https://world-nuclear-news.org/Articles/Romania-restarts-approach-to-new-Cernavoda-units [Accessed 7 November 2020].

WNN. 2021. 'Romanian Energy Policy Would See Nuclear Double'. Bucharest, 10 May. Available at: https://www.world-nuclear-news.org/Articles/Romanian-energy-policy-will-see-nuclear-double.

World Nuclear Association. 2021. 'Nuclear Power in China'. Country Profile, last updated March 2021. Available at: https://www.world-nuclear.org/information-library/country-profiles/countries-a-f/china-nuclear-power.aspx [Accessed 2 April 2021].

World Nuclear Association. 2021. 'Nuclear Power in the United Kingdom'. Country Profile, last updated February 2021 [Accessed 2 April 2021].

Xi, J. 2014. 'Statement by H. E. Xi Jinping President of the People's Republic of China at the Nuclear Security Summit'. The Hague, Ministry of Foreign Affairs of the People's Republic of China, 25 March. Available at: https://www.fmprc.gov.cn/mfa_eng/wjdt_665385/zyjh_665391/t1140583.shtml.

Zhang, B. 2019. 'State Transformation Goes Nuclear: Chinese National Nuclear Companies' Expansion into Europe'. *Third World Quarterly* 40 (8): pp. 1459–1478.

9
The Political Dimensions of Chinese Outward FDI and Their Implications for the Liberal International Order

Jan Knoerich

Introduction

Chinese international investments have surged at an exasperating speed in less than two decades and have spread to all parts of the world (Knoerich, 2015a), leaving pundits, policymakers, and everyone seeking to understand the implications of China's growing global presence desperate to catch up with fast-moving developments.[1] The extraordinary rapidity with which Chinese multinational enterprises have expanded globally has sparked portrayals of Chinese investments as part of an ambition for global systemic change and as an element of a Chinese 'grand strategy' to challenge the international order (Bhattacharya, 2016; Breuer and Johnston, 2019; Callahan, 2016; Fallon, 2015; Fasslabend, 2015; Leverett and Wu, 2016). Their connotation with money, power, and influence, and association with China's controversial Belt and Road Initiative (BRI), have made Chinese investments a suitable focus area of such claims. But while narratives of China upending the Liberal International Order may provide a convenient and catchy-sounding mental shortcut, especially when brought in connection with China's widely disliked authoritarian political system and state capitalist economic model, they are unlikely to adequately represent the actual complexities surrounding the global spread of Chinese capital. As Roy and Hu emphasize in the introductory chapter to this volume, more nuanced analyses are needed and have recently begun to emerge in the literature (Benabdallah, 2019; de Graaff, ten Brink, and Parmar, 2020; Jones and Zeng, 2019; Knoerich and Urdinez, 2019; Wu, 2018). In this chapter, I acknowledge the multifaceted nature of Chinese

[1] I would like to thank Yiqin Huang for research assistance, and Indrajit Roy, Jappe Eckhardt, Dimitrios Stroikos, and Elena Simona Davidescu for editing this book.

Jan Knoerich, *The Political Dimensions of Chinese Outward FDI and Their Implications for the Liberal International Order.* In: *Rising Power, Limited Influence.* Edited by: Indrajit Roy, Jappe Eckhardt, Dimitrios Stroikos, and Simona Davidescu, Oxford University Press. © Oxford University Press (2024). DOI: 10.1093/oso/9780192887115.003.0010

cross-border capital flows, adding some further nuance to the debates about the political dimension of Chinese investments and their influence on the Liberal International Order.

One significant point of nuance is that, when analysing Chinese cross-border capital flows, it is important to distinguish between what are effectively two different types of Chinese investments. The first type is the financing of large international projects, typically in the infrastructure and construction sectors, by Chinese development banks and other associated financing vehicles. These tend to comprise of sizeable loans issued to foreign governments with the backing and support of the Chinese state, often under condition that contracts for project delivery are handed to Chinese state-owned enterprises (SOEs). However, despite their involvement, multinational enterprises do not necessarily hold equity capital in the projects. Table 7.1 in Crawford's chapter to this volume provides several examples of such project finance in Europe. They include the Bar-Boljare motorway in Montenegro, which is financed by a loan of approximately 1 billion USD from the Export-Import Bank of China and was contracted to the China Road and Bridge Corporation (Hopkins, 2021). Another example is the Belgrade-Budapest railway upgrade, which is cofinanced by the Export-Import Bank of China and involves the participation of Chinese companies in the construction activities (Brinza, 2020). Many projects under the BRI involve this kind of project finance, and they have often been contentious because of the large size and funding capacity, the direct and frequently non-transparent involvement of governments, and concerns about inadequacies in project delivery in line with internationally accepted standards and norms. The Bar-Boljare motorway project, for example, has been viewed sceptically, as its economic viability and the ability of the government of Montenegro to repay the loan have been questioned (Hopkins, 2021).

The second type of Chinese investment involves foreign direct investment (FDI) that is not necessarily associated with project finance. These are investments made by companies and enterprises for the purpose of some form of long-term productive business activity, such as building and running a factory, acquiring a foreign company, establishing an overseas research and development (R&D) centre, or opening a sales office. While the companies conducting such FDI can be SOEs, and governments may offer backing for such investments, private firms are key players in this area, and it is normally the multinational enterprise making the investment and associated business decisions, rather than any government. Examples in Europe are Huawei's UK headquarters in Reading, or ChemChina's purchase of the machinery company Krauss Maffei in Germany.

Because of such differences, it is useful to distinguish between project finance and other forms of investment by multinational enterprises, and examinations of any implications Chinese investments might have for politics and the Liberal International Order should take this distinction into account. Due to the size of projects, their strategic importance, and complex financing schemes involving government loans, project finance by its very nature evokes considerations of influence, dependence, and political leverage. But the political dimension is different when multinationals acquire firms or establish factories, R&D centres, and sales offices. Answers to the questions of Chinese power and influence—outlined by Roy and Hu in the introductory chapter and which constitute a key line of inquiry in this volume—will differ depending on whether the focus of analysis is on project finance or FDI.

In this chapter, I focus on FDI that is unconnected with project financing—henceforth referred to simply as 'FDI'—and aim to identify the political impact of such Chinese outward FDI in the recipient countries where the investment is made, in order to infer what implications it has for the Liberal International Order. My examination will focus on Western Europe, given that such FDI has dominated Chinese investments in this region and contracted projects have been comparatively rare (Eastern Europe has received considerable amounts of project finance from China). Nevertheless, despite this focus on Western Europe, most of the analysis will have broader application.

Previous research on the impact of FDI in recipient countries has focused primarily on the economic and, to a lesser degree, social implications, including whether FDI accelerates processes of development and industrialization in less advanced economies. Its impact on politics has been much less studied. An illustration of this can be found in the World Investment Reports (for example UNCTAD, 2010, 2019), published annually by the United Nations Conference on Trade and Development (UNCTAD), the organization widely considered to be the focal point for FDI in the United Nations system. These reports cover many aspects related to the economic and social implications of FDI, yet they prefer to omit thorough consideration of political dimensions. In academic research as well, the study of economic and social impact far exceeds any consideration of political implications, resulting in claims that political, international relations and international political economy dimensions have been insufficiently examined or largely ignored (Abdelal, 2013; Babic, Fichtner, and Heemskerk, 2017). Arguably, the focus on the political implications of FDI has intensified considerably only since *Chinese* multinational enterprises emerged as investors, with FDI by companies from the United States and other Western economies having been much less politicized in the decades prior. Regardless of whether such politicization focused on Chinese investments is justified, more examinations of the impact FDI has on politics are certainly needed.

This chapter addresses this shortcoming by examining how the operations of Chinese multinational enterprises can have political implications in Western European countries. Drawing in part on notions of power and influence that have already been set out in this volume's introductory chapter by Roy and Hu, together with an amalgamation of insights on the politics of Chinese FDI compiled for this chapter, the following analysis focuses on five distinct aspects through which Chinese FDI could have a political dimension: structural power, referring to the collective ability of Chinese multinational enterprises to shape some of the broad structures of the international political economy; the direct influence and leverage China could have over individual countries receiving Chinese FDI; enhancements in Chinese (technological) competition resulting from investment activities; the misuse of FDI for national security purposes; and the use of FDI to enhance China's international soft power. For each of these aspects, the chapter identifies potential avenues of political impact in recipient countries, yet it also finds that there are considerable limitations in the extent to which Chinese multinationals effectively influence politics. Moreover, not all political implications are problematic, and Chinese FDI can even generate desirable political outcomes for recipient countries. Given these limitations, the chapter concludes that outward FDI cannot be considered as a particularly suitable economic activity to support a challenge of the Liberal International Order, though other types of investments or economic and political activities not examined in this chapter but covered elsewhere in this volume may have greater potential to achieve this.

FDI from a Political Perspective

FDI commonly involves a long-term commitment of capital by a company resident in one country for the purpose of conducting its business in another country, such as producing a good or delivering a service. The company assumes either partial or full ownership and control over this foreign enterprise. In its definition of FDI, the Organisation for Economic Co-operation and Development (OECD) points out that the investor has a lasting interest in this direct investment enterprise and a strategic long-term relationship with it, and therefore exerts considerable influence over its management and operations. Such influence also comes in the form of voting rights assumed by the investing company over decisions made by the direct investment enterprise (OECD, 2008).

This arrangement enables companies to expand their business abroad, but it can also be seen to have a political dimension. It gives foreign decision-makers the power over an entity's economic operations within a recipient country and allows a foreign company to hold assets of that country, including strategic assets such as technologies or iconic brands. FDI enables a company to conduct far-reaching operations in the recipient country affecting many people and stakeholders, including production, employment, sales, procurement, research, and further investment. In this position, the investing company does not only have an impact on the recipient country's economic and social progression, but might also seek to exert power over its employees, business partners, competitors, and other stakeholders. It might draw on political connections with its home government to advance its economic interests in the recipient country and might seek to directly influence the government of the recipient country through lobbying efforts. These and other examples show that foreign investors are not only economic entities, but can function as political actors. Some are very large—the biggest multinational enterprises have revenues that exceed the gross domestic products of entire countries (Babic et al., 2017), and with this comes considerable power and ability to influence governments and stakeholders.

Some have argued, in what has become known as the transnational capitalism perspective, that many of today's multinational enterprises, especially large ones such as Facebook, Google, Starbucks, and Walmart, have rid themselves of their attachment with their country of origin, instead becoming truly global, stateless actors that adapt their businesses considerably to local cultures and conditions (Babic et al., 2017; Gilpin, 2001; Strange, 1996). However, given that their entry into global markets through FDI has been comparatively recent, Chinese multinationals have yet to achieve such considerable erosion of their association with their country of origin.

Instead, the state-centric perspective, viewing multinational enterprises as products of the history, culture, institutions, values, and ideologies of their country of origin, even when they compete internationally, appears more applicable to Chinese companies. Advocates of this perspective see the multinational enterprise as mirroring its country of origin's economic, social, and political systems. They argue that managers and shareholders of most multinational enterprises are still residents in the country of origin, with financing and R&D still being concentrated there (Doremus, Keller, Pauly, and Reich, 1998; Gilpin, 2001). The nature and characteristics of the country of origin may therefore matter for the nature and extent of political power and influence an investor has in the recipient country. From the state-centric perspective, China's large economy, state capitalist model, authoritarian governance, and distinct culture will project itself onto the international operations of its multinational enterprises, including those investing in European countries.

What is likely to affect the investing company's political role in the recipient country is the extent to which it is under the influence of its home government. Aspects that could raise suspicions are state ownership, strong government intervention domestically, and concrete measures aimed at regulating the overseas investments of companies—all three are widespread in China. China has a vast amount of SOEs, its largest companies and largest international investments are state-owned, and around half of Chinese outward FDI has been made by SOEs (MOFCOM, 2019). The Chinese government has engaged in detailed regulatory intervention in the overseas activities of Chinese firms, including through requirements for approval of overseas investments, easing or tightening of regulatory restrictions, financial support, information and guidance on outward investment, and investment insurance schemes. The primary aim of these measures has been to selectively support those investments that promise to generate beneficial outcomes for China's own economic development and catch-up (Knoerich, 2016a; Luo, Xue, and Han, 2010; Sauvant and Chen, 2014). While these home-country measures have been elaborate in China, it is worth pointing out that many other countries, including advanced industrialized countries, have also adopted various kinds of measures to regulate and promote their outward investors (Sauvant et al., 2014; UNESCAP, 2020). Similarly, while the number and size of SOEs is particularly large in China, many other countries have them as well (Babic et al., 2017). Evidence of governments systematically using these measures and their SOEs to achieve international political aims has yet to surface at a large scale.

A concern often raised specifically with regards to China is the extent to which its government is directly involved in Chinese companies, both state-owned and private. There are claims that no Chinese company could defy orders imposed by Beijing, even when it comes to handing over foreign technologies or sensitive information to the Chinese government. Further ammunition for such concerns has come from the recent introduction of party cells in every enterprise in China (Hornby, 2017). However, there is insufficient concrete evidence of significant state influence over strategic decisions in companies and of Beijing forcing Chinese companies to hand over sensitive information. In 2017, China enacted the National Intelligence Law, which foresees the handing over of data and systems for national security reasons as a possibility, but it is worth noting that the US Clarifying Lawful Overseas Use of Data (CLOUD) Act of 2018 places similar obligations on companies such as Facebook or Twitter (Haskell-Dowland, 2020).

When FDI as an economic activity is used by a government to achieve political and foreign policy objectives, it becomes an instrument of economic statecraft. But certain conditions would need to be met for a government to effectively utilize FDI to achieve political objectives: a state would need to have a certain degree of control over the multinational enterprises to be able to intentionally manipulate their actions, and the activities of the enterprises would need to be effective in generating the political and security externalities envisioned by the government (Norris, 2016). Both are far from guaranteed, as companies, including many SOEs, are independent economic actors that are usually driven by considerations of profitability rather than any political imperative, and the security externalities of interest to a government may be antithetical to the business objectives of an enterprise. Yu confirms this in her chapter to this volume when she suggests that the interests of SOEs do not necessarily align with those of the Party-state. The opaqueness of the Chinese government's role vis-à-vis its enterprises certainly has led to suspicions that it might have the intention to use them for strategic purposes, but concrete evidence is lacking. Accordingly, an in-depth understanding of how FDI is used as an instrument of economic statecraft has yet to emerge in the literature.

The Political Impact of Multinational Enterprises

The political implications of FDI have to date been insufficiently conceptualized and under-theorized. It is certainly possible for multinational enterprises, collectively and individually, to have political impact, and in the following paragraphs I set out to discuss some of the ways in which FDI affects politics. Particularly pertinent, however, are questions that concern the extent of this impact, whether it is positive or negative, and under what circumstances it occurs, and these are aspects I also consider. I focus my analysis on five distinct aspects: structural power, influence, (technological) competition, national security, and soft power.

Structural power

The country that has produced by far the largest number of multinational enterprises and highest amount of FDI is the United States (US). US multinationals dominate in the global economy in a huge variety of sectors and are unlikely soon to be matched by any contenders (Starrs, 2013). Although Chinese outward FDI has been growing fast, its scale is still a fraction of US investments (Knoerich, 2015a). In 2019, the total outward FDI stock of US multinationals had reached 7.7 trillion USD, or 22% of the world total, while the corresponding figures for China were 2.1 trillion USD and 6%, according to UNCTADstat data. In the United Kingdom, US multinationals held almost 600 billion GBP in outward FDI positions as of 2018 and were the leading investors in the country, whereas China ranked twentieth with 9.5 billion GBP in investments (Office for National Statistics, 2020). Data on non-European Union (EU) foreign investments by total assets in EU countries for 2016 similarly indicate that 61.8% accrued to US and Canadian firms, with a mere 3% owned by companies from China, Hong Kong, and Macau (European Commission, 2019).

While states and governments establish the international political context in which companies conduct their business, firms can be actively involved in shaping this context, especially through informal relations between businesses and government (Abdelal, 2013). Their large number and international dominance have privileged US multinationals in their ability to affect political outcomes internationally. They have been able to draw on the support of their home government's hegemonic position, economic diplomacy, and leadership in the international governance of trade and investment. US multinationals have exerted global influence and shaped the structures of the global economy, its international markets, production networks, and financial systems (Babic et al., 2017; Malkin, 2020). Susan Strange referred to such an ability to shape some of the structures of the international political economy as 'structural power', which consists of the capacity to exert control over security, the production of goods and services, the system of finance and credit, and the creation and possession of knowledge (Strange, 1987). It has been argued that multinationals from the United States have enjoyed massive structural power over international production and the system of finance and credit (Malkin, 2020).

US multinationals collectively enjoy structural power thanks to their massive scale and global dominance, and other countries are unlikely to acquire similar powers any time soon at a global level. It might be conceivable that multinationals from countries such as China manage to exert some structural power in confined geographical spaces favourable to China (Malkin, 2020). Roy and Hu have mentioned in their introductory chapter how China attempts to enhance its structural power in South-East Asia. However, this would keep any broader global influence limited. One would need to speculate about a very distant and hypothetical future to imagine a scenario in which Chinese multinationals replace US companies globally in ways that endow them with similar amounts of structural power.

Influence

Although US multinationals are likely to remain globally dominant for an extensive period of time, multinationals from other countries such as China might still be able to exert meaningful influence over some countries where they have a strong presence. A massive amount of inward FDI from one country, such as China, could induce policymakers in the recipient country to alter their approaches to domestic and foreign policy issues, quite possibly in ways that favour the home country's interests. Concerns have been raised especially about the possibility that China might enjoy this kind of influence, because of its unique political characteristics, geopolitical situation, and resultant differences in policy priorities and ambitions (Meunier, Burgoon, and Jacoby, 2014). Taken together, the chapters in this book by Boni, Crawford, Jakimów, Stroikos, and Szunomar offer mixed assessments of the degree of Chinese influence in European countries, even when focusing on broader economic diplomacy and project finance rather than FDI.

In its simplest form, an increase in political influence could result from the intensification of relations between the recipient and home countries that would naturally accompany large-scale FDI inflows. Beyond this, there might be concrete incentives for governments to shift policy directions, when they believe such a move facilitates the attraction of FDI from a specific country. This can be acute when there is a strong need for foreign financing, such as in Europe after the Anglo-American financial crisis of 2008, or it can occur in circumstances where specific domestic constituencies or elites are to benefit from the inflow of capital (Lim and Mukherjee, 2019). Jakimów's chapter in this book describes how Chinese investments promoted an increase of Chinese advisors to politicians in the Visegrad countries, as well as broader interaction between Chinese businesses and politicians in those countries.

Strong international competition for a country's investments could also shift the stance of policymakers. There has certainly been considerable interest and competition for Chinese FDI in European countries (Knoerich and Miedtank, 2018; Knoerich and Vitting, 2018, 2021), which could induce policy actions aimed at appeasing China. The 'Golden Era' between the UK and China, launched under David Cameron to intensify Sino-UK commercial relations and attract more Chinese investment, implicated a friendlier discourse about China in UK policy circles to make the UK China's best partner in the West. At the time of the 'Golden Era', the UK was particularly keen to lead the West in joining China's controversial Asian Infrastructure Investment Bank (Knoerich and Urdinez, 2019).

Another possibility is that governments adapt their domestic laws and regulations to the presence of certain types of investors, such as Chinese multinationals, leading to modifications in the regimes governing the conduct of business (Trinkunas, 2016). There have been fears of the political influence associated with Chinese FDI resulting in the relaxation of labour, environmental, and social standards (Meunier, 2014). Reliable evidence of such a 'race to the bottom' in standards still needs to emerge, however.

While FDI can be accompanied by increased political influence, the actual strength of such influence and leverage remains unknown. FDI can be economically important for countries and specific regions within them, especially when it creates jobs, but the total amounts invested are rarely huge. They usually accumulate to a few billion US dollars annually, which is minute compared to the trillions of dollar transactions made for the purposes of cross-border portfolio investments. Individual large projects in key industries, such as in energy, natural resources, or critical infrastructure, could result in some strong leverage in particular issue areas, especially as projects of such nature tend to require the involvement of governments. Greece's veto in 2017 on a shared EU position towards human rights in China at the United Nations Human Rights Council could be cited as an example, as it followed the acquisition by the China Ocean Shipping Company of a stake in the Piraeus Port (Knoerich and Miedtank, 2018), and other Chinese investments in Greece as discussed in Stroikos's chapter. But to achieve consistent leverage in broad and important areas of domestic or foreign policy, the amounts invested through FDI may be insufficient, especially when taking into account that recipient economies tend to receive FDI from many source countries whose influence may cancel each other out. Even more unusual would be situations in which FDI is used for coercive forms of leverage. All this suggests that outward FDI is a rather less promising avenue for China to exert direct leverage and influence over other countries.

There is a tendency to portray influence and leverage via FDI as something purely negative, though this may not always be justifiable. Whether the outcome is positive or negative may rather depend on the issue and policy that is influenced, and who makes the judgement about the desirability of the policy shift. For example, whether the neoliberal and open-border mentalities spread by US multinationals and their government is something desirable will be judged differently depending on an individual's particular outlook on politics. China's political influence in Western countries is more likely to be viewed as broadly negative, seen to induce less favourable policy outcomes, weaker laws, and lower standards, though an informed judgement would still need to be made about the particular issues at stake.

Competition

FDI has the potential to affect the economic competitiveness of a nation and its technological edge over other countries. Relative economic and technological strengths are guarantors for prosperity and national security, as they endow countries with greater powers in the international system and can be transformed into military capabilities. By its very nature, FDI brings additional capital to a country which, in most cases, is invested in a lasting business activity that can generate employment and economic benefits. Many kinds of FDI bring technologies and know-how to recipient countries for use in production processes or to be sold on host country markets, and in Europe foreign companies often use FDI to invest in R&D. Greenfield investments aimed at establishing a new enterprise such as building a factory or an R&D centre are particularly beneficial as they generate new employment and economic activities. Most FDI should therefore strengthen the competitiveness of a country, and such benefits have been found for many types of Chinese FDI aimed at a lasting economic activity in European countries (Knoerich, 2012; Knoerich and Vitting, 2021). China's Huawei Technologies has, for instance, invested billions in the UK over the past decade in offices and R&D centres and employed thousands of local staff.

Despite these positive political implications, concerns have been raised about the potential of FDI to undermine competition in the recipient country and strip it of technological assets. Such concerns have focused on takeovers of companies in recipient countries, as they do not necessarily generate employment and additional economic activity whilst potentially allowing the acquirer to strip the assets of the firm it acquired and transfer them back to its home country. The pursuit of strategic assets in recipient countries has been a common activity associated with FDI, including by US multinationals in Europe and elsewhere. But the more recent emergence of Chinese multinationals as international investors has brought to the front the concerns about strategic asset-seeking FDI, as China's policies have strategically promoted such FDI to achieve technological catch-up (Knoerich, 2016a). China is the first large non-Western source of global FDI and a strategic competitor to most major FDI recipient countries, including countries in Europe. Its multinationals might try to repatriate technological assets and know-how, including potential dual-use technologies, back to China at the expense of European firms and their economies' competitive advantages (Knoerich, 2015b; Meunier, 2014). Major deals such as Midea's takeover of German industrial robot manufacturer KUKA or ChemChina's acquisition of Swiss pharmaceutical company Syngenta, both in 2017, have raised concerns about the negative implications of such takeovers. The response by European governments and the European Commission was to tighten procedures for screening non-EU investments.

But there is insufficient concrete evidence overall of the suspected negative implications occurring at a significant scale. While know-how transfer after acquisitions often forms part of ordinary business activities by Chinese, US, and other multinationals, Chinese multinationals are actually known to leave the companies they acquire in Europe untouched and in the hands of local management, and even aim to improve the performance of their target companies (Knoerich, 2010, 2016b). Magnitudes of Chinese acquisitions in Europe also remain comparatively modest. In 2017, just 6.5% of non-EU mergers and acquisitions (M&A) in the EU were from China, Hong Kong, and Macau, with almost half (46.4%) undertaken by US and Canadian firms (European Commission, 2019).

What cannot be ruled out is the possibility that outward FDI, even just through the profits made from doing business in Europe and the R&D activities by Chinese companies on European soil, will over time help strengthen Chinese multinationals and the Chinese economy. But outward FDI will unlikely be the main factor enabling China to leapfrog in its economic and technological development—domestic factors in China, such as inward FDI, economic policies, and innovation performance, are much more pertinent.

National security

Some types of FDI, especially those in sensitive sectors and critical infrastructure, are a potential threat to national security or public order, a concern that is elevated if the investing multinational comes from a non-allied country, a strategic competitor, or a potentially hostile state. For most countries in the West and Europe, China has been viewed in those terms, and Chinese investments have had to endure above-average scrutiny for national security threats. Investment screening has been tightened in many countries, including European countries, to improve the assessment of potential security implications of takeovers by firms from China and elsewhere.

There are various ways in which an investment might impact national security. A foreign presence of a company might facilitate a home country's commercial and government espionage, surveillance, and intelligence gathering in the recipient country. Expatriates posted from the home country could function as spies, and investments in information and communication (ICT) technologies, such as those by Huawei Technologies in Europe, could become vehicles to transfer private and confidential information into Chinese hands (Knoerich, 2015b). Chinese social media applications hold sensitive data of consumers in the US and Europe which might not be safe from the tentacles of the Chinese Communist Party. For this reason, the short video app TikTok, which has millions of users in the United States, was targeted by US President Donald Trump in 2020, and Beijing Kunlun Tech was forced in 2019 to resell the gay dating app Grindr, which it had purchased in 2016–2018. The video surveillance technologies produced by Hikvision, a Chinese firm with investments globally, have been scrutinized for similar privacy concerns.

Investments that are sited near strategic locations have also aroused suspicions. The attempted purchase in 2011 of land in Iceland (close to the strategically important Arctic region) by Chinese investor Huang Nubo, and Ralls Corporation's unsuccessful purchase in 2012 of four wind farms close to a military site in Oregon, United States, are two examples. Similarly, the construction and operation by two Chinese companies of a space monitoring station in Argentina, seen to be located in a strategically opportune location, raised concerns about its potential misuse for military purposes, but was eventually approved (Urdinez, Knoerich, Ribeiro, 2018).

Beyond surveillance, intelligence gathering, and espionage, investments in some sectors can result in a foreign company's control over parts of a country's critical infrastructure, opening up the possibility of foreign powers sabotaging associated equipment for military purposes. In sectors such as the nuclear industry, where safety is paramount and reliability of services provision needs to be guaranteed, ownership by a company from a strategic competitor or potentially hostile state could increase the risk of foreign interference and reduce national security. These issues were under consideration in 2016 when British Prime Minister Theresa May re-evaluated the minority participation by the China General Nuclear Power Group in constructing and operating the UK's Hinkley Point C nuclear power plant in Somerset, before eventually approving it. Telecommunications infrastructure and chips could also be tampered with to interfere with or undermine vital communications systems needed for the basic functioning of societies, which explains Huawei's frequent difficulties in many European countries. Concerns about the use of investments for military purposes have also been raised about Chinese purchases of German airports, such as the Frankfurt Hahn airport, though the risks have been considered manageable (Cristiani, Ohlberg, Parello-Plesner, and Small, 2021).

Overall, the number of investments associated with such threats is low, even if the amount of capital can be substantial in individual cases. Often, the security threat refers to a remote possibility (such as blowing up a nuclear power plant) and would unlikely be realized at a large scale without major war ensuing. In fact, economic exchanges have the potential to promote peace (Copeland, 2015), and so could the economic interdependence resulting from Chinese FDI. The stakes for the Chinese of any major conflict with a country in which its multinationals are strongly invested would also be high, as it would put these investments and its citizens in the recipient country at risk (Knoerich, 2015b).

Soft power

FDI can become a vehicle to enhance a country's soft power, that is, its ability to shape the preferences of others through attraction, persuasion, and seduction (Nye, 2004), with potential implications for political views and actions among people and politicians in the recipient country. Through the establishment of its foreign subsidiary, FDI puts in place conditions that foster economic integration, strengthen partnerships, and contribute to the home country's image. The positive impact FDI can have on the economy and employment in recipient countries can create much goodwill and lay the foundation for mutually beneficial long-term economic partnerships. Philanthropic engagements by the investor in the recipient countries could further enhance the home country's positive image, as could its advertisements and commercials. The recipient country's political elite might support investments with positive messaging, especially if the home state is a large source of foreign investment. At the same time, FDI can also have negative implications (for example, laying off employees, closing down factories, or even involving illicit activities) and lead to conflicts in an investor's relationships with project partners, employees, and other local stakeholders. The result could be negative perceptions of the country from where the investments originate. In Europe, a mix of such positive and negative sentiments about Chinese investments is observable among policymakers, the media, companies and their employees, and other stakeholders (Knoerich and Vitting, 2018). Thus, FDI can strengthen or weaken a country's image and soft power. Chinese investments in many places have contributed to a positive image of China, though the Chinese government has been keen to monitor the overseas operations of its multinationals to prevent them from engaging in activities that harm China's reputation (Morgan, 2019).

An extreme case in which country image and FDI can help project soft power is a situation where the economic properties of a country and its multinationals offer inspiring examples to emulate, and governments in countries receiving these multinationals' investments become inclined to follow the economic and potentially even political approaches of the investors' home country (Lim and Mukherjee, 2019). This could at times have applied to US multinationals, which have successfully exported US business practices and functioned as ambassadors of shareholder capitalism. Recently, the Chinese government has become more confident in promoting its own 'wisdom' on how to develop and prosper, amid rising international interest in China's experience of successful economic development, especially among developing countries (Goodburn and Knoerich, 2021; Knoerich, Mouan, and Goodburn, 2021; Jiang, 2019). Yet, China and its multinationals are still far from being considered a major model to emulate and are especially not viewed in this way in Europe.

At a more individual level, FDI enables and facilitates the interaction and mutual exchanges between people, managers, personnel, business partners, and other relevant stakeholders from the home and recipient countries. Sometimes exchanges among personnel are specifically cultivated, as has happened in Chinese acquisitions in Germany and the United Kingdom (Liu and Meyer, 2020). As such exchanges happen over a long period of time, they fuel mutual understanding and engagement, though conflicts could also emerge that spur resentment. Ultimately, these relationships can function as platforms to exchange values, perspectives, and political views. The exchanges are bi-directional processes in which each side has some influence on the other and both sides get to know each other better. For example, Chinese expatriates and workers might share their perspectives in Europe while Europeans explain their own values and viewpoints to the Chinese. Multiple factors can influence the nature of these exchanges, such as hierarchies among people, the identities of individuals, the number of people involved in conversations, and the location of the exchanges. An exchange of thoughts will be different when it occurs in the European subsidiary or the Chinese parent company. Managers and leaders in a company will have a stronger voice when sharing opinions than employees. The result could be an enhancement of China's soft power in Europe by influencing the hearts and minds of Europeans; at the same time, the Chinese side will be influenced as a result of its integration with a European subsidiary. The net outcome of such interactions is unknown and subject to speculation (Knoerich, 2015b).

Specific sectors may also provide favourable conditions for expansion of a foreign country's soft power through FDI. A good example are media investments channelling messages in line with the perspectives of the home country to consumers in order to influence their opinions. The China Global

Television Network (CGTN), the international arm of state-owned China Central Television that is seen as a mouthpiece for the Chinese Communist Party, has opened regional offices in Chiswick Park, London, as well as in Nairobi and Washington, D.C. Due to concerns about its political messaging, the US Department of Justice issued a letter in late 2018 ordering the company to register under the Foreign Agents Registration Act (FARA) as an agent working for a foreign principal. In February 2021, the UK media regulator Ofcom also temporarily revoked CGTN's right to broadcast in the country, due to concerns that the TV news service channel was editorially controlled by the Chinese Communist Party (Nilsson, 2021). These kinds of situations are likely only to emerge in a few specific sectors that have the necessary properties to facilitate Chinese soft power. Services FDI should be more susceptible to be used for this purpose.

In sum, FDI provides China with avenues to increase its soft power in recipient countries, yet there appear to be many limitations. Investments are unlikely the main aspect that determines a country's image elsewhere, and people tend to be subject to a cacophony of different messages from numerous sources. FDI might even contribute to a negative image of China, or the Chinese might themselves become subject to recipient country influences.

Conclusions: Implications for the Liberal International Order

To return to the main theme of this book, what, then, are the implications of China's growing outward FDI for the Liberal International Order? As was already specified at the beginning of this volume, the Liberal International Order refers to an open, rules-based, and progressive international regime. It involves a system promoting economic openness (in particular for trade), international cooperation, especially through multilateral institutions, and the global spread of liberal values and institutions, such as human rights, representative democracy, and the rule of law. This is an international order built under the hegemonic leadership of the United States in close partnership with its allies (Ikenberry, 2012, 2018; Stephen and Skidmore, 2019). Despite not having been a partner in building this order, China embraces many of its rules-based and economic openness elements, though it still allows itself some flexibility to advance its own industrial policies. It has an ambivalent approach to the multinational institutions created by the Western powers, though as Jones argues in her chapter, China could also be seen as filling some gaps in the existing system. What China rejects outright is the commitment to political principles such as liberal values and democratization (Malkin, 2020).

FDI feeds on the economic openness component of the Liberal International Order, and China's support for the internationalization of its multinationals is testament to its endorsement of this component, although China does exhibit some tendencies to regulate and control outward FDI. Another indicator of its commitment to the economic openness component is China's position as one of the top three signatories of international investment treaties in the world (according to UNCTAD's investment policy hub) and its growing ambition to incorporate more liberal provisions in its investment treaties. This includes the conclusion of the EU-China Comprehensive Agreement on Investment in late 2020 (which, however, has yet to be ratified).

Nevertheless, outward FDI may still be a vehicle for strengthening China's political leverage, possibly aimed at influencing other countries and the institutions of the Liberal International Order as well as building up a protective bulwark against efforts to transfer liberal values and democratization to China. This chapter has outlined various avenues of potential political impact in recipient countries, yet it also acknowledged numerous limitations in the extent to which Chinese multinationals effectively influence politics in those countries.

Historically, the Liberal International Order has both facilitated the global spread of US multinationals and been a product of their structural power. For Chinese multinationals to influence the prevailing order at a large scale, they would need to acquire considerable structural power themselves, yet Chinese multinationals are unlikely to match the dominance of US companies or even surpass them any time soon. This limits their ability to collectively mount any meaningful challenge to the Liberal International Order. At a more modest level, outward FDI could aid China in expanding its political influence over specific other countries and their leaders. This is certainly possible when the aim is to achieve specific objectives in a few issue areas, but to enjoy consistent leverage in broad and important areas of domestic or foreign policy, the amounts invested through FDI in any particular country may still be insufficient. In the areas of competitive catch-up, national security, and soft power, outward FDI can help expand China's political influence, yet here as well many limitations present themselves when it comes to big political ambitions and changes to the prevailing international system. In sum, each of the five dimensions outlined in this chapter are interesting and noteworthy as avenues of political influence, yet outward FDI cannot be considered as a particularly suitable economic activity to support a challenge of the Liberal International Order.

The political dimension of FDI might not only have negative implications, but may well yield positive outcomes for recipient countries. Chinese FDI might contribute to the competitiveness of both China and the recipient countries, can promote peace but occasionally be a risk to national security, and might channel political influence in both directions between the recipient country and China. The ultimate balance on these matters has yet to be determined.

While this chapter concludes that outward FDI is not a particularly promising instrument to mount a challenge to the Liberal International Order (should China wish to do this), other types of investments or economic and political activities emanating from China may well pose more substantial threats to Europe and the international order. The purpose of this chapter was to delineate the particular role played by FDI as a specific type of investment and international economic activity, excluding project finance and ignoring other aspects, some of which are covered in other chapters of this volume. The way things currently look, it might not even need China to take down the Liberal International Order. The rise of populism within the birthplaces of the Liberal International Order itself—Britain and the United States—is itself a threat to this order from within (Fukuyama and Muggah, 2018; Mearsheimer, 2019; Patman, 2019).

No matter what the future brings in international politics, one issue this chapter has clearly demonstrated is the need for further in-depth research on the political impacts of FDI. This includes theoretical and conceptual development of the political and security dimensions of FDI, and concrete empirical research to detect and measure its political impact, possibly with reference to each of the five aspects examined in this chapter. Such research could focus on Chinese outward FDI, although studies of other countries would be of equal value, as there is a general knowledge deficit on the political and security dimensions of FDI that requires urgent scholarly attention.

Bibliography

Abdelal, R. 2013. 'The Profits of Power: Commerce and Realpolitik in Eurasia'. *Review of International Political Economy* 20 (3): pp. 421–456.

Babic, M., J. Fichtner, and E. M. Heemskerk. 2017. 'States versus Corporations: Rethinking the Power of Business in International Politics'. *The International Spectator*, 52 (4): pp. 20–43.

Benabdallah, L. 2019. 'Contesting the International Order by Integrating It: The Case of China's Belt and Road Initiative'. *Third World Quarterly* 40 (1): pp. 92–108.

Bhattacharya, A. 2016. 'Conceptualizing the Silk Road Initiative in China's Periphery Policy'. *East Asia* 33 (4): pp. 309–328.

Breuer, A., and A. I. Johnston. 2019. 'Memes, Narratives and the Emergent US–China Security Dilemma'. *Cambridge Review of International Affairs* 32 (4): pp. 429–455.

Brinza, A. 2020. 'China and the Budapest-Belgrade Railway Saga'. *The Diplomat*, 28 April.

Callahan, W. A. 2016. 'China's Belt and Road Initiative and the New Eurasian Order'. Policy Brief 22/2016. Norwegian Institute of International Affairs.

Copeland, D. C. 2015. *Economic Interdependence and War*. Princeton: Princeton University Press.

Cristiani, D., M. Ohlberg, J. Parello-Plesner, and A. Small. 2021. 'The Security Implications of Chinese Infrastructure Investment in Europe'. The German Marshall Fund of the United States Report. September 2021.

European Commission. 2019. Commission Staff Working Document on Foreign Direct Investment in the EU: Following up on the Commission Communication 'Welcoming Foreign Direct Investment while Protecting Essential Interests' of 13 September 2017. Brussels, 13 March.

de Graaff, N., T. ten Brink, and I. Parmar. 2020. 'China's Rise in a Liberal World Order in Transition—Introduction to The FORUM'. *Review of International Political Economy* 27 (2): pp. 191–207.

Doremus, P. N., W. W. Keller, L. W. Pauly, and S. Reich. 1998. *The Myth of the Global Corporation*. Princeton: Princeton University Press.

Fallon, T. 2015. 'The New Silk Road: Xi Jinping's Grand Strategy for Eurasia'. *American Foreign Policy Interests* 37 (3): pp. 140–147.

Fasslabend, W. 2015. 'The Silk Road: A Political Marketing Concept for World Dominance'. *European View* 14 (2): pp. 293–302.

Fukuyama, F., and R. Muggah. 2018. 'How Populism Is Poisoning the Global Liberal Order'. *World Economic Forum*, 6 February.

Gilpin, R. 2001. *Global Political Economy: Understanding the International Economic Order*. Princeton, NJ: Princeton University Press.

Goodburn, C., and J. Knoerich. 2021. 'Importing Export Zones: Processes and Impacts of Replicating a Chinese Model of Urbanization in Rural South India'. *Urban Geography* 43 (10): pp. 1496–1518.

Haskell-Dowland, P. 2020. 'A Storm In a Tiktok'. *East Asia Forum*, 30 August.

Hopkins, V. 2021. 'Montenegro Calls for EU Help Over $1bn Chinese Highway Loan'. *Financial Times*, 11 April.

Hornby, L. 2017. 'Communist Party Asserts Control Over China Inc'. *Financial Times*, 3 October.

Ikenberry, G. J. 2012. *Liberal Leviathan: The Origins, Crisis, and Transformation of the American World Order*. Princeton: Princeton University Press.

Ikenberry, G. J. 2018. 'The End of Liberal International Order?'. *International Affairs* 94 (1): pp. 7–23.

Jiang, Y. 2019. 'Chinese Wisdom: New Norms for Development and Global Governance'. In *China's 19th Party Congress: Start of a New Era*, edited by K. Brown, pp. 177–203. London: World Scientific Publishing Europe.

Jones, L., and J. Zeng. 2019. 'Understanding China's "Belt and Road Initiative": Beyond "Grand Strategy" to a State Transformation Analysis'. *Third World Quarterly* 40 (8): pp. 1415–1439.

Knoerich, J. 2010. 'Gaining from the Global Ambitions of Emerging Economy Enterprises: An Analysis of the Decision to Sell a German Firm to a Chinese Acquirer'. *Journal of International Management* 16 (2): pp. 177–191.

Knoerich, J. 2012. 'The Rise of Chinese OFDI in Europe'. In *Chinese International Investments*, edited by I. Alon, M. Fetscherin, and P. Gugler, pp. 175–211. Basingstoke: Palgrave Macmillan.

Knoerich, J. 2015a. 'China's Outward Investment Surge'. In *World Scientific Reference on Globalisation in Eurasia and the Pacific Rim—Volume 1: Foreign Investment*, edited by D. A. Dyker, pp. 273–298. Singapore: World Scientific Publishing.

Knoerich, J. 2015b. 'The Role of High Technology in Mainland China's Outward Investment into Taiwan: Economic, Security and Cultural Dimensions'. In *Cross-Taiwan Strait Relations in an Era of Technological Change: Security, Economic and Cultural Dimensions*, edited by P. I. Crookes and J. Knoerich, pp. 96–117. London: Palgrave Macmillan UK.

Knoerich, J. 2016a. 'Has Outward Foreign Direct Investment Contributed to the Development of the Chinese Economy?' *Transnational Corporations* 23 (2): pp. 1–48.

Knoerich, J. 2016b. 'Why Some Advanced Economy Firms Prefer to Be Taken Over by Chinese Acquirers'. Columbia FDI Perspectives, No. 187, 21 November 2016.

Knoerich, J., and T. Miedtank. 2018. 'The Idiosyncratic Nature of Chinese Foreign Direct Investment in Europe'. *CESifo Forum* 19 (4): pp. 3–8.

Knoerich, J., L. Mouan, and C. Goodburn. 2021. 'Is China's Model of SEZ-Led Development Viable? A Call for Smart Replication'. *Journal of Current Chinese Affairs* 50 (2): pp. 248–262.

Knoerich, J., and F. Urdinez. 2019. 'Contesting Contested Multilateralism: Why the West Joined the Rest in Founding the Asian Infrastructure Investment Bank'. *The Chinese Journal of International Politics* 12 (3): pp. 333–370.

Knoerich, J., and S. Vitting. 2018. 'Controversies and Contradictions about Chinese Investments in Europe'. *EuropeNow* 18.

Knoerich, J., and S. Vitting. 2021. 'The Distinct Contribution of Investment Promotion Agencies' Branch Offices in Bringing Chinese Multinationals to Europe'. *Journal of World Business* 56 (3): 101187.

Leverett, F., and B. Wu. 2016. 'The New Silk Road and China's Evolving Grand Strategy'. *The China Journal* 77: pp. 110–132.

Lim, D. J., and R. Mukherjee. 2019. 'What Money Can't Buy: The Security Externalities of Chinese Economic Statecraft in Post-War Sri Lanka'. *Asian Security* 15 (2): pp. 73–92.

Liu, Y., and K. Meyer. 2020. 'Boundary Spanners, HRM Practices, and Reverse Knowledge Transfer: The Case of Chinese Cross-Border Acquisitions'. *Journal of World Business* 55 (2): 100958.

Luo, Y., Q. Xue, and B. Han. 2010. 'How Emerging Market Governments Promote Outward FDI: Experience from China'. *Journal of World Business* 45 (1): pp. 68–79.

Malkin, A. 2020. 'Challenging the Liberal International Order by Chipping Away at US Structural Power: China's State-Guided Investment in Technology and Finance in Russia'. *Cambridge Review of International Affairs* 33 (1): pp. 81–104.

Mearsheimer, J. 2019. 'Bound to Fail: The Rise and Fall of the Liberal International Order'. *International Security* 43 (4): pp. 7–50.

Meunier, S. 2014. 'Divide and Conquer? China and the Cacophony of Foreign Investment Rules in the EU'. *Journal of European Public Policy* 21 (7): pp. 996–1016.

Meunier, S., B. Burgoon, and W. Jacoby. 2014. 'The Politics of Hosting Chinese Investment in Europe—An Introduction'. *Asia Europe Journal* 12 (1): pp. 109–126.

MOFCOM. 2019. *2018 Statistical Bulletin of China's Outward Foreign Direct Investment*. Beijing: China Commerce and Trade Press.

Morgan, P. 2019. 'Can China's Economic Statecraft Win Soft Power in Africa? Unpacking Trade, Investment and Aid'. *Journal of Chinese Political Science* 24 (3): pp. 387–409.

Nilsson, P. 2021. 'Chinese State Broadcaster Regains Right to Broadcast in the UK'. *Financial Times*, 9 April.

Norris, W. J. 2016. *Chinese Economic Statecraft: Commercial Actors, Grand Strategy and State Control*. Ithaca and London: Cornell University Press.

Nye, J. 2004. *Soft Power: The Means to Success in World Politics*. Cambridge, MA: Public Affairs.

OECD. 2008. *OECD Benchmark Definition of Foreign Direct Investment*. Paris: Organisation for Economic Co-operation and Development.

ONS. 2020. *UK Foreign Direct Investment, Trends and Analysis: August 2020*. Office for National Statistics, 3 August.

Patman, R. 2019. 'The Liberal International Order and Its Populist Adversaries in Russia, UK and USA'. In *Populism and World Politics: Exploring Inter- and*

Transnational Dimensions, edited by F. Stengel, D. MacDonald, and D. Nabers, pp. 277–303. Cham: Palgrave Macmillan.

Sauvant, K. P., and V. Z. Chen. 2014. 'China's Regulatory Framework for Outward Foreign Direct Investment'. *China Economic Journal* 7 (1): pp. 141–163.

Sauvant, K. P., P. Economou, K. Gal, S. W. Lim, and W. Wilinski. 2014. 'Trends In FDI, Home Country Measures and Competitive Neutrality'. In *Yearbook on International Investment Law & Policy 2012–2013*, edited by A. K. Bjorklund, pp. 3–107. New York: Oxford University Press.

Starrs, S. 2013. 'American Economic Power Hasn't Declined—It Globalized! Summoning the Data and Taking Globalization Seriously'. *International Studies Quarterly* 57 (4): pp. 817–830.

Stephen, M. D., and D. Skidmore. 2019. 'The AIIB in the Liberal International Order'. *The Chinese Journal of International Politics* 12 (1): pp. 61–91.

Strange, S. 1987. 'The Persistent Myth of Lost Hegemony'. *International Organization* 41 (4): pp. 551–574.

Strange, S. 1996. *The Retreat of the State: The Diffusion of Power in the World Economy*. Cambridge: Cambridge University Press.

Trinkunas, H. 2016. 'Renminbi Diplomacy? The Limits of China's Influence On Latin America's Domestic Politics'. *Geoeconomics and Global Issues*, Paper 3, The Brookings Institution.

UNCTAD. 2010. *World Investment Report 2010: Investing in a Low-Carbon Economy*. New York and Geneva: United Nations.

UNCTAD. 2019. *World Investment Report 2019: Special Economic Zones*. Geneva: United Nations.

UNESCAP. 2020. *Outward Foreign Direct Investment and Home Country Sustainable Development*. Studies in Trade, Investment and Innovation, 93. Bangkok: United Nations.

Urdinez, F., J. Knoerich, and P. F. Ribeiro. 2018. 'Don't Cry for Me "Argenchina": Unraveling Political Views of China Through Legislative Debates in Argentina'. *Journal of Chinese Political Science* 23 (2): pp. 235–256.

Wu, X. 2018. 'China in Search of a Liberal Partnership International Order'. *International Affairs* 94 (5): pp. 995–1018.

10

Catalyst for Stasis?

China's Engagement with Developing States and its Influence on International Development Assistance

Catherine Jones

Introduction

This volume considers China's influence in Europe through its economic investments. In this chapter, I argue that this influence is evident not only in how China directly engages with states within Europe, but that China's engagement with the international development architecture and its investments in developing states also produces effects—tantamount to influence—in Europe.

China's role in providing aid and infrastructure assistance continues to attract attention and scholarship. China's engagement with developing states, particularly in Africa, has been seen as being instrumental in the People's Republic of China (PRC, hereafter China) gaining the UN Security Council seat from the Republic of China (hereafter Taiwan) in 1971. More recently, attention has been focused on China's creation of and engagement in formal multilateral forms of development and infrastructure assistance.

The debates on how China engages with existing international trade and financial institutions and practices have been broadly considered in terms of rule-breaking, rule-making, or rule-changing (see, for example, Lee, Chan, and Chan, 2012; Hopewell, 2015: 327–332; Wang, 2017). More recent scholarship in this area has further refined these categorizations, highlighting the role China plays in shaping practices from outside institutions (Hopewell, 2019).

In the context of this book China's demonstrated agency in creating changes to the broader aid and investment architecture is particularly relevant. China remains outside the Organisation for Economic Cooperation on Development–Development Assistance Committee (OECD–DAC) countries, but it has an effect on the decisions they make. In this regard, this

Catherine Jones, *Catalyst for Stasis?*. In: *Rising Power, Limited Influence.* Edited by: Indrajit Roy, Jappe Eckhardt, Dimitrios Stroikos, and Simona Davidescu, Oxford University Press. © Oxford University Press (2024).
DOI: 10.1093/oso/9780192887115.003.0011

chapter considers influence to come in different forms: direct and indirect. Other chapters of this volume assess the direct forms of influence that China has by acting in or with European states. This chapter instead considers how Chinese investments in the developing world have consequences in Europe and therefore generate indirect Chinese influence.

Significantly for this volume, this shaping happens in two political locations: through China's actions in partnership with the aid recipient, and through China's engagement with European partners in investments in Europe where lessons from aid practices and Foreign Direct Investment (FDI) in low-income states are being attempted to be replicated at the same time the EU and its member states seek to learn from the demonstrated practices of China in its aid engagement and apply lessons learned to their own agreements with China. As a result, understanding the role China plays in aid and investment in developing countries is essential underpinning work in understanding relationships between China and Europe in investment, particularly in relation to the Belt and Road Initiative (BRI).

Background

Understandings of China's approach to international development have broadly fallen into two arguments. On the one hand, China is clearly striving to be an agenda-setter—at least in Asia, and potentially further afield (Ekman, 2015: 4). In the development space this ability to set the agenda has been widely acknowledged. As far back as 2011, then UK development secretary Andrew Mitchell stated, 'Chinese investors, Brazilian social entrepreneurs and Indian bloggers now rival Oxford and Oxfam in setting the development agenda' (Mitchell, 2011; see also Jones, 2019). As a result, China's entry as a significant development actor has been seen as shaping and setting a (new) development agenda for over a decade. According to these arguments, China is a challenger to the existing architecture.

On the other hand, a smaller group of scholars (Jones, 2019; Loke, 2018) and commentators make the argument that China may be instrumental in modifying what already exists within established development architectures and is creating parallel complementary approaches. China in this sense is a modifier. This characterization, then, draws on the debate indicated above regarding China as a rule-breaker, maker, or changer (Lee, Chan, and Chan, 2012).

At the intersection of these two sets of arguments lies the example of the Asian Investment Infrastructure Bank (AIIB) and other Chinese-inspired multilateral institutions. The creation of the AIIB, the New Development Bank (NDB), and the Belt and Road Initiative (BRI—formerly known as One Belt, One Road—OBOR) has further spurred discussion and analyses that argue that China is challenging the current aid architecture which has been dominated by Western powers through the Organisation for Economic Cooperation and Development (OECD), guided by the Development Assistance Committee (DAC), and engagement with the Bretton Woods institutions (see, for example, Hameri and Jones, 2018; Liao, 2015; Peng and Tok, 2016; Reisen, 2015; Ren, 2016; Stephen and Skidmore, 2019). This chapter makes a distinction: the aid architecture is being challenged, China is a key development actor, but that does not mean China is challenging the existing liberal order of development.

Within these analyses there is an excellent focus on how the AIIB and other Chinese-led institutions arise from frustrations with the Western liberal approach to development (for example, Liao, 2015), and although there is a common observation that the inspiration for creating these new China-centric approaches was this frustration, it is also becoming clear that—at least in the first years of existence—the functional operations of these new approaches mimic the existing banks (Hameri and Jones, 2018; Wilson, 2019).

The quality of the empirical work across these articles is not in dispute. What is missing from these analyses is a common framework to assess the nature or scope of the challenge that China's actions present. For example, Beverley Loke (2019) argues that China is not seeking to challenge US hegemony or the Liberal International Order wholesale, but rather to be recognized as being central, whereas Stephen and Skidmore argue that 'the AIIB stands in a relationship of *partial accommodation and partial challenge* to the LIO' (2019: 65, emphasis in the original).

As a result, we have a collection of literatures all seeking to understand China's role in international aid provision and its functional contribution to enhancing infrastructure. But, within this broad objective we have several foci: What is China functionally doing? What does China want to achieve politically? Is China a challenge to Western or liberal aid provision? Is China actively seeking to challenge or undermine the effectiveness of aid provision by other actors?

In the introduction to this volume, Hu and Roy set out a clear framework for understanding here. In particular, they outline that China's power may be conceptualized as being resource based or influence based. They note also the significance of intentionality, that China's power—demonstrated through its investments—produces consequences, but not all of these consequences may be intended. Hence, it is not straightforward to claim that because China has produced a consequence (in European states approaches to investment in the developing world) this was China's intention. Similarly, Hu and Roy point out that influence does not infer there is a conflict of interests. Although, it should be noted that identifying influence is methodologically more straightforward when such a conflict exists. This element of influence is developed in this chapter by arguing that China's presence as a development actor has catalysed actions that European states and development scholars had already identified as being necessary. Hence, China's influence here was to accelerate a process, rather than change its direction.

This chapter seeks to engage with this debate on the nature and objective of China's role in aid and infrastructure and does so by framing it in terms of whether China is challenging the status quo of development assistance. It presents a new schema for analysis, dividing out different types of challenge that China could instigate, but it also seeks to reflect that how China integrates its approaches within the existing architecture is affected by the architecture as well as by China's actions. Hence our analyses need to take into account that both cogs are turning, not just one.

In this context, the argument is made that through these developments China is a catalyst for a form of stasis. In making this argument a differentiation is made that this 'stasis' is premised on an understanding that the liberal international aid architecture is always evolving, it needs to adjust for lessons learnt, to new opportunities and new ideas. Hence, rather than understanding the liberal order as an entity with fixed contents and institutions, it is an organism of practices and norms that change incrementally in response to a variety of inputs. It therefore is not a static constant entity, but one that is constantly adjusting.

China's role in this adjustment is to change the tempo (both in terms of speed of change and intensity of input) of adjustments in some directions, but also to fill in gaps that emerge in this architecture—importantly gaps that would otherwise have to be filled by liberal or Western actors and that hamper a range of concerted development activities. For example, in providing support for education (particularly of women and girls) in schools, there is a created gap in further, higher, and tertiary education provision, and this created gap is partially filled by China's approach to scholarships for degrees. This provision by China allows and facilitates other actors to continue to focus on school education. In essence, China has enabled liberal development actors to continue their agenda, although they may also adjust what they are doing in light of additional provision. This in essence means China's presence as a development actor provides evidence of gradual incremental innovation that is generated by other aid actors responding to China's presence rather than these changes being caused by China. But, China's presence is not solely in a 'filling' capacity. In the places we see innovation and change, non-status approaches are the result of China's presence widening existing fractures or fissures in global consensus in aid, rather than radically overhauling the OECD-DAC/Bretton Woods approach. I argue that understanding the places where China maintains the status quo, or widens existing fissures, is essential in understanding the relationship to Europe in terms of investment.

In developing this argument, the chapter separates out different ways of 'seeing' China's challenge and maps this to different identification of 'causes': passive, permissive, catalytic, entrepreneurial. The chapter then explores the implication that, if a challenge is being created, it is necessarily normatively bad. This chapter makes the argument that the presence of China as a trigger for change (or an input for incremental adjustment) may actually benefit and force specialization, improvements, re-evaluation, and new approaches within the existing aid architecture, rather than posing a destructive challenge to it.

China As a Challenge to International Aid Praxis

There have been three distinct phases or focal points in the debate on China's engagement with the international aid architecture. The first phase was centred on China's relations with states, particularly those who could help China to achieve its objective of claiming the seat in the United Nations Security Council,. Subsequently, this discussion of China's engagement with African states has both deepened and become more specific. See, for example, Alden (2007); Brautigam (1998, 2011); Dent (2011); and Taylor (2009, 2011).

The second phase or grouping of China's aid engagement was to focus on China's perceived challenge to or ability to sustain the international aid architecture and particularly the aid practices of the Bretton Woods system (Goldstein and Lardy, 2005; Wang, 2015; Wu, 2018). China's engagement with the Bretton Woods institutions encompasses a huge range of topics and almost all of them court controversy. For example, China's currency pegging, changing World Bank and IMF voting shares, and WTO membership have all risen to the fore in gaining international attention. At least in part there is a concern that China will challenge or compete with the practices and approaches of these institutions, by providing and provoking an alternative to the rules of global governance (see Wu, 2018).

The final—but related—aspect of China's engagement with the development architecture is in its development of challenger institutions—the BRI and the AIIB. From the debates on China's challenge to the Bretton Woods and OECD aid architecture, it is not only that China challenges in bilateral ways, but that China institutionalized its alternative to the existing frameworks, objectives, and definitions of development (Jones, 2019: 258).

The World Bank is operating in a world of increasing diversity of actors; it is not only new powers as individual agents that contribute to this multiplicity, but also the manner of their engagement with each other, and the importance of regional approaches to development (Subacchi, 2008). As noted by Sophie Harman and David Williams (2014), the World Bank is increasingly concerned about the rise of regional fledged development actors. Among these competing actors are the new BRICS bank or New Development bank (Bracht, 2013; Trevisani, 2013), the AIIB, and the BRI.

Within these debates it is common for China to be presented as a challenger or a changer of the existing development architecture (see for example Mawdsley, 2007). Moreover, it is presented or implied that China's engagement is a normative bad. These conclusions contain three important assumptions. First, that China does something substantively different in terms of the aid it provides. Second, that what it does is unwelcome, unhelpful, or contrary to the existing approaches adopted by the OEDC–DAC states. Third, it assumes the aid architecture and its approach is in stasis rather than evolving in response to new approaches, critiques, and challenges. However, this form of argument is being increasingly challenged, and scholars including Wang (2017) and Wu (2018) increasingly indicate that China's role is more nuanced, supporting the continuation of some aspects of global financial institutions but reforming or rebalancing others.

Is China's approach different?

A fundamental recurring theme of these debates revolves around the question 'how different is China?' Particularly concerning the so called Beijing Consensus (Halper, 2010; Peerenboom, 2007; Ramo, 2004) or China model (Breslin, 2011; Zhao, 2010), there are claims that 'The Chinese have subsequently walked through an open door with an alternative philosophy that makes few demands on the internal root and branch of client states' (Halper, 2010: 36; see also Jones, 2019).

This argument makes three assumptions about China's approach: (1) China has an alternative philosophy or teleology of what counts as development; (2) that the liberal order states make no demands of client states; and (3) that there were already weakness and problems in the aid architectures and practices (for a longer discussion see, Jones, 2019: part 3). The first two parts of this argument are supported in the literature on China's new institutionalized approach to aid and investment. As Liao puts it: 'In fact, the AIIB's Articles of Agreement have remarkably similar (and broad) operating guidelines to banks within the Bretton Woods framework, but bar members from influencing political affairs' (2015). Wang (2015: 4) puts it more starkly, positioning the role of the AIIB as neither revolution nor affirmation: 'the AIIB does not constitute a new Bretton Woods moment or a total triumph for China in the broad sense'. Other authors adopt a similar approach in considering the 'coherence' of China's approach with other approaches to development finance and identifying that scholars have overemphasized the challenge that rising powers present (Heldt and Schmidtke, 2019: 1180). A crucial nuanced point here is that the challenge or the change that China does present is that whereas China's approach doesn't seek political influence, it does place longer-term economic demands on states.

The third element is of particular interest as it suggests that rather than China having a deliberate intention or agency over change or at least the most feasible, there were pre-existing issues that have made China's approach appealing. In consequence, it is not necessary for China to have an alternative guiding philosophy to be 'distinct and different' in how it enacts its aid policies—it just needs to do different things. If this is the case, it should affect how we conceptualize China as a development actor and subsequently how coordination activities take place. Consequently, the aim of this paper is not particularly concerned with related (and in some cases overlapping) debates surrounding the China model/Beijing Consensus; rather it looks in more detail at the type of agent China is in the wider context of aid infrastructure. As such, this paper broadly agrees with the trend in the literature that seeks to outline the nuance of China's position by presenting a framework through which China's agency can be consistently assessed. It therefore develops aspects of the introduction developed by Hu and Roy in this volume in considering intentionality of consequences of influence and conflict of interests.

Is the aid system static?

The third element above, that China has walked through an open door, suggests that both China's own agency and the context in which it is acting are both key components in any change we perceive in the liberal international architecture. A problem with the existing analyses is that they struggle with being able to capture that both parts of interaction are important in understanding change.

According to the rules of association with the OECD, all states have to sign up to a common aid architecture which includes a set of criteria of what constitutes official development assistance. Up to 2017 this was:

'The DAC defined ODA as "those flows to countries and territories on the DAC List of ODA Recipients and to multilateral institutions which are:

i. provided by official agencies, including state and local governments, or by their executive agencies; and
ii. each transaction of which:
   - is administered with the promotion of the economic development and welfare of developing countries as its main objective; and
   - is concessional in character and conveys a grant element of at least 25% (calculated at a rate of discount of 10%)"'. (OEDC, no date)

Since 2017 this definition has been updated to include further specifications and greater nuance:

'Official development assistance flows are defined as those flows to countries and territories on the DAC List of ODA Recipients and to multilateral development institutions which are:

i. provided by official agencies, including state and local governments, or by their executive agencies; and
ii. each transaction of which:
   - is administered with the promotion of the economic development and welfare of developing countries as its main objective; and
   - is concessional in character. In DAC statistics, this implies a grant element of at least (see note 4).
     - **45 per cent** in the case of bilateral loans to the official sector of LDCs and other LICs (calculated at a rate of discount of 9 per cent).
     - **15 per cent** in the case of bilateral loans to the official sector of LMICs (calculated at a rate of discount of 7 per cent).
     - **10 per cent** in the case of bilateral loans to the official sector of UMICs (calculated at a rate of discount of 6 per cent).
     - **10%** in the case of loans to multilateral institutions (see note 5) (calculated at a rate of discount of 5% for global institutions and multilateral development banks, and 6% for other organisations, including sub-regional organisations) (see notes 6 and 7)'. (OECD, no date)

This change in itself demonstrates that the liberal countries' approach to aid is not static, but responds to a changing field of development activities. One such activity is the arrival of China as a development and investment actor. However, it is not the only important factor.

Looking at China's importance in this change from the variation or scaling of the component of grants and separating out different sectors of types of assistance, this appears to mimic the approach to official assistance that China has adopted. Specifically, the action of reducing the 'gift' or grant component and increasing the economic cooperation activities and investments with developing states (Brautigam, 2010; Jones, 2019: pt. 3; Tan-Mullins et al., 2010: 876) seems to replicate the commercial approach of China. As a result, understanding these dynamics would have an implication for understanding China's FDI engagement in Europe.

Alternative reasons for the change in the aid definition are hard to find, but they include the reasons of the DAC countries themselves. The UK government committed itself to spending 0.7% of GNI (gross national income) on official development assistance by 2013. The UK, along with other developed states, has consistently met this obligation. However, the change in definition by the OECD of what official assistance is has allowed different types of economic and other engagement to be counted as aid—for example the UK sought to ensure that its contribution to peace and security in conflict areas was also able to be counted as 'aid' (Bond, 2016). However, the new methodology of calculating what counts as ODA has also changed, resulting in the production of incomparable data between pre- and post-2017 definitions. Significantly, it also means that it appears Western states are giving less in aid (Reliefweb, 2019). This means of calculating the amount of ODA may bring the OEDC approach more in line with the approach to calculating Chinese ODA—where commercial investments are excluded (Brautigam, 1998: 211, 2011: 168–172. For a longer discussion of the problems of calculating Chinese aid, see Jones, 2019: 200–202).

The change in the OECD–DAC definition of aid doesn't appear to have a direct link to any requests or specific actions by China. But instead it is the result of an internal four-year-long negotiation between states to change the definition and calculation of ODA. Yet, the movement in how the definition and calculation methodology of ODA could bring the DAC countries actions closer to the aid modalities of China. A question then arises of how do we account for China's effect here?

The actions of the UK government since the change in definition of ODA, in particular the merging of the Department for International Development (DfID) with the Foreign and Commonwealth Office (FCO), appears to confirm this impetus, so that in keeping the same headline figure for aid of 0.7% of GNI, different international activities are counted in rather than counted out. Hence making it easier to meet international obligations without adding more aspects to development assistance. Despite the potential there has still been a reduction in the assistance provided by DAC members since 2017. Indeed, the UK's commitment to contributing 0.7% of GNI to development was reduced to 0.5% during the COVID-19 pandemic.

A key criticism of Chinese assistance has been that it explicitly furthers the interests of the Chinese government, whereas the charitable or grant aspect of ODA assistance was ostensibly to distance the gift from the interests of the sender state. This claim was always a fallacy but, in the last decade from 2010 to 2020, successive DAC countries have sought to more explicitly demonstrate the link between their aid and their interests. For example, in explaining the importance of the merger of these two departments into the Foreign Commonwealth and Development Office, the government announced: 'This is exactly the moment when we must mobilise every one of our national assets, including our aid budget and expertise, to safeguard British interests and values overseas' (Gov.UK, 2020). This approach to making the interests of Western countries clear echoes the words of the German Chancellor in response to the announcements of the Forum on China-Africa Cooperation (FOCAC) III, that 'European policy towards Africa should not be based on "charity arguments" as ... in the past but on our "stalwart interests"' (quoted in Taylor, 2011: 74; see also Jones, 2019: 229). Why is it now necessary for Western governments to use ODA to more explicitly champion their own interests? Again it is clear that a correlative argument can be made that this change is in response to the presence of China and an aid giver, but the causal claim is less evident.

So far in this discussion, I have only highlighted the correlation of actions of the DAC in terms of aid to those of China. However, it is also important to factor in that it has been well noted in the literature that it is not only China (not an DAC member) that has different approaches to aid and how it is allocated. Brautigam (2011: 80) noted that both South Korea and Japan operated systems of aid that were recipient-led and also adopted assistance practices similar to China's recipient-led shared risk approach prior to their membership of the DAC group. Contrary to the argument in China's challenge to Liberal Norms (2019), where it was claimed that changes in aid modalities in the OECD triggered by South Korea and Japan were likely to have occurred when those states joined, I would add a rejoinder or modifier to that argument, that the direct cause of the change in the OECD definition may have been the demonstrated experience of Japan and South Korea, but that catalyst for the need to make the change could plausibly be China.

This section has demonstrated two important things: (1) that in understanding China's effects of the liberal aid architecture, it is essential to develop a new conceptual framework to enable different types of causal effects to be disaggregated; and (2) within this framework it is vital to acknowledge that the 'effecting agents' are both in motion, the international aid system is also developing and adjusting at the same time China is acting the aid space.

China as a Catalyst for Change? A Conceptual Framework

One issue arising from this—very brief—review of the relevant literatures is causation. Across these literatures it becomes clear that the problem of causation is alive and well in exploring China's relationships here. Looking at China as a development partner or a challenger in providing investments, the most obvious approach is to adopt a view of causation associated with Hume (Hollis, 2008: 49; see also Jones, 2019)—A caused B to act in a particular way. However, as noted in the introduction to this volume (Hu and Roy) and in considering difference forms of causation (see Kurki, 2008: 296–297; Wendt, 2003: 495; see also Jones, 2019: 16), it is clear that in developing debates on the effect of China's use of material power and its influence, is not equal to arguing that these effects reflect the intentional outcome that China sought.

In line with that framework and the wider conception of causation discussed above, this chapter argues that it is China's presence rather than its intention that allows consideration of China as a 'cause' or the influencer of changes in practices and policies. In this sense identifying China's presence as the cause of any changes in approach is difficult, and in the data we are only likely to see a correlation of timing rather than a specific binary link between China's actions and any changes in the investment architecture.

As a result of these different relationships and different approaches to causation, it is possible to identify three possibilities for understanding how China engages with these institutions:

(1) China is providing alternative ideological or pragmatic methods to determine how to do aid; the presence of this alternative then challenges the principles that underpin the practices of Western institutions and investment actors;
(2) China, by just providing an alternative venue for seeking loans and finance, contributes to the negation of the effectiveness of these institutions' strategies, rendering changes/modifications more likely;

(3) The presence of China acts as a catalyst for demonstrating that these institutions are simply no longer necessary or 'fit for purpose' in the globalized world of today, and consequently they must adjust and adapt their own approaches.

In parallel with these differential 'inputs' that China as an investment actor might have, there are also a multitude of effects that we might want to consider as a response to this. So, in addition to considering the type of agent China is, there is—whether implicit or explicit—a tendency to assume changes or outcomes are the result of China's actions rather than a correlation to China's behaviours or practices.

This chapter makes the argument that although China is an agent and is a trigger or catalyst for responses within investment architecture across Europe, the effect that is having is to curtail or limit changes that might be increasingly liberal and politically tied development investments, and in some places and development locations China fills in development gaps that enable the continuation of liberal approaches to investment. As such, it contributes to maintaining a status quo.

It is evident from these three possible outcomes of the literature that they are in part premised on the type of causation that is sought when looking at China.[1]

Framework, data, and research issues

The data in this paper draws heavily on open-data sources. In the past few years new databases have been developed to aid researchers exploring engagements of different actors in countries. The International Aid Transparency Index (IATI, Extractive Industries Index (EITI), Gap Minder (2020), and aid data (Aidata, 2020) give a good picture of both the 'gaps' in the data and 'gaps' in the interlinks between projects. The discussion and exposure of these gaps may then enable better 'coordination' between partners, but also may enable smaller donors to contribute small interstitial projects that have a significant transformative effect.

One significant area for discussion in this paper is how to understand the issues relating to China as a cause of change/challenges to existing bank practices and how to identify China's presence being merely correlative to changes

[1] Adopting an Aristotelian four-causes approach, it becomes evident that some of the challenge presented by challenge is through formal causes rather than efficient causes. For a greater discussion of the distinction between these, see Aristotle (1993: Books 4–6); Kurki (2008: 296–297); and Wendt (2003: 495).

Table 10.1 Types of causes and definitions

Type of Cause	Definition
Catalyst	Accelerates trend or changes that had previously been identified in the aid literature or by development actors.
Permissive	The presence of an alternative actor taking on some projects (for example building roads) enables other types of projects by other actors.
Entrepreneur	Developing new ideas for how to approach development or aid projects. This approach encompasses ideas that include presenting a new alternative that is deliberate and geared towards China mapping out a 'new' world order.
Passive	An actor doing actions that are necessary for its (China's) own growth and development of future. Its other actors or effects are therefore outside its immediate concerns.

already taking place. In seeking to overcome this problem, this paper suggests a typology for what kind of effect China may be having.

Moving the discussion away from partner or competitor is important in setting out alternative means to engage with China as well as for identifying 'gaps' in coordination. Consequently, this paper puts forwards four possibilities for understanding China and the bank and therefore awareness of the risks of creating gaps (see Table 10.1).

Opening up this different approach to understanding China's aid engagement also opens up space to discuss gaps in development and how to engage China in filling them. Importantly, it is essential to recognize that these possibilities are not mutually exclusive. It is possible for China to be a catalyst in the area of debt sustainability but also a permissive cause that enables the effects of catalysed actions to come about.[2]

In moving towards looking at the data in this area three different elements are explored: infrastructure, education, and debt sustainability.

Probative Analysis of the Data

This section provides an initial discussion of the above framework in relation to data currently available on infrastructure projects, education, and debt sustainability and management. This section illustrates the utility of the above framework in better understanding the nature of challenge or contest that China presents to the liberal order.

[2] This point then bridges discussions of multiple Chinas in foreign policy making.

Infrastructure projects

China is cited in the literature as being a big contributor to African infrastructure projects (Davies et al., 2008; He, 2010; Reisen and Ndoye, 2008). More recently, the development of the Asian Investment Infrastructure Bank and the Belt and Road Initiative have become focal points for China's infrastructure projects. According to reports in The Economist (2022), China accounted for 31% of all infrastructure projects in Africa. They note that according to figures from Deloitte this is up from 12% in 2013. Indeed there has been a seeming reversal of contributions from the Deloitte data; *The Economist* reported that in 2020 'western firms were directly responsible for just 12% or so (compared to 37% in 2013)' (The Economist, 2022). These figures are seemingly borne out by Kang-Chun Cheng's (2022) research for Africa Report, where the 30% figure is repeated but also supported by claims that China's provision of these infrastructure projects is filling in significant gaps for populations.

As these figures indicate, it is not that infrastructure projects are not a concern of Western or OCED-DAC donors, but that their contributions to infrastructure are dwarfed by the commitments of China. Similarly, it is not that multilateral development banks are becoming increasingly of interest for development by traditional donors (Harman and Williams, 2014). The key point here is that these infrastructure projects are one point of engagement between Bretton Woods and China (Foster et al., 2008; He, 2010: 153). However, they are also a site of potential missing links in the projects to develop consistent development over the continent. These gaps can be seen to emerge in two areas: the narrowing of the range of activities and places of projects, and the 'after completion' stage of projects.

Gaps in the range and geography of projects

Infrastructure projects can include information and communications (mobile phones and internet access are central here), mining, oil, and gas projects, and development of rail and road connections. Some of these projects are clearly linked—to extract mined products it is necessary to have roads and rail links that connect sites of mining to ports. While China may be doing this to ensure the 'development' of these industries' connections across the countries involved, ensuring that populations can transport goods is also necessary. As noted by PIDA (Programme for Infrastructure Development in Africa), gaps in infrastructure development are putting a break on the continent's development (PIDA, 2014). According to this report, 'The road access rate in Africa is only 34%, compared with 50% in other parts of the developing world, while transport costs are 100% higher' (PIDA, 2014). The problem caused by this infrastructure 'gap' is demonstrated in the visual presentation of infrastructure projects' data plotted against per capita income on Gapminder (Gapminder 2020).

One solution to this problem is developing coordinated activities with China in tri-lateral relations between China and traditional donors. However, these activities so far suggest that there is a move towards 'copying China' rather than 'filling in the gaps'. For example, in looking at a map of infrastructure in Africa there is still an absence of a road route across the continent (both East/West and North/South). Whilst it should be recognized that this is at least partially the result of political/security concerns, this too presents an opportunity—the presence of skilled peace-builders should be working to help connect and stabilize parts of the region, rather than treating security problems as a separate issue.

In addition, the need to develop road and rail links is directly concerned with developing internal markets and trading a wider range of products (and extending tourist revenues). However, in order for this commercial project to be viable it is necessary to ensure that there is still concern regarding the 'policy and environmental' aspects of development. That is, the bank (and other BW institutions) need to ensure that whilst they may seek to coordinate with China on infrastructure projects, they still need to develop new ways for enhancing governance projects, to increase the appeal of African states to private investors in new sectors, which in turn would provide other incentives to develop connections continent-wide (PIDA 2014). PIDA already has plans for infrastructure projects that run until 2040; however, these projects are costed at 360 billion USD, and at least part of this money needs to come from private investors. This opens the door to Chinese-style investments and the utilization of Chinese companies to develop projects. However, there is also a need to prevent some of the potential problems in China's development approaches (for example a lack of transfer of training and skills to local workers in order to maintain projects) (PIDA, 2014: 13).

This links to a 'lesson learnt from China' in a sense, as there are many critiques of China's asymmetrical development (particularly concerning the growing economic inequalities, as well as weaknesses in governance of financial organizations. There have also been concerns from private investors regarding the robustness of the rule of law). Thus, there is also a need to prevent these problems arising in Africa—which means that in coordinating with China in Africa there is a need to ensure that the BW institutions find new ways to promote robust governance structures. Indeed, statements by the Chinese leadership concerning the potential export of the Beijing Consensus have been very candid concerning the limitations and problems of China's development and the limitations this presents for its application in other states.[3]

In terms of infrastructure projects China may be seen as a catalyst for new projects to be started, but it is also an entrepreneur in how it approaches infrastructure projects.

Education

In education there is also the potential for a large gap to emerge. As with infrastructure China has adopted a different approach to the BW institutions. China's focus in education related to aid programmes has to focus on university- and tertiary-level aid programmes. However, the focus of many BW partners has been primary education. In looking at data from Gapminder it is evident that education provision at the primary level has been successful; however, levels of education achieved at the secondary level, or even criteria such as eight-grade maths, fall off.[4] As a result there is an obvious gap emerging; China is providing aid to support tertiary provision, but there are a number of students within countries that are being lost in the gap between primary and secondary education and thus the numbers that are eligible to engage with higher-level jobs is greatly reduced.

If we look at Ghana, we can see these problems. According to Aid Data (in 2014), Ghana received approximately 11% of aid flows from China. In education, China has thirteen projects. Of these seven are targeted at tertiary-level education and these include all bar one of the high-ticket items of donations (Aid Data, 2017). Yet in looking at the data from Gapminder, Ghana is still a low performer in maths to the eighth grade, and its literacy rates of people ages 15–24 are at 66% (not the lowest on the continent but still significantly lower than other states (Aid Data, 2017; Dreher et al. 2021; Dreher et al 2022).

What does this approach to aid provision in education demonstrate about China's agency as a challenger or catalyst? In looking at the three potential types of effects that China's approach could be having, China does appear to adopt a different method of education aid assistance, but this doesn't inherently undermine the approach or Western or European investors. In this field it is not even offering an alternative, but instead and addition to funding and

[3] Chinese leadership statements.
[4] Gapminder graphs.

investment available from traditional donors, nor does it appear to be demonstrating a flaw, absence, or central problem with the approaches of traditional donors. In this area, then, China's provision of education assistance actually appears to help to maintain the status quo, whereby Western/European investment can be targeted at primary education and China's aid can support tertiary education. In this way they are mutually supporting each other to achieve a common goal.

Debt management/sustainability

In 2019 it was argued that in addition to different approaches to providing aid (for example, recipient-led, with economic risk rather than political conditionality) and as a consequence of these different approaches China also provides an alternative approach to debt management (Jones, 2019: part 3). This is often associated with arguments about the 'non-conditionality' of China's aid and assistance in contrast to the political conditionality imposed by traditional donors.

In seeking to calculate and make decisions about investments, the World Bank uses a number of indicators, among them the Country Policy and Institutional Assessment (CPIA). According to the World Bank, 'The CPIA rates countries against a set of 16 criteria grouped in four clusters: (i) economic management; (ii) structural policies; (iii) policies for social inclusion and equity; and (iv) public sector management and institutions' (World Bank, 2020). The CPIA is therefore a reflection of the link between the politics and policies of recipient countries and their eligibility of investment and aid. This index also underpins the assessment by some individual donors—for example the former Department for International Development (DfID) in the UK (Tribe, 2016).

The role of the CPIA in DfID's (now the Foreign, Commonwealth and Development Office), Needs-Effectiveness Index (N-EI) is to inform and assess the potential effectiveness of aid by considering the environment into which aid is provided (Tribe, 2016). The CPIA therefore is a tangible metric that links the philosophy of Western aid provision to the practice of giving—it makes a claim that different forms of governance are better or worse for making aid more effective (Jones, 2019: 226–227). However, CPIA has long been subject to critical reviews (Arndt and Oman, 2008) for its link between good policy environments and the effectiveness of aid. For example, China—as a developing country—would have performed poorly on the CPIA index, but it has demonstrated considerable success in terms of development and poverty reduction. As a result of both continuing critiques and evidence from states including China, the balance in the CPIA has been made (Alexander, 2010). Indeed, since 2011, the CPIA has rebalanced some of the sixteen indicators in the CPIA, and it has been argued that this was as a result of pressure for at least a debate for this index to become more transparent.

The presence of China as an aid contributor has the potential to help countries change their own position in the CPIA and therefore move from not qualifying for IMF or World Bank loans to qualifying. An example of this is Tonga. China's investment in Tonga meant that it could satisfy existing loans despite an absence of changes to economic or political structures (IMF, 2013: 2; Jones, 2019). Similarly, according to Brautigam, the presence of contracts between China and the Democratic Republic of Congo in 2007–2008 helped to persuade the IMF and World Bank to sign off on debt sustainability, even though the state didn't meet the normal conditions to do so (1998: 22–23; Jones, 2019: 227)

This change has been associated with China but not caused by it. Indeed, the agency of China here is as an example of a developing state rather than only as a development provider. Importantly, the underpinning rationale of aid has not been challenged by the change to the CPIA, but only a minor modifying tweak in how the methodology works. As a result, in looking at the framework for analysis China's presence in the aid scene (both as developing state and donor) seems to have amplified the calls that already existed in relation to the CPIA rather than triggering new changes: it has acted as a catalyst for change. Secondly, it has not overturned either the methodology of Western investment or its practice, but modified the assessment of how investment takes place: it hasn't changed the status quo. Perhaps the most important consideration here is not whether China challenges the status quo or not, but rather how China and traditional donors can work more effectively together to achieve development outcomes (Reisen and Ndoye, 2008: 42).

Conclusion

This chapter makes the argument that China's presence as a development actor means that it is a catalyst that allows for the some so-called liberal patterns of aid and investment to continue. It seeks to demonstrate that rather than being a direct cause of changes in the Western aid and investment practices, it pursues actions that correlate with these changes—it is a catalyst for action, not the impetus of action.

Similarly, this chapter makes the argument that by filling in gaps in the development architecture, China actually enables the continuation of patterns and types of investment preferred by Western states. For example, China provides specific education to tertiary students, which fills a gap in the UK approach that supports primary education specifically to girls.

Joining the gaps necessitates a more aware realization of how other actors approach development, but this is not the same as ensuring coordination with them. Moreover, it is not just development actors that need to be brought into this picture; state-building participants also need to be on board. The UNPKO needs to be aware of regional development projects with a security angle, and this is happening in the emerging new department of the Foreign, Commonwealth and Development Office in the UK.

Importantly, particularly when looking at infrastructure gaps, private as well as public projects are necessary for filling in gaps. These will involve engagement with and understanding of the many different actors that contribute to these projects (these may be many actors on China's side, but also on the BW side). All of these actors will engage with or contribute to projects in different ways with different incentives. One of the great benefits of China's engagement is that infrastructure projects are happening and are back on the agenda of the BW institutions. However, one significant downside is the potential for fracturing consensus between development partners among the traditional donors who may be required to work even more collaboratively. A further problem might be that as climate change adds to stress on infrastructure provisions, a new 'gap' may emerge that needs to be filled in relation to evaluating whether existing infrastructures are fit for a climate changed world (for example, dams, roads, flood defences), which may involve more coordinated practices among all donors.

Do investment partners need to form a consensus in order to effectively pursue development? One argument here is that traditional donors don't have to formulate a 'new' consensus that includes all new donors, but there does need to be enhanced awareness of projects and gaps that need filling. But one of the dangers of China's presence is that it fractures the development agenda developed since Paris and Accra; China changes the incentives of all of these actors, and this may be a formula for projects without an immediate financial outcome being side-lined (particularly concerning governance). This would present a glass ceiling for development across the continent in terms of internal developments, which raises the risks of the problems China currently faces in Western China.

Gap-filling requires both dialogue and coordination, but it also requires the maintenance of a conviction that policy and institutional form still matter and should be a concern of BW institutions—although there will necessarily be some need for re-evaluation of how this is incentivized in target states as a result of the presence of China as a permissive developer. This paper has therefore argued for: a movement away from the binary approach to looking at China as a development actor; an acceptance that China's agency as well as the agents involved in development may not provide easy causal chains; finally there needs to be awareness of the gaps created not just by China's presence, but also by the reaction of BW institutions to China's presence.

What does this tell us about China's overall agency? I have argued in this chapter that there is evidence that China is a permissive cause of changes in the practice of aid; it has catalysed action by traditional donors that has long been identified as being necessary in order to make aid more effective. However, in acting in this way China is supporting developing states by filling in gaps in the types of investment and nature of projects that recipient states can request, this in turn facilitates the continuation of the approaches adopted by traditional donors. At the same time, China's provision of aid may also create new gaps that need to be filled. But overall, China is a catalyst for statis rather than revolution.

Bibliography

AidData. 2017. Global Chinese Official Finance Dataset, Version 1.0. Retrieved from http://aiddata.org/data/chinese-global-official-finance-dataset.

Aidata. 2020. https://china.aiddata.org/ [Accessed 21 September 2020].

Alden, C. 2007. China in Africa, Zed Books.

Alexander, N. 2010. 'The Country Policy and Institutional Assessment (CPIA) and Allocation of IDA Resources: Suggestions for Improvements to Benefit African Countries'. Henrich Boll Steifing, Commissioned by Development Finance International, 16 August.

Aristotle. 1993. *Metaphysics*. Books 4–6. Oxford: Clarendon Press.

Arndt, C., and C. Oman. 2008. 'The Politics of Governance Ratings'. Maastricht Graduate School of Governance Working Paper MGSoG/2008/WP003, April.

Bond. 2016. 'OECD Redefines Aid'. 25 February. Available at: https://www.bond.org.uk/news/2016/02/oecd-redefines-aid [Accessed 21 September 2020].

Bracht, C. 2013. 'Will the BRICS Bank Deliver a More Just World Order'. *The Guardian*, 8 May. Available at: http://www.theguardian.com/global-development-professionals-network/2013/may/08/brics-development-bank [Accessed 14 March].

Brautigam, D. 1998. *Chinese Aid and African Development.* Basingstoke: Macmillan Press.

Brautigam, D. 2010. 'China, Africa and the International Aid Architecture'. African Development Bank, Working Paper Series 107, April.

Brautigam D. 2011. *The Dragon's Gift.* Oxford: Oxford University Press.

Breslin, S. 2011. 'The "China Model" and the Global Crisis: From Friedrich List to a Chinese Mode of Governance'. *International Relations* 87 (6): pp. 1323–1343.

Cheng, K.-C. 2022. 'China is Delivering over 30% of Africa's Big Construction Projects. Here's Why'. The Africa Report, 16 March. Available at: https://www.theafricareport.com/183370/china-is-delivering-over-30-of-africas-big-construction-projects-heres-why/ [Accessed 12 November 2022].

Chien-Huei, Wu. 2018. 'Global Economic Governance in the Wake of the Asian Infrastructure Investment Bank: Is China Remaking Bretton Woods?'. *Journal of World Investment and Trade* 19: pp. 542–569.

Collier, P., and D. Dollar. 2001. 'Can the World Cut Poverty in Half? How Policy Reform and Effective Aid Can Meet International Development Goals'. *World Development* 29 (11) pp. 1787–1802.

Collier, P., and D. Dollar. 2002. 'Aid Allocation and Poverty Reduction'. *European Economic Review* 46: pp.1475–1500

Dalgaard, C.-J., H. Hansen, and F. Tarp. 2004. 'On the Empirics of Foreign Aid and Growth'. *The Economic Journal* 114 (496): pp. F191–F216, F208–9.

Davies, M., H. Edinger, N. Tay, and S. Naidu. 2008. *How China Delivers Development Assistance to Africa.* Centre for Chinese Studies, University of Stellenbosch.

Dent, Christopher M. ed. 2011. *China and African Development Relations.* London: Routledge, Contemporary China Series.

Dreher, A., Fuchs, A., Parks, B. C., Strange, A., & Tierney, M. J. 2022. *Banking on Beijing: The Aims and Impacts of China's Overseas Development Program.* Cambridge, UK: Cambridge University Press.

Dreher, A., Fuchs, A., Parks, B. C., Strange, A., & Tierney, M. J. 2021. Aid, China, and Growth: Evidence from a New Global Development Finance Dataset. *American Economic Journal: Economic Policy* 13 (2), 135-74.

The Economist. 2022. 'How Chinese Firms Have Dominated African Infrastructure'. 19 February. Available at: https://www.economist.com/middle-east-and-africa/how-chinese-firms-have-dominated-african-infrastructure/21807721 [Accessed 12 November 2022].

Ekman A., "China setting the agenda(s)?", *European Union Institute for Security Studies' Brief* (March 2015) downloaded from https://www.google.com/url?sa=t&rct=j&q=&esrc=s&source=web&cd=&ved=2ahUKEwiml_SwjI-BAxUMQ8AKHdfVAMsQFnoECA0QAQ&url=https%3A%2F%2Fwww.iss.europa.eu%2Fsites%2Fdefault%2Ffiles%2F25%2520April%25202016.

pdf&usg=AOvVaw2GcBsEXXMAhMaeZPzm6qFQ&opi=89978449 last accessed 3 September 2023.

Foster, V. W. B., C. Chen, and N. Pushak. 2008. *Building Bridges: China's Role as Infrastructure Financier in Sub-Saharan Africa.* Washington D.C.: World Bank.

Gapminder. 2020. https://www.gapminder.org/ [Accessed 21 September 2020].

Goldstein, M., and N. R. Lardy. 2005. 'China's Role in the Revived Bretton Woods System: A Case of Mistaken Identity'. *Institute for International Economics, Working Paper* WP05–2: pp. 1–20.

Gov.UK. 2020. 'Press Release: Prime Minister Announces Merger of Department for International Development and Foreign Office'. Available at: https://www.gov.uk/government/news/prime-minister-announces-merger-of-department-for-international-development-and-foreign-office [Accessed 21 September 2020].

Halper, S. A. 2010. *The Beijing Consensus: How China's Authoritarian Model Will Dominate the Twenty-First Century.* New York: Basic Books.

Hameiri, S., and L. Jones. 2018. 'China Challenges Global Governance? Chinese International Development Finance and the AIIB'. *International Affairs* 94 (3): pp. 573–593.

Harman, S., and D. Williams. 2014. 'International Development in Transition'. *International Affairs* 90 (4): pp. 925–941

He, W. 2010. 'China's Aid to Africa: Policy Evolution, Characteristics and Its Role'. In *Challenging the Aid Paradigm: Western Currents and Asian Alternatives*, edited by Jens Stilhoff Sörensen, pp. 138–165. Palgrave Macmillan: Basingstoke, 2010.

Heldt, E. C., and H. Schmidtke. 2019. 'Explaining Coherence in International Regime Complexes: How the World Bank Shapes the Field of Multilateral Development Finance'. *Review of International Political Economy* 26 (6): pp. 1160–1186.

Hollis, M. 2008. *The Philosophy of Social Science: An Introduction.* Cambridge: Cambridge University Press.

Hopewell, K. 2015. 'Different Paths to Power: The Rise of Brazil, India and China at the World Trade Organization'. *Review of International Political Economy* 22 (2): pp. 311–338.

Hopewell, K. 2019. 'Power Transitions and Global Trade Governance: The Impact of a Rising China on The Export Credit Regime'. *Regulation & Governance*, 15: 634–652: pp. 1–19.

Huse, M. D., and S. L. Muyakwa. 2008. *China in Africa: Lending, Policy Space and Governance.* Norwegian Campaign for Debt Cancellation: Council for Africa.

IMF. 2013. 'Tonga: Joint IMF/World Bank Debt Sustainability Analysis 2013'. 2 July.

IMF and International Development Association. 2004. 'Debt Sustainability in Low-Income Countries: Further Considerations on an Operational Framework and Policy Implications approved by Gobind Nankani and Mark Allen'. 10 September.

Available at: http://siteresources.worldbank.org/INTDEBTDEPT/PolicyPapers/20279458/DSfullpapersept.pdf [Accessed 2 April 2012].

Jones, C. 2019. *China's Challenge to Liberal Norms*. Basingstoke: Palgrave Macmillan:

Kurki, M. 2008. *Causation in International Relations: Reclaiming Causal Analysis*. Cambridge: Cambridge University Press.

Lee, P. K., G. Chan, and L.-H. Chan. 2012. 'China in Darfur: Humanitarian Rule-Maker or Rule-Taker?'. *Review of International Studies*, pp. 423–444. Cambridge University Press.

Liao, R. 2015. 'Out of the Bretton woods: How the AIIB is different' Foreign Affairs, published 27 July 2015, available https://www.foreignaffairs.com/articles/asia/2015-07-27/out-bretton-woods last accessed 3 September 2023.

Loke B. 2018 China's economic slowdown: implications for Beijing's institutional power and global governance role, *The Pacific Review*, 31:5, 673-691. DOI: 10.1080/09512748.2017.1408674

Mawdsley, E. 2007. 'China and Africa: Emerging Challenges to the Geographies of Power'. *Geography Compass* 1 (3): pp. 405–421.

Mitchell, A. 2011. 'Emerging Powers'. Speech at Chatham House, 15 February. Available at: http://www.dfid.gov.uk/News/Speeches-and-articles/2011/Emerging-powers/ [Accessed 28 November 2011].

OECD. no date. Official development assistance – definition and coverage, https://www.oecd.org/dac/financing-sustainable-development/development-finance-standards/officialdevelopmentassistancedefinitionandcoverage.htm last accessed 3 September 2023.

Peerenboom, R. 2007. *China Modernizes: Threat to the West or Model for the Rest?* Oxford: Oxford University Press.

Peng, Z., and S. K. Tok. 2016. 'The AIIB and China's Normative Power in International Financial Governance Structure'. *Chinese Political Science Review* 1: pp. 736–753.

PIDA. 2014. 'Closing the Infrastructure Gap is Vital for Africa's Development'. Available at: http://www.afdb.org/fileadmin/uploads/afdb/Documents/Generic-Documents/PIDA%20brief%20closing%20gap.pdf [Accessed 16 March 2014].

Ramo, J. C. 2004. *The Beijing Consensus*. London: Foreign Policy Centre.

Reisen, H. 2015. 'Will the AIIB and the NDB Help Reform Multilateral Development Banking?'. *Global Policy* 6: pp. 297–304.

Reisen, H., and S. Ndoye, 2008. 'Prudent Versus Imprudent Lending to Africa: From Debt Relief to Emerging Lenders'. OECD Development Centre Working Paper No. 268, February.

Reliefweb. 2019. 'Development Aid Drops in 2018, Especially to Neediest Countries'. 10 April. Available at: https://reliefweb.int/report/world/development-aid-drops-2018-especially-neediest-countries [Accessed 21 September 2020].

Ren, X. 2016. 'China as an Institution-Builder: The Case of the AIIB'. *The Pacific Review*, 29 (3): pp. 435–442.

Schiere, R. L. N., and P. Walkenhorst, eds. 2011. *China and Africa: An Emerging Partnership for Development*. Tunisia: African Development Bank.

Stephenm M. D., and Skidmore D., The AIIB in the Liberal International Order, *The Chinese Journal of International Politics*, Volume 12, Issue 1, Spring 2019, Pages 61–91. DOI: 10.1093/cjip/poy021

Stephen, M. D., and D. Skidmore. 'The AIIB in the Liberal International Order'. *The Chinese Journal of International Politics*, ISSN 1750-8924, Oxford University Press, 12 (1): pp. 61–91. DOI: 10.1093/cjip/poy021

Subacchi, P. 2008. 'New Power Centres and New Power Brokers: Are They Shaping a New Economic Order?'. *International Affairs* 84 (3): pp. 485–498.

Tan-Mullins, M., G. Mohan, and M. Power. 2010. 'Redefining "Aid" in the China–Africa Context'. *Development and Change* 41: pp. 857–881.

Taylor, I. 2009. *China's New Role in Africa*. Boulder, CO: Lynne Rienner.

Taylor, I. 2011. *The Forum on China-Africa Cooperation*. London: (FOCAC), Routledge.

Trevisani, P. 2013. 'The BRICS Planning to Create Alternatives to the IMF And World Bank'. *Wall Street Journal Online*, March 22. Available at: http://online.wsj.com/article/BT-CO-20130322-714171.html [Accessed 14 March 2014].

Tribe, M. 2016. 'Quantifying Aid Allocation: A Critical Review of the DFID Needs-Effectiveness Index'. *Global Policy*. Available at: https://onlinelibrary.wiley.com/doi/full/10.1111/1758-5899.12362 [Accessed 28 September 2020].

Wang, H. 2015. 'The Asian Investment Infrastructure Bank: A New Bretton Woods Moment?'. CIGI Policy Brief, No. 59. Available at: https://www.cigionline.org/publications/asian-infrastructure-development-bank-new-bretton-woods-moment-total-chinese-triumph?utm_source=Newsletter&utm_medium=Web%20Archive&utm_campaign=CIGI%20WorldWide [Accessed 13 April 2021].

Wang, Z. 2017. 'The Economic Rise of China: Rule-Taker, Rule-Maker, Rule-Breaker?'. *Asian Survey* 57 (4): pp. 595–617.

Wendt, A. 2003. 'Why the World State Is Inevitable'. *European Journal of International Relations* 9 (3): 491–542.

Wilson, J. D. 2019. 'The Evolution of China's Asian Infrastructure Investment Bank: From a Revisionist to Status-Seeking Agenda'. *International Relations of the Asia-Pacific* 19 (1): pp. 147–176.

World Bank. 2020. 'Data Catalog'. Available at: https://datacatalog.worldbank.org/dataset/country-policy-and-institutional-assessment [Accessed 28 September 2020].

World Bank. 'Country Policy and Institutional Assessment'. Outline available at: https://datacatalog.worldbank.org/search/dataset/0038988/Country-Policy-and-Institutional-Assessment [last accessed 5 October 2023].

World Bank and the IMF. 2012. 'Revisiting the Debt Sustainability Framework for Low-Income Countries, approved by Otaviano Canuto and Siddhardth Tiwari'. 11 January. Available at: https://www.elibrary.imf.org/view/journals/007/2012/098/article-A000-en.xml [last accessed 5 October 2023].

Zhao, S. 2010. The China Model: can it replace the Western model of modernization?, *Journal of Contemporary China*, 19:65, 419-436. DOI: 10.1080/10670561003666061

Zhao, C.-H. 2012. 'China Export Import Bank'. OUCAN Conference Oxford, 14 March.

Conclusion

Chinese Investments, European Agency, and the Liberal International Order

Indrajit Roy, Jappe Eckhardt, Simona Davidescu, and Dimitrios Stroikos

Few themes have gripped students of development in recent years as much as 'the Rise of China'. Whether it is that country's success in lifting record numbers of people from absolute poverty or its emergence from a rural backwater to the workshop of the world, China's meteoric 'rise' has dazzled supporters and critics alike. China's growing international presence and overseas investments highlight not only the durability of globalization, but also the growing role of the state in promoting it. These investments were arguably spurred by the 2008 global financial crisis. The crisis also resulted in such multilateral institutions as the World Bank turning critical of previous market-led development paradigms it had itself advocated. Chief Economist Justin Yifu Lin went on to advocate a 'global Marshall Plan' (Yifu Lin and Wang, 2013). Both the United States and China encouraged overseas investments, especially in infrastructure (Tooze, 2018), but also in other sectors. Such a rare convergence of ideas and practices led to the consolidation of a 'global growth coalition' (Schindler and Kanai, 2019) that includes multilateral development banks, multinational corporations, consultancies and think tanks, as well as states across the Global South and Global North.

The award of the Nobel Prize in 2008 to Paul Krugman for his pioneering work on economic geography and uneven development validated the growing emphasis on infrastructure. As Chief Economist of the World Bank, Yifu Lin (2012) theorized a 'new structural economics'. According to this perspective, governments interested in development enhance their comparative advantage by deliberately investing in infrastructure, both hard and soft. Infrastructure is, after all, 'one more component of an economy's (factor) endowment' (Yifu Lin, 2012: 111). Purposeful investments in infrastructures reduce transaction costs and enable economies to reach new frontiers beyond

Indrajit Roy et al., *Conclusion.* In: *Rising Power, Limited Influence.* Edited by: Indrajit Roy, Jappe Eckhardt, Dimitrios Stroikos, and Simona Davidescu, Oxford University Press. © Oxford University Press (2024). DOI: 10.1093/oso/9780192887115.003.0012

manufacturing, he suggested. The World Development Report 2009 bore the imprint of these ideas. Titled 'Reshaping Economic Geography', the Report directed attention to spatially connective investments to ensure an inclusive development even if economic growth was to be unbalanced (World Bank, 2009: 25).

The ideas about global investments in soft and hard infrastructure brewing in the World Development Report were already being applied in China. Adam Tooze (2018) noted the dramatic decline in demand for its exports in the wake of the financial crisis and the state's response. The Chinese government launched an unprecedented spending program that 'was the first truly large-scale fiscal response to the crisis worldwide' (Tooze, 2018: 243). China's investments were initially focused on domestic infrastructure in its western region and 'carried the entire world economy' (Tooze, 2018: 251). By 2013, this stimulus assumed a global dimension with the inauguration of the Belt and Road Initiative (BRI) which was subsequently hitched onto the Chinese state's narrative of creating a Sino-centric world order.[1]

China's overseas foreign direct investment in 2020 stood at 153.71 million USD, ranking a global first for the first time.[2] Since 2012, China has become one of the top three countries in terms of the OFDI flows. Driven by its 'Going Out' strategy and Belt and Road Initiative, China is expected to continue the expansion of its OFDI footprints. Through overseas investment, China can not only boost its economy, but also further project its power by leveraging its economic strength. Between 2003 and 2012, China's OFDI flow to Europe tripled with a general uptrend, standing at 7.04 billion USD in 2012. Between 2013 and 2019, the flow has fluctuated. China's OFDI flow in Europe recorded its highest of 18.46 billion USD in 2017. These flows have spurred existential anxieties in Europe (Meunier, Burgoon, and Jacoby, 2014: 119). Critics have suggested that China was 'invading' Europe (L'Express, 2011), taking it over (Bordet, 2011), and 'buying' it up by fomenting a 'scramble' for the continent (Godement and Parello-Plesner, 2011: 1).

In the wake of these anxieties, the present volume focuses on China's expanding footprint in Europe. Chinese investments in Europe are significant for several reasons. They upend the usual direction of financial flows

[1] Beyond China, the United States' Treasury Department offered fourteen of its central banks almost unlimited access to US dollars (Tooze, 2018). Cheap capital and low interest rates spurred investments in infrastructure. A major destination of such investments were the so-called emerging markets, which financial institutions, sovereign wealth funds, and pension funds assessed to be worthwhile (Clark, 2017; Torrance, 2009).

[2] All the data are compiled from the Statistical Bulletin of China's Outward Foreign Direct Investment, an annual report compiled jointly by the Ministry of Commerce of the People's Republic of China, National Bureau of Statistics, and State Administration of Foreign Exchange. Data refers to mainland China only; Hong Kong and Macao are excluded.

from the 'developed countries' of the Global North to the 'developing countries' of the Global South, which have underpinned the international order. The growing volume of overseas investments originating in China, which continues to be labelled a 'developing economy', while unabashedly authoritarian and with the state permeating its economy, threatens to disrupt the liberal foundations of the international order. Furthermore, Europe prides itself on and is widely considered the champion of the Liberal International Order (LIO). The increasing volume of economic investments originating in one of the world's most resilient authoritarian regimes towards a Europe where liberal values are increasingly besieged, at times from within, offers us pertinent insights into the ways in which China's actions interact with responses from other states to influence the international order.

Anxieties about Chinese overseas investments have been compounded by its global pronouncements and hawkish actions. Since 2012, the Chinese government led by President Xi Jinping has largely abandoned its traditional foreign policy strategy of *taoguang yanghui* (keeping a low profile) and embraced a new strategy of *fenfa youwei* (striving for achievement) (Foot, 2014; Sørensen, 2015; Yan, 2014). China's domestic behaviour is not always an endorsement of liberal globalization, given its high degree of state intervention in the economy, the limited market access for foreign investors, and its human rights violations. Moreover, China has become more assertive, if not completely aggressive, particularly regarding the issues and events taking place in the Asia-Pacific region. A recent example is the growing tension between China and the US in the South China Sea where China continues to build artificial islands and conduct military exercises, whilst the US strengthens its cooperation with other countries in the region (Geaney, 2020; Tangen, 2020).

In recent years, the country has portrayed itself as a staunch champion of liberal globalization. And yet, these attempts do not seem to be successful in moulding public opinion in favour of China. Findings from the 2022 Pew survey on global public opinion reveal historic highs in unfavourable views of China among respondents in Europe (Pew Research, 2022). In the wake of the pandemic, such unfavourable views may be gleaned across the continent in countries as disparate as Sweden (82%), Netherlands (75%), Germany (74%), United Kingdom (69%), France (68%), Italy (64%), Spain (63%), Belgium (61%), Poland (55%), Hungary (52%), and Greece (50%). These figures stand in stark contrast to favourable views of China dominating public opinion in each country two decades ago. Frustrated by a lack of progress on improvement in China's market access and human rights practices, a new consensus among EU members against China appears to have emerged

(Oertel, 2020). Notably, in 2019, although the EU referred to China as a 'negotiation partner and an economic competitor', it also considered China as 'a systemic rival promoting alternative models of governance' (European Commission, 2019: 1). China's growing assertiveness in its neighbourhood and beyond, alongside the misinformation during the COVID-19 pandemic, have only exacerbated unfavourable views of that country in Europe (Pew Research, 2020).

The contributors to this volume are motivated by a significant puzzle that lies at the heart of China's ascendance: the gap between its growing economic, military, and cultural resources and the conversion of those resources into meaningful global influence. A consideration of this puzzle in turn led us to ask three crucial questions. (1) Does China, in fact, want to challenge the international order? (2) Do China's expanding overseas investments have unintended consequences on the international order? And (3) How does European agency interact with Chinese influence to (re-)shape the Liberal International Order? Answering these questions compels us to direct detailed attention to the ways in which China's power affects the policy choices and decisions of other countries, instead of focusing on scorecards that enumerate its political, economic, and cultural resources. Reflecting on these questions on China's power requires us to move away from understandings of power as resource to power as influence, which relates resources to outcomes. The contributors to this volume assert that to assess China's impact on the international order, we must appreciate the ways in which its growing power resources are translated into actual policy influence. Here, we find helpful the crucial distinction offered by Evelyn Goh (2014, 2016) between an understanding of power that is limited to enumeration of resources and latent capability, towards an understanding of power that focuses on its effective exercise, or influence, on the preferences and behaviour of other actors.

Harnessing insights from Goh's understanding of power as influence, our volume builds on a political economy literature that situates states within the 'broader field of social relations' (Overbeek, 2004: 114). Following M. D. Stephen, we use the concept of 'state-society complexes' (Stephen, 2014b: 919) to appreciate the embeddedness of states in configurations of social power. In emphasizing the value of state-society relations to the liberal world order, our contributors implicitly endorse 'second image' explanations that highlight domestic politics as a source of cooperation and conflict in global politics. Such explanations help us appreciate the agency of state and social actors in Europe while negotiating with their Chinese counterparts.

Indeed, the contributions to this volume serve as useful reminders that the use of China's power is entwined with the agency of state and social actors in Europe. They urge us to recognize that discussions on China's influence are impossible without a consideration of accountability, intentionality, and subjectivity of European actors. Furthermore, European actors are socially embedded. Analysts writing about the politics of Chinese investments in Europe (or anywhere else for that matter) ignore the local social context at their own peril. This volume thus contributes to the growing body of literature that emphasizes the role of agency in international affairs and global politics[3].

China and the International Order

The two contributions in Part One reflect on what China wants in relation to the international order. These two chapters reflect on Chinese intentionality vis-à-vis the liberal underpinnings of the international order and caution against the widely prevalent assumption that China seeks to overthrow it. Both contributions recognize that, as a resurgent power, we can expect Chinese actors to influence the international order in their favour. Such expectations entail that they may want to bolster rather than overthrow this order. However, their actions may well have unintended consequences of undermining some elements of the international order. Alternatively, they may want to revise specific aspects of it rather than aim for its complete overthrow.

Chapter 1 by Yu Jie directs attention to the question of what order is and whether China seeks to influence international order. In doing so, she argues that the notion of a singular international order is misleading. Multiple orders exist and revolve around specific issue areas as a result of the complex terrain of international politics. China supports some of these orders and opposes others. Besides, China's attitude towards specific orders can be characterized by shifting positions. Consequently, the question of whether China challenges the LIO depends greatly on which order is being considered. Yu urges us to move beyond such binary conceptual misunderstandings.

More specifically, Yu's chapter critically considers the extent to which Chinese companies, mainly state-owned enterprises (SOEs), have emerged as a challenge to the LIO by looking at the dynamic relationship between the Chinese companies and the Chinese central government in the context of the pursuit of the Belt and Road Initiative (BRI). In contrast to the prevailing simplistic assumption in Europe that Chinese SOEs act on behalf of the state

[3] See, for example, insightful discussion in Colin Wight (2004), Hagman and Péclard (2010), and Mohan and Lampert (2012).

informed by geopolitical considerations as part of an effort to enhance Beijing's political influence, she argues that reality has been more complex. The corporate interests of the SOEs involved in the BRI are not always aligned with those of the Party-state.

Building on the Bureaucratic Politics Model, Yu illustrates the ways in which decision-making processes in China are increasingly pluralistic. Various stakeholders and interest groups compete for influence, located both inside and outside of the formal foreign policymaking process, with implications for the implementation of the BRI. She emphasizes the significance of different types of bargaining between key actors, including bargaining between the central government institutions and the SOEs. An important aspect of this process is 'competitive persuasion', which entails competition between SOEs to formulate persuasive arguments on which policy or project under the BRI should be endorsed by the government. Furthermore, Yu suggests that there is a notable recalibration of the BRI as a result of Beijing's attempt to narrow down its priorities and refocus on its neighbourhood, which is likely to lead to less overseas economic activities from Chinese SOEs.

Chapter 2 by Ran Hu drills further into the actual working of the BRI to problematize the assumption that it represents a coherent global strategy. He investigates the formulation of the BRI between 2013 and 2015 from the perspective of state transformation. His findings suggest that the existing IR-based literature exaggerates the monopoly of the Chinese state and ignores China's fragmented policymaking process characterized by the tussles between decentralization and recentralization. In fact, the BRI started with incoherent and messy practices and discourses concerning two separate (sub-)regional proposals (the maritime Belt initiative and the land-based Road network). A series of recentralizing measures initiated by the central government made BRI into one relatively coherent, but still very vague and broad, initiative aligned with grand declarations about China's strategic goals. Hu argues that the fragmented policymaking process caused by the interplay between decentralization and recentralization emasculates the Chinese government and prevents it from developing a precise and coherent strategy for the BRI, far less to challenge the LIO.

Chinese Influence and European Agency: The Liberal Order Strained

In Part Two of the volume, we turn our attention to cases of friendly bilateral relations between China and EU member states and candidate countries, which potentially strain the liberal order. The chapters in this section investigate possibilities of China's investments in Central and Eastern Europe creating a multiplier effect that intensifies and mobilizes converging preferences in China's favour. Highlighting the agency of European actors, these contributions document the central importance of political elites and business groups in these countries—rather than vaguely referencing China's power—that embrace and/or consolidate illiberal politics.

The chapters by Ágnes Szunomár and Nicholas Crawford explore and challenge these claims of economic gains, while making a strong case for the importance of political rationale, instrumentally used by leaders across the region to back up domestic policy and ideological agendas. Despite similar contexts and legacies, there is no consistent approach across the region, but there is evidence of stronger ties with some illiberal regimes and leaders. Both chapters place under the spotlight the agency of domestic politicians from small countries in CEE and the Western Balkans, demonstrating also the limits of the EU's liberal rules.

Szunomár's chapter, Chapter 3, shows that friendly relations between China and Hungary and emphasis on economic benefits pre-dated the illiberal turn under the Orbán governments. The puzzle here is that despite evidence of limited economic benefits and an increasing trade deficit, as well as some major infrastructure projects being delayed or too costly, the relationship between the two countries did not change, but was further reinforced by Hungary's discourse of 'turning towards the East'. The chapter looks at the extent to which domestic elites in Hungary are using the relationship with China as a bargaining chip when there are tensions between the EU and Hungary. This alignment of illiberal rationale between China and Hungary could be contributing to fragmentation within Europe, potentially undermining the LIO. This is not stemming from the Chinese-Hungarian relations, but is exploited by self-interested domestic elites in Hungary for the purpose of their own survival. In this case, China's persuasion via economic inducement does not need to be effective in practice, as long as the elites and the media in both countries frame it in terms of economic benefits. Hungary's illiberal stance can undermine the coherence of the EU's discourse based on LIO norms from within, particularly when the EU adopts a critical stance on China's human rights abuses and treatment of national minorities such as the Uyghurs and other Muslims, and a tit-for-tat game of sanctions ensues (Brzozowski, 2021).

Crawford explores similar questions regarding the economic benefits of the cooperation between China and the small states in the Western Balkans in Chapter 7. The evidence presented points towards a less ambitious and influential economic diplomacy from China in this region, largely resembling a 'short-term organised economic opportunism'. The chapter shows that there are three main ways in which China pursues its economic diplomacy in this region: by supporting Chinese engineering and construction interests, while often encouraging the circumventing of competitive tender processes; by promoting the growth of its largest firms; and by stepping in when other avenues for funding have failed. The interesting puzzle is to see how governments in the region have diverged in terms of their engagement with China and whether this has translated into a weakening of their alignment with EU norms. Their diverse trajectories show the importance of domestic elites' preferences and strength of institutions, as well as how far along they are in the process of EU accession. The Western Balkan states play a difficult balancing act on the global stage, of maintaining their ambition of integration into LIO institutional structures such as NATO and the EU, while not being openly critical of China on issues of 'core interest'. Crawford shows that, with the exception of Serbia, the Western Balkan states prefer to adopt a position of silence on issues related to China's illiberal policies. The case of Serbia's increasingly closer ties with China happening alongside illiberal domestic policies and politics is similar with the findings from Szunomár's chapter on Hungary. The key difference, however, is that Hungary is following this path as an EU member state bound by EU liberal norms, while this position seems likely to move Serbia further away from a potential EU accession and convergence with EU rules.

Through her contribution in Chapter 6, Malgorzata Jakimów focuses on the Visegrád Group (V4) of four Central-Eastern European (CEE) states, Czechia, Hungary, Poland, and Slovakia, that make up the core countries of the cooperative format between China and Central and Eastern European Countries (known also as the '17+1'), which was established by China to promote its engagement with the region under the BRI. Her chapter explores the process of de/resecuritization of China in the context of the V4 countries through an investigation of the extent and limits of China's normative impact in the region from 2012 to 2018. This period witnessed an unprecedented increase in interactions between China and the V4 countries. One of the most important aspects of this process was the role of personal relationships between influential politicians in the V4, who promoted closer political and economic relations with Beijing, and Chinese high officials, exemplified by Polish president Andrzej Duda, Czech president Miloš Zeman, and Hungarian Prime Minister Victor Orban. This was accompanied by the process of China's desecuritization in the region, characterized by the adoption of China-promoted language and norms.

However, over the last few years, several factors, such as disappointment with Chinese investments in the region, the role of the United States as a security provider vis-à-vis Russia, domestic political realignments, and China's handling of the pandemic, have led to the resecuritization of China in the region (with the exception of Hungary), which in turn spearheaded the loss of Beijing's normative influence. Although Jakimów is careful to highlight that China's engagement with the region has elicited different responses from each of the V4 countries, this resecuritization trend serves to illustrate the limitations of China's normative influence, which is mediated by domestic interests of the V4 countries. The dynamic tension between desecuritization and resecuritization vis-à-vis China and the V4 countries illustrates the nuanced ways in which the LIO is strained in the region.

In Chapter 5, Dimitrios Stroikos offers a comprehensive overview of the economic, political, and strategic factors that shape Sino-Greek relations in order to assess China's influence on Greece. Reflecting the conceptual framework of this volume, the chapter examines the extent to which China's influence has led to the emergence of new preferences or the consolidation of existing preferences within Greece. This is important, considering that Greece is usually seen as a quintessential example of how Beijing has been successful in exerting political influence over smaller countries as a consequence of its economic power and investments in strategic sectors, such as ports. In this regard, in addition to paying attention to the role of domestic actors and domestic political considerations, the chapter calls for the need to move beyond an analysis that focuses solely on the dyadic relationship, which helps to illustrate how Athens is trying to manage Beijing's influence. While it is plain that China has emerged as a significant economic partner of Greece, Stroikos shows that China attained some political benefits when Greece was more vulnerable and susceptible to Chinese pressure during the Eurozone crisis. However, the chapter argues that there are increasing constraints on the nature of China-Greece relations as a result of international imperatives, such as the recent shift in the EU's China policy and the emergence of US-China strategic rivalry. At the same time, China's influence is constrained by local and domestic resistance, typified by recent developments pertaining to the Piraeus port.

Filipo Boni cautions against assuming that expanding Chinese investments challenge the LIO in Chapter 4. Through a focus on the specific case of Sino-Italian investment relations, he assesses the ways in which China's increasingly close economic relations with Italy have translated into actual political influence within the country. His starting point is that China is actively trying to advance its (illiberal) visions on key issues among Western political parties and leaders. He suggests that if, by doing so, China would be able to increase its political clout in a country like Italy, a founding member of the EU and a G7 country, this could have significant implications for the liberal order. However, he concludes that claims that Italy's engagement with China has led to significant policy shifts are exaggerated. This is not to say that there is no influence. In fact, his empirical evidence suggests that China has found a willing ear among the leadership of the Five Star Movement (*Cinque Stelle*), which is one of Italy's main political parties. That is, the core narratives advanced by China seem to have influenced the position of the Five Star Movement on some of the most pressing current international issues. So, Boni provides a nuanced account of China's influence on (Southern) European countries by showing that, although the country's political influence seems to be increasing, there is also mounting opposition against such influence.

Chinese Influence and European Agency: The Liberal Order Strengthened

The contributions in Part Three examine the alternative position: that China's bilateral investments in Europe strengthen, rather than strain, the international order, *including* its liberal aspects. Through the analysis of the bilateral energy relations between China and the UK and China and Romania, Simona Davidescu's study offers evidence of how China's investments strengthen liberal institutional commitments to sustainability. Jan Knoerich's study on Chinese foreign direct investments demonstrates China's commitment to rules-based financial transactions. Taking a broader view, Catherine Jones' study shows that China's presence as a development actor means that it acts as a catalyst to enable the continuation of liberal patterns of aid and investment.

The potential reshaping of global energy governance anchored in the LIO is relevant to Davidescu in Chapter 8, which illustrates the dilemma EU member states are facing about Chinese investments in key infrastructure projects, deemed crucial to national security, such as nuclear power plants. The most promising investments in Europe for the state-owned China Guangdong Nuclear (CGN) were located in the United Kingdom and Romania. The chapter traces the shifting fortunes of these projects and the policy reversals that followed, as the framing of the issue moved from economic benefits to security and political considerations. Both countries went from a 'golden era' of bilateral relations with China to a 'deep freeze', albeit at a different pace and with different constellations of domestic actors supporting these infrastructure projects. The policy change has not been easy or complete in the case of the UK, due to the lock-in effects of prior decisions and the importance of the partnership between CGN and the French Électricité de France (EDF). In the case of Romania, the emergence of the US as an alternative investor and the domestic priorities linked to NATO and EU membership have been crucial for understanding the sudden policy reversal. However, the case of Hinkley Point C has already been used by Hungary to make a case for Russian investments into nuclear power (Lindstrom, 2021), although Russia's war in Ukraine has made this a contentious issue.

Knoerich suggests that Chinese outward FDI may not pose as much of a threat to the LIO as is sometimes assumed. In Chapter 9, he focuses on the political impact of Chinese outward FDI in recipient countries and asks what, in turn, its implications are for the LIO. He helpfully identifies five ways through which China and/or Chinese firms could exercise political influence: structural power of Chinese MNCs; direct influence over individual countries receiving Chinese FDI; enhancements in Chinese (technological) competition because of FDI; FDI as a way to further Chinese national security interests; and FDI as a way to enhance China's international soft power. Knoerich shows that China uses all these ways as avenues to attempt to influence recipient countries, yet also finds that there are in fact considerable limitations in the extent to which Chinese MNCs are in practice able to effectively influence politics. He also suggests that in fact not all the political implications of Chines FDI are necessarily problematic, and that there could even be positive political implications for countries at the receiving end of Chinese FDI flows.

Jones looks at the field of development aid and asks whether China is challenging the status quo of development assistance in Chapter 10 by traditional European and other Western donors and, as such, is influencing the international order. She shows that Chinese investments in the developing world have consequences for European development programmes but that its influence is subtle and indirect and does not challenge or undermine the liberal order. That is, China's growing importance as a provider of aid has led traditional donors to make sure that their development assistance is more targeted and effective. However, as such steps to better target aid and improve effectiveness had already been identified by Western states and development institutions as being necessary, China has merely played a role in accelerating this process of change rather than changing the direction of development aid. As such, Jones suggests that China's presence as an important development actor means that it is a catalyst that allows for the liberal patterns of aid and investment to continue.

Chinese Power, European Agency, and the Vicissitudes of the Liberal International Order

Defined as a cluster of interlocked economic, trade, and security associations based on the conviction that states will move progressively towards liberal democracy and strengthen liberal values such as civil liberties, human rights, and the rule of law (Bettiza and Lewis, 2020; de Graaf et al, 2020; Ikenberry, 2018), the LIO is premised on both the economic benefits enabled by the emergence of liberal values and the inherent attractiveness of these values as compared to other forms of governance and social organization. Although China's recent rise has received growing attention for its potential threat to the LIO, it has not been perceived to threaten the attractiveness of liberal values in Europe. The global COVID-19 pandemic fundamentally challenged this premise. The economic resilience and competence claimed by China's authoritarian government sparked a 'global battle over the coronavirus narrative' (Apuzzo, 2020; He, 2020; Hong, 2020; Wong and Mozur, 2020) and its implications for the LIO (Huang, 2020). In the wake of the pandemic, China initiated a series of diplomatic initiatives, which comprised delivery of medical support, the promotion of the Health Silk Road, and the recalibration of the BRI to aid recession-hit European economies. Commentators have worried that the narrative that Chinese-style authoritarianism is more successful appears to be gaining ground (Kundani, 2021; Nibblett, 2021), thereby challenging, diluting, and eventually revising the LIO. By focusing on pronouncements and actions of its state and social actors, Yu and Hu advise caution against assumptions that China possesses a coherent plan to revise the LIO.

Departing from studies that measure China's power in terms of its military prowess and economic resources, other contributors to this volume are attentive to that country's in/ability to influence political elites, business interests, and multilateral institutions in their favour. They find that Chinese investments contribute to a 'multiplier' effect that aligns with and amplifies converging preferences with certain European states. Chinese investments also influence states through 'persuasion', which entails economic inducement: this helps China to influence perceptions in its favour when European countries are undecided as to whether or not China is a threat. A related mode of influence pertains to China's attempts to prevail over countries hosting investments in international forums.

The contributors to this volume find limited glimpses of all three modes of influence. Ágnes Szunomár's study (Chapter 3) of the 'special relationship' between China and Hungary demonstrates the 'alignment and amplification of preferences' between the illiberal rationales of the two countries. Filippo Boni's study (Chapter 4) finds an uptake among some (not all) political elites in Italy of China's narratives on key issues such as Xinjiang and Hong Kong, suggesting the operation of 'discursive persuasion' at work. Elements of 'preference multiplying' and 'persuasion' are evident in Dimitrios Stroikos' study (Chapter 5) of China-Greece relations from 2016 to 2019, when on a few occasions Greece's position diverged greatly from EU's China policy. Drawing on her study of China's involvement in the Visegrád group of Central and Eastern European (CEE) countries, Malgorzata Jakimów's study (Chapter 6) finds evidence of 'institutional shaping' through the adoption of some (not all) China-promoted norms by these countries. Similar evidence of 'institution shaping' is offered by Nicholas Crawford's study (Chapter 7) of the Western Balkans, although it is only Serbia's foreign policy that appears to converge with China's. However, they each note the limits of such influence.

Indeed, European agency is a crucial focus in each of these studies. The agency of these actors in mediating the influence of Chinese investments not only on the continent but on the LIO is illustrated through the in-depth case study approach taken in each of the contributions. The strain to which the LIO is subjected is not only caused by the resilience of China's authoritarian regime and its overseas investments, but by the domestic dynamics within European nation-states. Likewise, the cases that illustrate the ways in which the LIO is strengthened also document the agency of European actors such as multinationals (Knoerich, Chapter 9), governments (Davidescu, Chapter 8), and donors (Jones, Chapter 10).

The contributions in this volume emphasize the ways in which a focus on agency complements conversations about power in global politics. Blending insights on power as influence (Goh, 2016) with perspectives on agency (Lampert and Mohan, 2018), these contributions urge us not to neglect the accountability, intentionality, and subjectivity of actors in international relations. Such actors refer not only to political elites, bureaucrats, and others in government as the prevailing literature tends to assume (Wight, 2004), but also to diverse actors beyond formal state institutions such as business interests, civil society groups, and trade unions, among others (Hagmann and Péclard, 2010). This focus on agency enables an appreciation of the ways in which the influence of established and emerging powers, great power rivalries, and interstate conflicts and global cooperation is mediated through domestic politics.

Avenues for Further Research

This volume offers rich and novel insights into the politics of Chinese investments in a sub-set of European countries, yet there is much scope for further research in this important area.

Firstly, there is ample scope for more systematic comparative work. Such comparative work could still focus on Sino-European investment relations but extend the analysis to China's relations with other European countries not covered. Although the volume includes chapters on Chinese investment in most geographical areas of Europe, as well as chapters looking at Europe as a whole, further research could look at countries not covered such as France, the Benelux, and Scandinavian countries. What is more, there is also room for more explicit comparative analyses. Scholars could for instance look at the issue of the uptake of Chinese narratives as discussed by Boni in Chapter 4 and assess the susceptibility of European political parties to such narratives in a wider set of countries. Or they could use the framework developed by Knoerich in Chapter 9 to more systematically detect and measure the political impacts of China's outward FDI on recipient countries in Europe. An interesting question such work could look at is under what conditions China is most likely to wield influence. One way to study this comparatively is by combining insights from the framework developed by Roy and Hu (in the introduction to this volume) and the comparative capitalism (CC) literature (Nölke 2019). The CC literature allows scholars to explore whether different capitalist systems and their institutional configuration in Europe are more/less prone to be influenced by China (see, for example, De Ville and Vermeiren, 2016). Another way by which future comparative work could build on this volume is by comparing the influence of Chinese investments in Europe with that of other emerging and more established powers. This would allow us to assess difference and/or similarities in the political drivers and implications of Chinese investments with that of other powerful actors in the international order. Scholars could also explore any differences between China's influence in Europe to that in other political and economic contexts such as Africa, Latin America, North America, and so forth, to explore for instance whether the power of the investment partners matters for China to have influence.

Further comparative research can also take as a point of departure the chapters by Szunomar in Chapter 3 and Crawford in Chapter 7 and look at the importance of regime type and ideology for understanding bilateral relations with China, and could enquire why not all democratic backsliding or illiberal regimes in the EU or candidate countries (or outside Europe) have a rapprochement with China similar to that of Hungary. Similar questions could be raised about the relationship of these countries with Russia, at a time when a strengthening of Chinese-Russian relations could potentially be a significant threat to LIO and lead to the reshaping of global power relations.

Secondly, scholars could draw on the burgeoning literature on global value chains (GVCs) and global production networks (GPNs) to further develop this research agenda (see, for example, Gerreffi et al. 2005; Yeung and Coe 2015). There are various elements in this body of work, which could be fruitfully explored further by scholars interested in Chinese investments and their implications for the liberal order. Previous research has shown that the growing importance of GVCs/GPNs has increased the political power of 'foreign' actors in domestic politics, either because of the importance of their markets/supplies to local industry, or because of the weight of their investments in local economies (see Curran and Eckhardt, 2022 for an overview of this literature). Yet, these policy interventions have been controversial and have in recent years led to increased concern about the negative impacts of globalization and the GVCs which underpin it, contributing to a backlash against foreign trade and investment in the West (Curran and Eckhardt 2020; Rodrik 2018). An interesting question to explore is how these developments have affected the (in)ability of China, as a central actor within many GVCs, to exercise political influence abroad through its investments. What is more, the US-China trade war, as well as the COVID-19 pandemic, have led to debates on a restructuring and de-Sinicization of GVCs, and analysis of the economic implications of this development has already started (Dong and Xia 2020). The political implications have not been explored in much detail yet, although research suggests that a generalized increased distrust of foreign GVC actors, especially from China, is emerging (Henderson and Hooper 2021). It would be interesting to explore whether this has increased the 'Liability of Foreignness' of outside interests such as China seeking to impact on domestic politics, and whether it is swinging the pendulum of policymaking on trade and investment back once again towards the dominance of national actors (Curran and Eckhardt 2022). Such work could look at Sino-Europe investment relations, but could also explore Chinese investments in other parts of the world. Beyond political economy, the cultural and racial dynamics underpinning such investments could also be explored.

Thirdly, as many of the contributions in this volume have shown, the investment relations between China and Europe (and Chinese investment relations elsewhere for that matter) are very complex and multifaceted. This complexity is due to *inter alia* the overlap between investment and other policy areas, but it is also because of the sheer number of actors and institutions involved in and affected by decision-making at different levels of governance. The rich research agenda on regime complexity could help scholars to assess how the 'rising density of institutions, policies, rules and strategies to address' global issues (Alter 2022: 375) impacts on Chinese investments and, in turn, their influence on the international order. There is surprisingly little work which has looked at the investment regime through a regime complexity lens, and scholars have only recently started to look at China's role in complex regimes (see, for example, Wang 2021).

Fourthly, the agency of state and social actors emphasized by the contributions to this volume offer a further area of future research. Agency becomes important when it is denied, a common occurrence in accounts of China's meteoric rise and growing worldwide footprint: overtly structural accounts deny European agency and merely reproduce political nihilism that precludes a future in which such agency can be realized in transformative ways. Of course, we must be careful not to reify agency, as that could run the risk of reversing the analytical lens too far. Further research needs to be attentive to the diverse ways in which states and social actors in Europe assert their agency vis-à-vis Chinese investments on the continent. After all, agency is not only about 'embodied intentionality' (Wight, 1999: 132) or the autonomous ability to chart one's own course, as is commonly understood. A fuller understanding of agency recognizes that agents are 'agents of something', a perspective that recognizes social context, especially 'the socio-cultural system into which persons are born and develop' (Wight, 1999: 133). The formulation of agency recognizes the possibility of individuals reproducing and/or transforming the socio-cultural system into which they are born. Because not all agents are equally placed or positioned, they negotiate differently with the broader systems into which they are embedded. Such variations make it essential to situate its operation within the broad spectrum of state-society relations.

Fifthly, closely linked to the consideration of power as influence in the context of discussing China's growing profile in Europe via investments is the issue of the resilience of the influence of the United States. In this way, for all the debates about the decline of the US-led international order as a result of China's arrival as an authoritarian alternative to liberal values and practices, the picture that emerges from the contributions to this volume concerning China's influence over Europe is rather mixed, at a time when many European countries are looking for the United States as a security provider and reliable partner thanks to increasing geopolitical uncertainty. In this way, building on the findings of this volume, further studies can benefit from considering the influence of the United States vis-à-vis China on Europe to assess the endurance of US power understood in terms of influence when compared with the achievements and limitations of Chinese power and influence.

Finally, further studies can ethnographically investigate the interactions of power and agency made possible by the proliferation of Chinese investments in Europe. Ethnographic investigations into the social life of infrastructure have blossomed in recent years as a field in which investigators explore and examine, at once, the necessities of mediated and modern life, the material ordering of social relations, and the hopes and imaginations attending to global connections that underpin much contemporary politics.[4] A parallel literature directs attention to the materiality and agency of the infrastructure of modern life, including the vast networks that both entangle and isolate human and nonhuman powers, highlighting the complexes of material connections, actions, and reactions that only eventually, and contingently, come to gain wider social meaning.[5] The indispensability of infrastructures to contemporary social, economic, political, and cultural life is taken for granted in both strands of the literature, opening up further questions about how people engage with, and negotiate, dispute, challenge, or comply with infrastructure programs, especially the smaller-scale schemes, interventions, and pilots that are often the precursor to large-scale projects. Further research on the social appropriations 'from below' of Chinese investments in Europe will enrich our understandings of their everyday political economies. Such studies will be indispensable to understanding the true nature and extent of China's influence on the lives of people in Europe and beyond.

Bibliography

Alter, K. J. 2022. 'The Promise and Perils of Theorizing International Regime Complexity in an Evolving World'. *The Review of International Organizations* 17 (2): pp. 375–396.

Anand, N. 2011. 'PRESSURE: The poliTechnics of water supply in Mumbai', *Cultural Anthropology* 26 (4): 542–654.

Apuzzo, M. 2021. 'Pressured by China, E.U. softens report on Covid-19 disinformation'. *The New York Times*, 6 January, 2021.

Bettiza, G. and D. Lewis. 2020. 'Authoritarian powers and norm contestation in the Liberal International Order'. *Journal of Global Security Studies* 5 (4): 559–577.

[4] See Anand (2011); Appadurai (1996); Ferguson (1999); and Larkin (2008).
[5] See Latour (2007); and Roy (forthcoming).

Bordet, M. 2011. 'La Chine rachète l'europe'. *Le Point*, 22 September. Available at: https://www.lepoint.fr/economie/la-chine-rachete-l-europe-22-09-2011-1380187_28.php [Accessed 17 May 2021].

Brzozowski, A. 2021. 'EU Efforts to Ratify China Investment Deal "Suspended" After Sanctions'. *Euractiv*, 5 May. Available at: https://www.euractiv.com/section/eu-china/news/eu-efforts-to-ratify-china-investment-deal-suspended-after-sanctions/.

Clark, G. L. 2017. The new era of global economic growth and urban infrastructure investment: Financial intermediation, institutions and markets. Available at SSRN: https://ssrn.com/abstract=2954616.

Curran, L., and J. Eckhardt. 2020. 'Mobilizing against the Antiglobalization Backlash: An Integrated Framework for Corporate Nonmarket Strategy'. *Business and Politics* 22 (4): pp. 612–638.

Curran, L., and J. Eckhardt. 2022. 'The Structure of International Trade, Global Value Chains and Trade Wars in the Twenty-First Century'. In *Research Handbook on Trade Wars*, pp. 27–46. Edward Elgar Publishing.

Dong, J., and L. Xia. 2020. 'De-Sinicization of Global Value Chain after COVID-19'. BBVA Research Report, 3 June, Madrid: BBVA. Available at: https://www.bbvaresearch.com/publicaciones/china-desinizacion-de-la-cadena-de-valor-global-despues-de-la-covid-19.

European Commission. 2019. EU-China Strategic Outlook: Commission and HR/VP Contribution to the European Council (21–22 March 2019).

Ferguson J. 1999. *Expectations of Modernity: Myths and Meanings of Urban Life on the Zambian Copperbelt*. Berkeley: University of California Press.

Foot, R. 2014. 'Doing Some Things' in the Xi Jinping Era: The United Nations as China's Venue of Choice'. *International Affairs* 90 (5): pp. 1085–1100.

Geaney, D. 2020. 'China's Island Fortifications Are a Challenge to International Norms'. *Defense News*. Available at: https://www.defensenews.com/opinion/commentary/2020/04/17/chinas-island-fortifications-are-a-challenge-to-international-norms/ [Accessed 14 May 2021].

Gereffi, G., J. Humphrey, and T. Sturgeon. 2005. 'The Governance of Global Value Chains'. *Review of International Political Economy* 12 (1): pp. 78–104.

Godement, F., and J. Parello-Plesner. 2011. *The Scramble for Europe*. European Council on Foreign Relations.

Goh, E. 2014. 'The Modes of China's Influence: Cases from Southeast Asia'. *Asian Survey* 54 (5): pp. 825–848.

Goh, E. 2016. 'Introduction'. In *Rising China's Influence in Developing Asia*, edited by E. Goh, pp. 1–23. Oxford: Oxford University Press.

de Graaff, N., T. ten Brink, and I. Parmar. 2020. 'China's Rise in a Liberal World Order in Transition—Introduction to the FORUM'. *Review of International Political Economy* 27 (2): pp. 191–207.

Hagmann, T. and D. Péclard. 2010. 'Negotiating statehood: dynamics of power and domination in Africa', *Development and Change* 41 (40): 539–562.

He, W. 2020. '"The battle of narratives": Coronavirus and the EU Infodemic'. *RUSI*, Available at https://www.rusi.org/explore-our-research/publications/commentary/battle-narratives-coronavirus-and-eu-infodemic [Accessed 10 December 2022].

Henderson, J., and M. Hooper. 2021 *China and European Innovation: Corporate Takeovers and Their Consequences*. Development and Change.

Hong, T. 2020. 'The battle for the coronavirus narrative'. *Yale Global Online*. 12 May 2020. Available at https://archive-yaleglobal.yale.edu/content/battle-coronavirus-narrative.

Ikenberry, G. J. 2018. 'Why the Liberal World Order Will Survive'. *Ethics and International Affairs* 32 (1): pp. 17–29.

Kundani, H. 2021. *Coronavirus and the future of democracy in Europe*. London: Chatham House, Accessed: https://www.chathamhouse.org/2020/03/coronavirus-and-future-democracy-europe.

L'Express. 2011. Comment la Chine envahit l'Europe. 4 February.

Lampert, B. and Mohan, G. 2018. 'A transformative presence? Chinese migrants as agents of change in Ghana and Nigeria'. In *Chinese and African Entrepreneurs: Social Impacts of Interpersonal Encounters Giese*, edited by Karsten and Marfaing, Laurence. Leiden: Brill, pp. 147–169.

Larkin B. 2008. *Signal and Noise: Media, Infrastructure, and Urban Culture in Nigeria*. Durham, NC: Duke University Press.

Latour B. 2007. *Reassembling the Social: An Introduction to Actor-Network-Theory*. Oxford, UK: Oxford University Press.

Lindstrom, N. 2021. 'Aiding the State: Administrative Capacity and Creative Compliance with European State Aid Rules in New Member States'. *Journal of European Public Policy* 28 (11): pp. 1789–1806.

Niblett, R. 2021. China emerges turbo-charged. *Foreign Policy* 239: 114.

Nölke, A. 2019. 'Comparative Capitalism'. In *The Palgrave Handbook of Contemporary International Political Economy*, edited by Timothy M. Shaw, Laura C. Mahrenbach, Renu Modi, Xu Yi-chong, pp. 135–151. London: Palgrave Macmillan.

Oertel, J. 2020. 'The New China Consensus: How Europe Is Growing Wary of Beijing'. European Council on Foreign Relations. Available at: https://ecfr.eu/publication/the_new_china_consensus_how_europe_is_growing_wary_of_beijing/ [Accessed 14 May 2021].

Rodrik, D. 2018. 'Populism and the Economics of Globalization'. *Journal of International Business Policy* 1(1): pp. 12–33.

Roy, I. forthcoming. 'Negotiating Power: Disputes over Electrification in an Indian Village'. *Modern Asian Studies*.

Schindler, S. and Kanai, J. 2019. 'Getting the Territory Right: Infrastructure-led Development and the Re-emergence of Spatial Planning Strategies', *Regional Studies*, https://doi.org/10.1080/00343404.2019.1661984.

Sørensen, C. 2015. 'The Significance of Xi Jinping's "Chinese Dream" for Chinese Foreign Policy: From "Tao Guang Yang Hui" to "Fen Fa You Wei"'. *Journal of China and International Relations* 3 (1): pp. 53–73.

Tangen, O. 2020. 'Is China Taking Advantage of COVID-19 to Pursue South China Sea Ambitions?'. *Deutsche Welle*. Available at: https://www.dw.com/en/is-china-taking-advantage-of-covid-19-to-pursue-south-china-sea-ambitions/a-53573918 [Accessed 14 May 2021].

Tooze, A. 2018. *How a Decade of Financial Crises Changed the World*. New York: Allen Lane.

Torrance, M. I. 2007. 'The Power of Governance in Financial Relationships: Governing Tensions in Exotic Infrastructure Territory'. *Growth and Change*, 38 (4), 671–695.

De Ville, F., and M. Vermeiren. 2016. 'The Eurozone Crisis and the Rise of China in the Global Monetary and Trading System: The Political Economy of an Asymmetric Shock'. *Comparative European Politics* 14 (5): pp. 572–603.

Wang, H. 2021. 'Regime Complexity and Complex Foreign Policy: China in International Development Finance Governance'. *Global Policy* 12: pp. 69–79.

Wight, C. 2004. 'State agency: social action without human activity', *Review of International Studies* 30 (20): 269–280.

Wight, C. 1999. 'They shoot dead horses don't they? Locating agency in the agent-structure problematique', *European Journal of International Relations* 5(1): 109–142.

Wong, E., and Mozur, P. 2020. 'China's "donation diplomacy" raises tensions with U.S.'. *The New York Times*, 14 April 2020.

World Bank. 2009. *World Development Report 2009: Reshaping Economic Geography*. Washington, DC: World Bank.

Yan, X. 2014. 'From Keeping a Low Profile to Striving for Achievement'. *The Chinese Journal of International Politics* 7 (2): pp. 153–184.

Yeung, H. W. C., and N. Coe. 2015. 'Toward a Dynamic Theory of Global Production Networks'. *Economic Geography* 91 (1): pp. 29–58.

Yifu Lin, J. 2012. *The Quest for Prosperity: How Developing Economies Can Take off*. Princeton: Princeton University Press.

Yifu Lin, J., and Wang, Y. 2013. Beyond the Marshall Plan: A global structural transformation fund (Background Research Paper submitted to the High Level Panel on the Post-2015 Development Agenda) Retrieved from https://www.post2015hlp.org/wp-content/uploads/docs/Lin-Wang_Beyondthe-Marshall-Plan-A-Global-Structural-Transformation-Fund.pdf.

Index